Urban Green Belts in the Twenty-first Century

Edited by

MARCO AMATI
Macquarie University, Australia

ASHGATE

Published by
Ashgate Publishing Limited
Gower House
Croft Road
Aldershot
Hampshire GU11 3HR
England

Ashgate Publishing Company
Suite 420
101 Cherry Street
Burlington, VT 05401-4405
USA

Ashgate website: http//www.ashgate.com

British Library Cataloguing in Publication Data
Urban green belts in the twenty-first century. – (Urban
  planning and environment)
  1. Greenbelts 2. City planning – Environmental aspects
  3. Cities and towns – Growth
  I. Amati, Marco
  307.1'216

Library of Congress Control Number: 2008924311

ISBN: 978-0-7546-4959-5

Typeset by TJO Typesetting, Prenton, Wirral

Mixed Sources
Product group from well-managed
forests and other controlled sources
www.fsc.org Cert no. SA-COC-1565
© 1996 Forest Stewardship Council
FSC

Printed and bound in Great Britain by
MPG Books Ltd, Bodmin, Cornwall.

Contents

Figures

Tables

Notes on Contributors

Marco Amati is Director of the planning programme in the Graduate School of the Environment, Macquarie University, Sydney, Australia. His research interests are on green belts, urban growth and Japanese, Australian and UK planning systems.

Alon Bassok is a doctoral candidate in the department of Urban Design and Planning at the University of Washington. His research examines the linkages among growth management, transportation and public health.

Meinhard Breiling is a senior lecturer at the Faculty of Architecture and Planning at the Technical University in Vienna. He received his PhD in landscape planning at the University of Applied Life Sciences in Vienna (BOKU). He worked for several years at the Department of Landscape Planning in Alnarp, Sweden and has been a guest professor at Tokyo University and University of Hyogo, Japan.

Michael Buxton is an Associate Professor in the School of Global Studies, Social Science and Planning at RMIT University, Melbourne, Australia. His research interests are green belts, peri-urban development, urban form, environmental policy and environmental theory.

Pasquale Dal Sasso engineer, is a Professor at the Department of Engineering and Management of the Agricultural, Livestock and Forest Systems of the University of Bari. He is a member of the Accademia dei Georgofili, author of more than 90 articles and two books. He has also been a coordinator of international projects related to landscape planning (Interreg Italia-Albania II; Interreg IIIB Grecia-Albania).

Kenya Endo is a PhD candidate at the Graduate School of Frontier Sciences, University of Tokyo. His research interests are landscape planning in the face of rapid urbanization at the edge of provincial cities in Japan.

Paolo Stefano Ferrario agricultural engineer, is a researcher at the Institute of Agricultural Engineering of the University of Milan. He is a specialist in Geographical Information Systems and a member of the Italian Agricultural Engineering Association and the Greenways Italian Association.

Ludger Gailing studied spatial planning at the University of Dortmund. Since 2003 he has been a research assistant at the Leibniz-Institute for Regional Development and Structural Planning (IRS) in Erkner near Berlin. His research focuses on regional forms of landscape governance such as regional parks and the development of cultural landscapes from a spatial and institutional perspective.

Christine Garnaut is Research Fellow and Director of the Architecture Museum, Louis Laybourne Smith School of Architecture and Design, University of South Australia. Her research focuses on aspects of South Australia's colonial and twentieth century planning and architectural history.

Robin Goodman is a senior lecturer in the Environment and Planning Program at RMIT University in Melbourne, Australia. She researches and teaches on issues surrounding sustainable strategic planning, transport and retail planning and planning history.

David Gordon is Associate Professor in the School of Urban and Regional Planning, Queen's University, Canada. His recent publications include *Planning Twentieth Century Capital Cities* (Routledge, 2006), *Planning Canadian Communities* (Nelson, 2007, with Gerald Hodge) and numerous articles on plan implementation and Ottawa planning history. He received degrees in urban planning and engineering from Queen's University, and the Doctorate in Design from Harvard.

Jekook Kim is a Research Fellow in Gyeonggi Research Institute. He has a PhD in Urban Planning from the Tokyo Institute of Technology which examined the relationships between the Urban General Plan and Planning Permissions.

Tae-Kyung Kim is a Researcher in Gyeonggi Research Institute. He has a PhD in City and Regional Planning from Ohio State University and studies land and housing issues.

Manfred Kühn studied city and landscape planning at the University of Kassel and graduated in 1988. He obtained a Dr. rer. pol. in 1993. Since 1996 he has been a scientific researcher at the Institute for Regional Development and Structural Planning in Erkner near Berlin. His main research interests include planning analysis of cities, suburban landscapes and regions. He teaches at the Institute for City and Regional Planning, Technical University of Cottbus.

Raffaele Lafortezza landscape ecologist, is a Research Associate at the Department of Plant Sciences, University of Cambridge, UK. He holds a PhD in Landscape Analysis and Design from the University of Bari and has authored a large number of articles on landscape ecological planning and GIS-based modelling.

Nicolas Laruelle has been the joint head of green belt studies at IAURIF (Ile-de-France Regional and Town Planning Institute, closely linked with the Ile-de-France Regional Council) with Corinne Legenne since 2003. He has been in charge of the reappraisal of the Paris-Ile-de-France green belt project.

Corinne Legenne is a landscape architect at IAURIF and joint head of green belt studies with Nicolas Laruelle. She has been in charge of studying the links between the uses of open space, the intensification of peri-urban life and the improvement of transportation networks.

Caroline Miller is a senior lecturer in the Planning Programme in the School of People, Environment and Planning at Massey University, New Zealand. Her research has focused on the planning and urban history of New Zealand from 1900 to the 1960s, the development of the planning profession and critiques of planning practice.

Gisa Ruland was educated as a landscape architect in Hanover, Germany and worked as principal investigator in several offices in Germany and Austria. She has worked at the Austrian Institute of Ecology, teaches in the Vienna University of Technology and finished her thesis in 2002 at the University of Hanover. Now she runs an office for environmental and open space planning in Vienna researching the design of high quality open space areas in cities, participation in planning and implementation processes of urban development.

Richard Scott worked for Canada's National Capital Commission as an environmental and regional planner for almost 20 years. He managed the development of the 1996 Greenbelt Master Plan. Richard is currently Waterway Heritage Planner with the Parks Canada Agency for the Trent-Severn waterway. He holds a masters degree in environmental studies from York University.

Giulio Senes agricultural engineer, is assistant Professor of GIS and Rural Landscape Planning at the Institute of Agricultural Engineering of the University of Milan. He is Vice-President of the Italian Greenways Association and of the European Greenways Association. He is member of the Accademia dei Georgofili and the Italian Agricultural Engineering Association and the Italian Association of Landscape Architects. He holds a PhD in Rural Engineering.

Alessandro Toccolini engineer and architect, is a Professor at the Institute of Agricultural Engineering of the University of Milan. He is President of the Italian Greenways Association, member of the Accademia dei Georgofili, member of the Italian Institute of Town and City Planning, the Italian Agricultural Engineering Association, the Italian Association of Landscape Architects and the American Society of Landscape Architects. Author of more than 100 articles as well as two books, he introduced the GIS and METLAND system of landscape planning to Italy.

Takashi Watanabe is an Associate Professor in the Faculty of Environmental Studies at Nagasaki University. His current interests include research on land use management methods, environmental attitudes, and the appraisal and assessment of natural settings in urban fringe areas.

Makoto Yokohari is a specialist in Japanese and international landscape planning. He is currently a professor at the University of Tokyo. For more than fifteen years his aim has been to question the application of Western urban planning techniques to Japanese cities and to develop new indigenous planning concepts for the Japanese landscape. He is active in a number of national-level projects such as representing Japan during Organization for Economic Cooperation and Development trade negotiations in the late 1990s.

Preface

Western visitors to Japan are often struck by the apparent disorder of land-uses in the urban fringe. Tiny patches of farmland dot an otherwise urban landscape of houses, shops, restaurants and small industries. This apparently haphazard pattern presents a challenge to the normative distinction between urban and rural. As a newly arrived PhD student at the University of Tsukuba in 2000 I frequently heard that the cause for this pattern was the 'failure' of green belt planning in Japan, which was then contrasted with stories about the UK planning's 'successes'. While such exchanges were more a part of welcoming small-talk than serious debate a search among Japanese journals revealed to me the deeply held belief that the UK's planning system, among others, held the answers for Japanese planners. From the 1950s onwards a small cottage industry of Japanese academics had produced a range of studies on the UK's planning methods and its history. There was, for example, detailed work on the processes and methods of public participation in the UK as well as surveys of Groundwork and other non-governmental activity. There was also a small body of largely laudatory studies of the history and application of the London green belt. No works had alluded to the green belt as a contentious issue and certainly not that it might be reformed, which seemed increasingly likely as my studies unfolded.

When I examined why the UK's green belt had remained a feature of planning for much of the post-WWII period, I began to think about the broader implications of the discourse of success and failure in planning. From the way these terms were used I realised that the question was less about the effect of the policy on land-use and more about its impact on planning as a discipline. In both Japan and the UK it seemed that the outcome of the green belt had been dictated by and contributed to the status of planning and the agency of planners. This has since formed the basis for other questions about planning, not only in Japan and the UK, but also in Australia and New Zealand.

As I neared the end of my write-up I realised that no book had compared international experiences of the green belt to open similar avenues for researchers. My initial idea was then fleshed out in discussions with Makoto Yokohari, Robert Freestone and my new colleagues at Massey University into a book proposal. I was then fortunate to be able to draw on the networks of the series editors, friends and colleagues who pointed me towards reviewers and, in some cases, authors. Since I first started asking for contributions a year and a half ago the work of editing this book has been a constant iterative process in the process of which I have learnt a huge amount about planning in different countries and the possibilities and limits of my own editing skills.

Currently, with a new Prime-Minister in place and with talk of an election, the UK's green belt reform appears to be less of a priority than it did during the autumn of 2004. I have also realised that although many UK academics are quick to point to a variety of negative impacts that are caused by the green belt – for example, a lack of affordable housing in the South-East, there is a great deal of admiration, if not affection, for the policy. Green belts are, after all, the final reminder of a time when such bold measures were possible and of the early post-WWII political consensus that created the planning system that is used today. It might be that in the end a similar consensus would be needed to dismantle the UK green belt.

M.A.

Palmerston North

November, 2007

Acknowledgments

In completing this book I have drawn on the goodwill, time and energy of a large number of people to whom I owe a great debt of gratitude. I wish in particular to thank my PhD supervisor Makoto Yokohari (University of Tokyo), Robert Freestone (University of New South Wales) and Gavin Parker (University of Reading) for their mentorship, encouragement and support without which I would not have had the confidence to write the book proposal let alone complete this project. I wish to thank all the reviewers of the chapters, who anonymously worked behind the scenes to improve the quality of each contribution and the authors for their enthusiasm and patience with my editing. Finally, my thanks go to my parents, my sister, Katharine and Lucia without whose love and support none of this would have been possible.

Note: although the term greenbelt is often employed for reasons of consistency the term green belt is used throughout this volume unless it is part of a title.

CHAPTER 1

Green Belts: A Twentieth-century Planning Experiment

Marco Amati

The general public creates an outcry if any attempt is made to invade this green belt and that is something we want to get into planning – the creation of public interest. We want to get them to know something of our work and support us in our activities (Abercrombie, 1948, 13)

The implementation of green belts in many countries can be regarded as one of the most internationally famous attempts to control urban growth. Green belts have ringed major cities to prevent them sprawling. Planners have used them to separate satellite 'new towns' from the urban core, safeguarding land for recreation, agriculture and forestry. Green belts have also provided sites for more utilitarian uses such as salvage yards, incinerators and quarries. In some places, areas of the green belt have suffered through illegal dumping or through neglect.

The popularity of green belts among planners during the twentieth century is due to the alignment of their attributes with some of the assumptions that underpinned modernist planning. These assumptions were that strict divisions between different land-uses could be unproblematically drawn, and that planners' actions could be justified by normative conventions and a search for universal truths.

As planners began to grapple with the messy realities of urban growth during the twentieth century, green belts gave them a tool to realise a normative geography that a city has natural limits, that urban and rural areas should be separated and that settlements should be balanced and evenly-spaced. Green belts were used as part of a project to construct a universal planning canon, being employed regardless of the contingencies that affect urban growth in different cities around the world. They also contributed to the construction of planning as a discipline, as the open space they preserved could be linked directly to a who's who of famous UK planners such as Patrick Abercrombie and Raymond Unwin (Gault, 1981).

Planning has changed considerably since the early post-WWII period when practitioners attempted to physically realise the ideas of high modernism (Taylor, 1998). As planners seek to direct the growth of cities towards sustainable patterns of land-use, how likely is it that they will continue to see a green belt policy as a useful tool for managing urban growth? Planners are no longer the all-powerful experts that they once were, nor can they rely on a consensus politics that will support such bold measures. The impact that green belts have on market processes sits uncomfortably with the neo-liberal strategies to deregulate government invoked in many countries during the latter part of the twentieth century (Evans, 2003; Healey, 1997, 15). Furthermore, a number of well-known alternatives to a green belt exist allowing planners to opt, for example for a green wedge, a greenway or a greenweb.

Despite these forces of change, green belts can be found next to fourteen cities in the UK, where they have remained a central plank of national planning policy for more than fifty years. Planners have successfully enforced green belts despite sustained periods of high development pressure particularly in the South-East of England. Green belts have garnered broad political support throughout successive changes of government, including the Thatcherite deregulation of the 1980s. Yet, as contributions to a recent special issue of *Journal of Environmental Planning and Management* and an article by Sir Peter Hall have discussed, the UK's green belts are by no means sacrosanct and a debate currently rages on their future in relation to housing and the urban fringe (Amati, 2007; Gunn, 2007; Gallent, 2007; Lloyd, 2007; Hall, 2007).

This book is concerned with attempts to reform the green belt as a reflection of the shifts away from modernist planning thought. Although it may contribute to the UK's green belt debate, the book's focus steers deliberately away from the large body of research that already exists on the UK, and towards work by international scholars and practitioners. The aim of bringing these works together is to use green belts as a lens through which to view the changes in planning during the twentieth century. At the same time, each of the following chapters contributes to the question of whether green belts remain a relevant or useful concept for the twenty-first century.

Any book that makes the green belt its central theme but fails to mention how the concept was developed and disseminated would be remiss and leave the reader unaware of its importance. Therefore, the aim of the present chapter is to unpack the reasons for the widespread implementation and popularity of the green belt among planners. Central to this history is that of UK planning and how it influenced other countries. It is argued that the popularity of green belts among planners internationally peaked from the early 1950s to the 1970s when the ideas of high modernism seemed practicable. At the same time, the green belt concept was transmitted to, or borrowed by, other countries. In some cases diffusion occurred along colonial channels, where attempts were being made to integrate elements of UK planning into indigenous systems. In New Zealand for example, Abercrombie's *Greater London Plan 1944* was widely read and it was common for planners to train in the UK or at least take Town Planning Institute (later Royal Town Planning Institute) exams until 1958.

In the following a brief sketch of the historical development of the green belt in the UK is provided, describing how pre-WWII planners invoked the green belt as a way of achieving the normative goals associated with preserving the landscape. A great deal of research already exists in this area (for example, Thomas, 1963; Sheail, 1981; Elson, 1986; Cherry, 1996; Matless, 1998), and the intention is not to repeat this work but to use it to unpack how Raymond Unwin and Patrick Abercrombie, two of the most internationally reknown planners, used the green belt to entrench preservationist values into the planning system. Secondly, it is shown how the success of the green belt was deliberately associated with the growing discipline of Planning. Thirdly, I focus on two aspects of modernist planning, the concealment of normative goals behind rational justifications and the search for a universal planning discipline, and discuss the extent to which the implementation of the green belt mapped onto these. Finally, I introduce the book's structure as a reflection of the changes that have taken place in planning since the early post-WWII period and summarise how each of the contributions fit into this.

The Pre-WWII Green Belt

The simple idea of surrounding an urban area with a band of undeveloped land has a variety of nineteenth century origins but first gained prominence through its association with the Garden Cities concept. To think of green belts is to think inescapably of Ebenezer Howard and his work *To-morrow: a peaceful path to real reform* (1898).

Despite the importance of the green belt in the UK's planning history, the origins of the term and its application have been diverse (Freestone, 2002). A number of similar schemes, such as parklands, parkways and greenways, flourished during the early twentieth century, spreading internationally via conferences, exhibitions and international lecture tours (Ward, 2002, 79). Each of these schemes have their individual histories and have shaped the development of different cities at various times.

While the green belt was one of several policies that planners in different countries could choose from, it was strongly supported in the UK by an active group of 'preservationists'. Preservationists sought to impose a normative model of settlement on the landscape, what Matless (1998) terms a 'morality of settlement', and to use the landscape to constitute citizens (Parker, 2006; Reeder, 2006, 60). Preservationists normatively asserted that a town should be clearly a town, and a village a village. They saw the adoption of green belts as a way of imposing an urban-rural polarity on an in-between landscape of urban fringe suburbs and ribbon development (Matless, 1998, 32).

The ideas of preservationists were woven into the UK's planning system during the pre-WWII period by a broad array of actors. The highly distinguished planner Patrick Abercrombie, writing about the *Council for the Preservation of Rural England* (CPRE), one of the most active preservationist groups that he co-founded in 1926, mentions:

> the local authorities, the owners, the farmers, the inhabitants; the users of the country, the ramblers, the campers, the motorists; the preservationists of the commons and footpaths, wild flowers, fauna, ancient buildings, trees, etc.; the National Trust; the women's institutes, the rural community councils, the architects, surveyors, engineers and town planners; the garden cities, housing and town-planning propaganda associations (Abercrombie, 1959, 228)

These were all to be coordinated, from however divergent angles, to achieve the common goal of preserving the countryside's existing beauty. Although these groups would have had disparate concerns, their support for the work of the CPRE is a reflection of the broad appeal of the preservationist cause.

Preservationist concerns also constituted the discourse of the influential *London Society* (Beaufoy, 1997), and were voiced by prominent politicians such as William Bull, Lord Meath, Neville Chamberlain and Herbert Morrison (Reeder, 2006, 58). They included the geographer, Lawrence Dudley Stamp, whose pioneering land-use survey of Britain contributed to the 1947 Town and Country Planning Act. Preservationists were able to count among their ranks, not only Patrick Abercrombie, but also planners such as Raymond Unwin and F. J. Osborn who all had enormous influence on the development of the UK's planning system.

Unwin, in particular, was a keen advocate for separating town and country deriding, in his widely read *Town Planning in Practice* 'that irregular fringe of half-developed suburb, and half-spoiled country which forms such a hideous and depressing girdle around modern growing towns ...' (Unwin, 1909, 156). The irony is that this could be used to describe London's present-day green belt.

As Unwin and Abercrombie's career and influence developed they were able to project their preservationist ideals onto the planning system through the implementation of a green belt. In 1929 Unwin became the chief planner of the Greater London Regional Planning Committee and published his *First report* proposing a 'green girdle' for the enjoyment of Londoners to compensate for the deficiency of open spaces. The implementation of his plan was prevented by a government financial crisis in 1931 (Miller, 1991, 189–209), and it was only in 1935 that the green belt could be finally implemented with the help of a London County Council scheme to buy land and the cooperation of an array of actors that shared preservationist concerns (Amati and Yokohari, 2007; Reeder, 2006, 64–5). Abercrombie wrote the enormously influential *County of London Plan 1943* and the *Greater London Plan 1944*) which were published to national and international acclaim (Forshaw and Abercrombie, 1943; Abercrombie, 1945). Both of these contained sections on the green belt and directly influenced central government thinking at a time when UK planning legislation was undergoing momentous changes as development rights were being nationalised through the 1947 Town and Country Planning Act (Garside, 2006).

The popularity of the green belt in the UK is demonstrated by its eventual integration into central government planning policy. Abercrombie's work in the 1940s influenced Duncan Sandys the Minister with responsibility for planning. He issued a Circular calling on all local planning authorities, county councils in England and Wales to consider submitting plans for a green belt in 1955 (Ministry of Housing and Local Government, 1955).

The implementation of the green belt in the UK can be seen as a fifty year struggle during which the popularity and fame of the concept steadily increased in line with its proponents' careers. Once the popularity of the green belt peaked it remained high for the first 20 years of the post-WWII period. The following explores the reasons for this popularity in greater depth.

Connecting the Success of the Green Belt to Planning

The incorporation of the green belt into the UK's central government policy as well as the support it gained from well-known planners inspired what Ward (2000) terms as the 'undiluted' borrowing of the concept by a number of cities during the post-WWII period. The following sections describe why the borrowing of the green belt was so wholesale. Firstly, UK planners trumpeted the success of the green belt to further the planning project. Secondly, the normative values articulated during the pre-WWII period and certain aspects of modernist, early post-WWII planning aided the implementation of the green belt.

By the mid-1950s the green belt could justifiably be called part of an international planning language. The ideas behind the green belt would have been recognisable from the pre-WWII attempts to preserve the existing greenery around other European cities such as Frankfurt, Berlin and Vienna (Ward, 2002, 84; Kühn and Gailing; Breiling and Ruland, this volume). The US federal government had employed a variant of the concept to build its three 'greenbelt towns' during the 1930s depression (Arnold, 1971). The use of green belts to separate satellite towns was a part of Communist Party policy for St Petersburg during the early 1930s (Anan'ich and Kobak, 2006). But it was through the propagandising work of British planners in the post-WWII period that the green belt concept was deliberately and rapidly spread.

During the 1940s to 1970s, UK planning was being held up as an example and UK planners were in demand. For example, Patrick Abercrombie toured Australia in 1948 on a month long visit sponsored by the British Council which also sponsored a *Town Planning in Britain Exhibition* that travelled to both Australia and New Zealand. Abercrombie also travelled to Hong Kong in 1947 advising on the planning of the city (Tang et al., 2007). F. J. Osborn travelled extensively acting as an international propagandist for the Garden Cities movement during the 1950s, 60s and 70s (Whittick, 1987).

In many cities green belts were attempted at this time. The New Zealand and Australian cities of Wellington, Christchurch, Brisbane, Melbourne and Sydney drew their inspiration for their green belts from the UK but also from earlier schemes such as Colonel Light's Adelaide Parklands (Amati, 2006; Low Choy and Gleeson, 1998; Freestone, 1992; Miller and Amati; Buxton and Goodman; Garnaut, this volume). Cities in East Asia such as Hong Kong and Tokyo both implemented their own versions of the green belt drawing on Abercrombie's work (Tang, 2007; Amati and Parker, 2007; Watanabe et al., this volume). Ottawa's green belt while being based originally on the work of F. L. Olmsted, also drew on Abercrombie's *Greater London Plan 1944* (Gordon and Scott, this volume).

The green belt was seen by planners as an achievement to be assiduously promoted – as the quotation from Patrick Abercrombie's 1948 speech at the University of Melbourne shows at the beginning of this chapter. The planning theorist Lewis Keeble, whose *Principles and practice of town and country planning* was standard reading throughout the English-speaking world during the 1950s and 1960s (Taylor,

1998), also saw the green belt as a way of furthering the aims of planning as a discipline:

> It is therefore desirable that great and persistent efforts should be made to publicise the achievements of Planning. These include the following: –
>
> The establishment and maintenance of Green Belts around the great cities; the overall success of these is far greater than the detailed local failures which have sometimes occurred (Keeble, 1961a, 90–91)

In other words, Keeble hoped that the green belts would carry the cause of planning forward, being, as Desmond Heap stated in his 1955 presidential address to the Town Planning Institute, its 'very *raison d'être*'. The Town and Country Planning Association, celebrating the UK government's incorporation of the green belt into national policy, were able to pronounce that 'one great nation has officially adopted one of the major principles of the garden city idea formulated by Sir Ebenezer Howard in 1898' (Elson, 1986, 14–15). F. J. Osborn was similarly delighted by the popularity of the green belt among the public: 'The sudden almost universal acceptance of the policy of dispersal, green belts and new towns is the most heartening thing that has happened in the history of planning' (quoted in Whittick, 1987, 91). In the late 1950s, B. J. Collins writing in the *Town Planning Review* could note a number of 'healthy signs': 'The salutary cry goes up in tones of horror, "This is Green Belt." It is a cause in which each authority and numberless individuals have made sacrifices for the sake of the future, and many of them now feel deeply opposed to any compromise' (Collins, 1957).

The satisfaction that these planners derived from succeeding to get green belts designated was linked to their concerns to further the planning project. The green belt provided a useful example, for planners to show what their discipline could achieve nationally and internationally

Green Belt as a Modernist Planning Policy

The early post-WWII period also saw the green belt being employed alongside modernist planning tools. This period can be characterised as one of 'middle modernism' because planners were forced to reach compromises with both the practicalities of implementing modernist ideals and the grounding of their subject in concepts that had been inherited from the pre-WWII era (Donald, 1992).

The green belt epitomised the normative goals that had seen it heralded as a solution to London's growth during the pre-WWII period. These were mixed with elements of modernist planning, such as the application of scientific analysis and the assumption that planning was based on universal truths, to produce a policy that was ideally suited to the planning *zeitgeist* of middle modernism. The pre-WWII normative aspirations that justified the green belt and modernist planning reinforced one another. The normative goals were based on the pre-WWII ideas of the preservationists and therefore vulnerable to attack, for that reason planners found it necessary to reinforce them with 'scientific' analysis. Such analysis was also employed because it was assumed that planners would eventually be able to uncover the logic of social systems (Beauregard, 1989; Sandercock, 1998). If planning was based on universal truths then it was reasonable to assume that the green belt could be just as effectively implemented around London as any other city. Drawing in particular on Lewis Keeble's widely read work these assumptions are unpacked.

A normative policy The preservationist norms that had been associated with the implementation of the green belt during the pre-WWII period were perpetuated through Keeble's work but also through Ian Nairn and Thomas Sharp's scathing critiques of urban growth (Nairn, 1955a,b; Bruegmann, 2000). At the time, the green belt intersected with preservationist norms in three ways. Firstly the rigorous separation of 'town' and 'country' in the green belt reflected the preservationist aversion towards hybrid landscapes but also overlapped with the modernist predilection for order. The binary separation was unquestioningly reapplied not only through the green belt alone, but also through other tools such as zoning policies. Secondly, the blanket prohibition on development imposed by the green belt fitted with master plans and comprehensive planning espoused by modernist planners (Taylor, 1998, 14–17). This also overlapped with the preservationist assumption that without restraint the countryside would be overrun with development. Thirdly the green belt was meant to keep settlements small. Since the foundation of planning as a discipline a rich body of knowledge had linked the size of cities to its inhabitants' health (Donald, 1992, 427–9). This assumption led planners to justify a maximum size for cities as they thought that there was a point beyond which cities would be unmanageable or uneconomic.

In Keeble's work the role of three norms is clearly evident (Keeble, 1961b, 71–5). To justify the preservation of open countryside for example, he assumes that residents should be able to access the countryside on foot in towns but use transport in cities. For a town therefore the maximum reasonable size would be a radius of two miles (3.2 km) which at a density of 20 person per acre (0.4 hectares) would give a population of 160,000. For cities where transport is available he calculated that the maximum size should be a 16 km radius, giving a city with a maximum population of 4 million (Keeble, 1961b, 72).

Although Keeble is ready to admit that these calculations are 'naïve' and that the facts are not 'scientifically ascertainable' this does not stop him from making an argument to impose this geography of towns and cities against a background of green spaces. He does not consider the alternative that inner urban green spaces may be an adequate substitute for the open country, that a city of more than 4 million could be manageable or that cities could be polycentric and have several large centres (Bogart, 2006).

A rationally determined policy The modernist planning project entailed an assumption that planners would be able to uncover the internal logic of social systems through the application of rational analysis. In other words, a rational planning decision could be reached unproblematically through the application of a scientific method and increasingly sophisticated technology for processing and gathering data.

Lewis Keeble recognised some of the political challenges that confronted green belt planners but it was simply assumed that with enough of the right kind of rational analysis these would be overcome. In his work *Town planning at the crossroads* Keeble displays a clear awareness of the politics of establishing a green belt. He notes, that among other difficulties, planners were faced with considerable uncertainty in drawing the boundary of the green belt. On the one hand a green belt was meant to be permanent, but on the other hand planners were expected to draw it on a development plan that would guide development over a 20 year period. This left planners with the responsibility for deciding a permanent boundary for the town when it was possible that after 20 years the needs of the town would have changed (Keeble, 1961b, 68).

Despite the obvious difficulty of gathering knowledge to make a decision on the location of the green belt boundary beyond a 20-year horizon Keeble was confident that with the application of technology these problems could be solved:

> If a survey of office mobility is urgently required, so too is a survey of the suitability of every town to receive increases of population, together with an estimate of how much it could receive ... I feel confident that in this, and in other parts of the planning field, the employment of electronic computors [*sic*] suitably programmed offers a completely new opportunity for determining planning problems susceptible of specific factual solution ... (Keeble, 1961b, 69)

Keeble's confidence about the role of rational analysis makes the political invisible in the complex process of establishing a green belt. Recent historical studies have shown the importance of politics during the establishment of the green belt in the 1930s. In particular, planners struck secret bargains with landowners or opportunistically changed the function of the green belt to gain politicians' support while publicly espousing the green belt as a solution for the chronic lack of open in London's East End (Amati and Yokohari, 2004, 2007).

In the case of the green belt 'scientific', knowledge and expert judgement were used to strengthen the legitimacy of urban growth restraint and the normative assumptions that underpinned it. Planners such as Keeble expressed confidence that the complex problem of determining a city's needs well into the future would be solved through the suitable application of rationally derived knowledge. The use of this analysis also considerably hid the complex web of normative assumptions that supported the implementation of the green belt as well as the political strategies that planners and other actors used to implement it.

A universal policy   The tendency to employ rational analysis led planners to assume that the results of their work could be universally and un-problematically applied regardless of the context that determines the success of any planning policy. The green belt was particularly susceptible to this assumption because it had been held up as a successful example of planning. For example, the apparent success of the green belt around London led Japanese planners to assume that it would work as well around Tokyo, regardless of the land reform that was re-shaping Japanese society during the 1950s and 60s (Amati and Parker, 2007). Furthermore, a green belt usually affected a large number of people, so appeals to its universality would have made implementation easier.

The appeal to the advantages of the green belt facilitated its dissemination beyond the UK. Planners variously invoked the long history, and therefore, the appeal of an urban form modelled on a medieval walled city. Collins (1957) commented that the green belt was to reflect 'the universal sentiment for a country setting for a town' (see also Unwin, 1909). Patrick Abercrombie also extolled the virtues of the British way of planning. In his lecture given at the University of Melbourne he spoke of an encircling green belt as being something that 'interests all planners'. He then continued, gently admonishing Melbourne's planners for allowing 'these houses dotted about on the urban fringe of the city. I think there should be some planning powers to prevent that sort of thing from happening. We say that you should determine a certain area beyond which the town should not spread' (Abercrombie, 1948).

The green belt was invoked as a universal solution to urban growth. This was a two-way process; while British planners extolled the virtues of the green belt, planners in other countries, inspired by Abercrombie's work, implemented the green belt expecting it to be as effective as it had been for London. A famous case of this occurred in 1956 when Tokyo's City Planning Committee borrowed the UK green belt concept to contain Tokyo's urban growth (Watanabe et al., this volume; Yokohari et al., 2000; Amati and Parker, 2007). The weakness of assuming that the green belt would be a universal solution was brought into sharp focus by the widespread landowner protests that the green belt policy caused. Tsubaki (2003) describes the visit to Tokyo of William A. Robson, Professor of public administration at the London School of Economics and a leading expert on London and its governance. He was invited by Minobe Ryokichi, the left-wing Tokyo governor in 1969, to review the planning of Tama new town and was highly critical calling it 'a fundamentally misconceived project'. Robson's ideal was that of an independent new town separated by a green belt. The reality in Japan however was considerably different because of the recent land reforms, uncontrolled development and the high post-WWII demand for urban housing (Amati and Parker, 2007).[1]

Overall, therefore, while the concept was deliberately spread by British planners keen to use the green belt as a 'poster-boy' for their nascent discipline, it was also copied wholesale by some cities. The green belt also fitted with the planning philosophy of 'middle modernism' during the early post-WWII period. The period

---

1   Indeed the attempted green belt implementation in Japan may well have undermined planning as a whole by making it seem overly focused on ideals. As one senior planning officer in the Tokyo Metropolitan government remarked: 'The choice is, do you leave the families in Tokyo to rot, whilst you build an ideal new town, or do you find them somewhere reasonable to live and solve what you can at the end' (quoted in Tsubaki, 2003).

from the early 1950s to the 1970s was one in which planners were confident that political problems would be eventually overcome by the application of enough 'scientific' analysis. It was also one in which planners could assume that universal planning-related 'scientific' laws existed, they simply needed to discovered and articulated. Other aspects of modernist planning such as master planning, which provided a blueprint for the whole city, were also suited to the green belt (Taylor, 1998, 14–17). All of these factors during the 1950s helped to reinforce the green belt concept and ensure its application internationally.

Is a 'Post-modern' Green Belt Possible?

The UK-based Critiques of the Green Belt

Despite the boost that the implementation of the green belt received from the proponents of modernism, and they received from it, from the 1960s an increasing number of, mostly British studies, have questioned the usefulness of the policy. Just as the vigorous promoters of the green belt were British figures such as F.J. Osborn, Raymond Unwin and Patrick Abercrombie, the most comprehensive critiques have also been British (see Freestone, 2002, for a review of these.

A number of well-known studies can be cited, starting with Sir Peter Hall's allusion to the problems of the green belt at the end of his book *London 2000* (Hall, 1963), followed up in a comprehensive study that showed that despite the government's containment strategies development had leap-frogged the green belt and had encroached on the surrounding countryside (Hall et al., 1973). More recent works include John Herington's review of the green belt policy and a vision for its future (Herington, 1991) and the study by Sir Peter Hall and Michael Breheny pointing out the future deficit of the South-East's housing (Breheny and Hall, 1996).

The irony of planners' enthusiasm to capitalise on the popularity of the green belt during the 1950s is that currently the misguided popularity of the green belt impedes its reform. Although green belts remain popular, widespread misunderstanding prevails over their purpose. Elson (1993, 137) reporting on a survey notes that although four out of five people agree that the green belts should be protected at all costs, people gave priority to preserving the special character of the green belt and providing green space for people to enjoy over the official aims of the green belt. Such is the popularity of the green belt in England that it is impossible to have a rational debate on its reform (Kliman, 2007).

One of the most active critiques of the green belt has been the Town and Country Planning Association (TCPA), which has tirelessly campaigned to achieve a rational and humane system of town and country planning since its foundation in 1899 (Hardy,1999). The TCPA was established as the Garden City Association with the sole aim of bringing Ebenezer Howard's Garden Cities vision to life. Since the late 1960s the TCPA has been highly active in supporting or publishing studies that have sought to reform the green belt. A motivating theme of these studies has been a concern with the societal effects of the green belt. In the TCPA publication *London under stress* Thorburn (1970, 74) proposed 'breaking the green belt' as part of a range of strategies to improve the housing conditions of people living in inner areas of London. More recently, the TCPA has focused on the issue of housing affordability in the South-East and the effect that the green belt has had on house prices (Holmans, 2001; Holmans and Whitehead, 2006). These studies culminated in 2002 with the call by the TCPA for a green belt reform (Town and Country Planning Association, 2002).

The most recent and forceful criticism of the green belt has come from the UK government's 'Barker reviews'. This independent review was instigated jointly by the Treasury and the Office for the Deputy Prime Minister. The Barker reviews are significant because of the depth of their analysis and because they indicate the interest that the Treasury is taking on the impact of urban restraint on South-East's competitiveness and housing affordability (see Amati, 2007, for a review).

Broader Shifts and the Structure of this Book

As this book will show, green belts, their critics and their reform are by no means confined to the UK. Four reasons for reform can be identified, which form the themes of the book. Underlying the four themes are broader changes in planning that have occurred since the early post-WWII period when the green belt was a part of the modernist planning project. A green belt reform is a necessarily complex task that can be prompted for a large number of reasons, so many of the chapters within this book could arguably fit into other parts. For similar reasons, the structure of the book does not aim to be a comprehensive review of all the reasons for reform but is there to signpost readers towards the authors' emphasis.

Part I – The coalition of the un-willing: landowners and the green belt   Although planners in the 1950s such as Lewis Keeble relied on their position as 'experts', as the previous section has shown they were keenly aware of the need for popular support to implement their plans. There is a tension between the position of planners as 'experts', removed from the political process and able to arbitrarily make decisions, and the need for policies to attract political support. Part I explores this tension by focusing on two cases where the green belt was imposed by experts and was then fiercely resisted.

Watanabe, Amati, Endo and Yokohari first detail the various green belt schemes that were employed to control Tokyo's growth between the 1920s until the 1960s. They highlight the role that landowners played in effectively resisting the green belt and the reasons for this. The authors go on to show that the story of greenspace planning around Tokyo does not end with the demise of the green belt. They describe the nascent urban agriculture movement in Tokyo's eastern suburbs, showing how central and local governments promoted this.

Kim and Kim also highlight the role of landowners in their history of the reform of the Korean green belt. They trace the history of the policy, from its inception during the Park dictatorship of the 1970s to the various attempts by successive democratic governments to implement an effective green belt reform after 1986. They show how the green belt distorted the land market and the rights of citizens under the Park dictatorship. They show how these distortions plague current reform attempts and describe the government's reliance on environmental evaluation as a way of 'de-politicising' the reform process.

Both chapters detail resistance to the green belt and eventual reform that has been driven by a recognition of the need to appease landowners. In both cases, the constitutional guarantee of landowners' rights gave them a powerful political voice to argue for green belt abandonment.

Part II – Falling out of favour: deregulation and green belts   The emphasis on master plans and expert planners during the early post-WWII era saw a significant role for the state in planning the green belt. The shift in public attitudes towards the role of planners has dovetailed with the neo-liberal inspired strategy to deregulate planning and its apparent interference with market processes. In this part the focus of the book is on the deregulation of the planning system to describe how this affects the implementation of the green belt. In both of the following chapters the authors point to how the green belt no longer becomes viable when the planning system is deregulated and the power of regional planners is stripped away.

In their chapter on Christchurch, Miller and Amati describe how the green belt was abandoned when the Resource Management Act (RMA) was passed at the end of a wave of government deregulation in 1991. The authors also point to the role that the reorganisation of local government activity and the redefinition of regional planning played in the abandonment of the green belt. Regional planning ceased to be an attempt to manage a core urban area with its surrounding hinterland and instead came to encompass a radically wider area and remit.

In their chapter about Melbourne, Buxton and Goodman point to the influence that changes in Victoria's State government has brought to the green belt/green wedge system. They trace the historical development of the system, showing how it remained an established part of planning until the shift to a neo-liberal government in the early 1990s. While they concede that the Labor governments were as ready to re-zone areas of Melbourne's green wedges as the government of the neo-liberal premier Jeff Kennett, the authors argue that the shift in government towards the right prompted planners to view the metropolitan strategy as irrelevant, considerably undermining the green belt/green wedge system.

Both chapters show that while a shift towards a deregulated planning regime does not necessarily entail an abandonment of green belt planning, it may undermine the green belt because it prompts a redistribution of power. The main organisation which supports the green belt can be removed or altered. Deregulation may also entail a considerable reorganisation of regional planning which can substantially weaken a green belt. Power can be taken from regional planning authorities and redistributed to district or city authorities but may also end up with national or state government, or in committees.

Part III – Re-forming greenery: from green belts to green nets   As Freestone (2002) describes, planners have had a variety of different greenspace policies at their disposal throughout the twentieth century. While these planning strategies have a long history in themselves, their popularity may be due to a questioning of the importance of strictly dividing urban and rural areas. This questioning has also prompted a re-evaluation of the functions of urban fringe areas, giving rise to such concepts as Continuous Productive Urban Landscapes (Viljoen et al., 2003; Gallent et al., 2006). Linear greenspaces can be more flexibly positioned than green belts and can be used as much for enhancing an ecological network as for preventing urban development. In this part, the book's focus is on the attempts that planners' have made to complement green belts with a system of greenways, green wedges, urban growth corridors and other linear planning tools.

In her chapter on Adelaide, Garnaut describes the history of the Parklands, one of the earliest and most influential attempts to implement a green belt. She introduces the themes and issues that have affected the progress of the Parklands and refers to their various functions. She then examines schemes that attempted to reserve an unbuilt-upon zone of open space and how these shifted towards a recognition of the importance of linear greenspaces such as river corridors.

Gordon and Scott, focus on Canada's national capital, Ottawa, and how its planning evolved over the first half of the twentieth century. They describe the diverse influences on Ottawa's planning including that of Abercrombie's *Greater London Plan 1944*. They then describe how the Ottawa green belt evolved from an urban containment measure to an open space and ecological feature of a regional plan. Finally, they present some lessons from Canada's half century of experience with green belt proposals for its national capital.

Bassok examines the growth policies around Washington State's Puget Sound area arguing that collectively they represent an alternative to a green belt. He describes the different policies whose overall aim is to preserve farmland that include the transfer of development rights, land trusts and urban growth boundaries that work together, forming a green belt overall. He then shows how the *Mountains to Sound Greenway* complements and intersects with these policies, arguing that the greenway prevents sprawl along the I-90 corridor but also has a heritage function by linking and preserving the identity of small towns.

Part IV — Works in progress: patching together a flexible green belt   Although the London green belt was held up as a paragon of modernist planning during the post-WWII period, its 1930s variant was far from ideal. It was patched together in a series of deals through the commitment of a broad range of activists, planners, landowners and councillors to the green belt as a cause. The first green belt was an assembly of former aristocratic estates, farms, airfields, commons and golf courses; a policy that was directed more through opportunity than grand-designs (Amati and Yokohari, 2007). Today's London green belt can also be seen as a patchwork of different policies (Amati and Yokohari, 2006). It is possible to imagine that the modernist 'blanket' green belt was a brief interlude in history. If a green belt were imposed today planners would not expect it to be the uniform or blanket restriction that their modernist predecessors favoured. Even Abercrombie never saw the green belt to be as permanent or inflexible as it has been during the last fifty years (Hall, 1995). In this part the authors present other examples of green belts that control urban growth flexibly and using a variety of policies.

Each chapter describes several cases of urban growth management where the green belt has been conceived as a patchwork of different spaces and may be softened in the face of changing demands for development. This approach may not concur with the ideal of a blanket control over development, but instead reflects the shifting political compromises that planners must reach in a world where bottom-up, rather than top-down policies are more likely to succeed.

Breiling and Ruland examine the case of the green belt around Vienna. They detail its implementation at the end of the nineteenth century and how it was based around the battle to preserve a nearby area of woodland. They show how the core area of green belt was gradually added to, with the green belt currently comprising a variety of different elements that range from the urban *kleingärten* to outlying areas of wetlands, woodland and meadows. This varied landscape is also reflected in the variety of, often overlapping, uses of Vienna's green belt. These include organic and small-scale to industrial-scale agriculture, areas for leisure, landscape preservation, tourism and ecology, which all enjoy different levels of protection. Finally, the authors introduce the role of international links in protecting the green belt, either through organisations such as UNESCO or through EU-level cooperation.

Like Vienna, Berlin's green belt also traces its origins to the end of the nineteenth century and currently consists of a patchwork of different spaces. In their chapter, Kühn and Gailing describe how planners who supported either the green belt or the radial models of development vied to have their plans implemented during the twentieth century. Berlin's urban growth was effectively restrained from 1961 to 1990 by the Berlin wall in the West and by a highly regulatory socialist planning regime in the East. The city therefore has a large amount of open space and a compact urban centre. To maintain this form, the State of Brandenburg has opted for a green belt but, as Kühn and Gailing note, this will consist of a mosaic of regional parks which do not have statutory force and rely on the local government to implement them. The results are by no means uniform but the regional parks have achieved some success in including citizens in a variety of tourism, recreational and ecological projects.

Senes, Toccolini, Ferrario, Lafortezza and Dal Sasso also pick up on the theme of regional parks in their chapter on Italy. They first trace the development of greenspace ideas in Italy and then describe the results of a study to show the effect of the *South Milan Agricultural Park*. The Park is as they describe an indirect measure and the municipalities have a certain amount of discretion to ignore it when defining planning schemes. Their study evaluates the effectiveness of a discretionary or flexible green belt which is promoted under the general discourse of agricultural protection. Despite this flexibility the authors argue that the Park is currently an effective instrument for growth control although several decades have to pass before its effects can be properly evaluated.

Finally, Laruelle and Legenne pick up on the theme of patches and a discretionary or flexible green belt in their study of the Ile-de-France green belt around Paris. They highlight the variety of landscapes that constitute the green belt, the long history of the project and the variety of tools that the regional council has to control growth. They conclude by describing the variety of linear and circular elements that currently make up the green belt around Paris.

The book shows that green belt reforms are occurring globally. It also shows that planners will continue to seek ways to control urban growth and preserve greenspaces, and displays the rich variety of tools and methods that they are developing to achieve their aims.

Overall, the chapters show that green belt concept has adapted despite the changes that have taken place in planning since the policy's hey-day of the 1950s. The chapters make it possible to argue that the green belt is still a relevant planning policy for the twenty first century, albeit as a drastically different flexible growth management tool that recognises a variety of interests.

References

Abercrombie, L.P. (1945), *Greater London Plan, 1944* (London: HMSO).

—— (1948), 'A great city', A lecture given at Wilson Hall, The University of Melbourne.

—— (1959), *Town and Country Planning* (Oxford University Press).

Amati, M. (2006), 'Ascribing changing values to suburban greenspaces: the inception of Wellington's green belt', in C. Garnaut and K. Round (eds.), 'The Adelaide Parklands Symposium. A Balancing Act: Past-Present-Future', Centre for Settlement Studies and the Bob Hawke Prime Ministerial Centre (Adelaide: University of South Australia), pp. 1–12.

—— (2007), 'From a blanket to a patchwork: The practicalities of reforming the London green belt', *Journal of Environmental Planning and Management*, 50(5), 579–94.

Amati, M. and Parker, G. (2007), 'Planned by farmers for farmers? Twentieth century land reform and the impact on twenty-first century Japan', in C. Miller and M.M. Roche (eds.), 'Past Matters: Heritage and Planning History Case Studies from the Pacific Rim', (London: Cambridge Scholars Press), pp. 172–94.

Amati, M. and Yokohari, M. (2004), 'The actions of landowner, government and planners in establishing the London green belt of the 1930s', *Planning History*, 24(1–2), 4–12.

—— (2006), 'Temporal changes and local variations in the functions of London's green belt', *Landscape and Urban Planning*, 75(1–2), 125–42.

—— (2007), 'The establishment of the London green belt: reaching consensus over purchasing land', *Journal of Planning History*, 6(4), 311–37.

Anan'ich, B. and Kobak, A. (2006), 'St Petersburg and green space, 1850–2000: an introduction', in P. Clarke (ed.), 'The European City and Green Space', (Aldershot: Ashgate), pp. 247–71.

Arnold, J.L. (1971), *The new deal in the suburbs: a history of the greenbelt towns* (Columbus: Ohio State University Press).

Beaufoy, H. (1997), '"Order out of chaos": the London Society and the planning of London 1912–1920', *Planning Perspectives*, 12, 135–64.

Beauregard, R.A. (1989), 'Between modernity and postmodernity: the ambiguous position of U.S. planning', *Environment and Planning D: Society and Space*, 7, 381–95.

Bogart, W.T. (2006), *Don't call it sprawl: Metropolitan Structure in the Twenty-First Century* (Cambridge University Press).

Breheny, M. and Hall, P. (1996), *The people – where will they go?* (London: TCPA).

Bruegmann, R. (2000), 'The Paradoxes of Urban Sprawl Reform', in R. Freestone (ed.), 'Urban Planning in a Changing World: The Twentieth Century Experience', (London: E & FN Spon), pp. 158–74.

Cherry, G. and Rogers, A. (1996), *Rural change and planning* (London: E & FN Spon).

Collins, B.J. (1957), 'A talk on green belts', *Town Planning Review*, 219–30.

Donald, J. (1992), 'Metropolis: the city as text', in R. Bocock and K. Thompson (eds.), 'Social and cultural forms of modernity', (London: Polity Press in Association with the Open University), pp. 417–71.

Elson, M.J. (1986), *Green Belts: Conflict Mediation in the Urban Fringe* (London: Heinemann).

—— (1993), *The effectiveness of green belts* (London: HMSO).

Evans, A.W. (2003), 'Shouting very loudly', *Town Planning Review*, 74(2), 195–212.

Forshaw, J.H. and Abercrombie, L.P. (1943), *County of London Plan* (London: HMSO).

Freestone, R. (1992), 'Sydney's green belt 1945–1960: stop laughing this is serious', *Australian Planning*, 70–77.

—— (2002), 'Greenbelts in City and Regional Planning', in K. Parsons and D. Schuyler (eds.), 'From Garden City to Green City: The Legacy of Ebenezer Howard', (Baltimore: John Hopkins), pp. 67–98.

Gallent, N., Andersson, J., and Bianconi, M. (2006), *Planning on the Edge* (London: Routledge).

Gallent, N. and Shaw, D. (2007), 'Spatial planning, area action plans and the rural-urban fringe', *Journal of Environmental Planning and Management*, 50(5), 617–39.

Garside, P.L. (2006), 'Politics, ideology and the issue of open space in London, 1939–2000', in P. Clarke (ed.), 'The European City and Green Space', (Aldershot: Ashgate), pp. 68–99.

Gault, I. (1981), 'Green Belts and the development plan system', in 'Green Belt Policies in Development Plans', (Oxford: Oxford Polytechnic Dept. of Town Planning, Working Paper Series), vol. 41, pp. 1–17.

Gunn, S.C. (2007), 'Green belts: a review of the region's responses to a changing housing agenda', *Journal of Environmental Planning and Management*, 50(5), 595–617.

Hall, P. (1963), *London 2000* (London: Faber).

—— (1995), 'Bringing Abercrombie back from the shades: A look forward and back', *Town Planning Review*, 66(3), 227–42.

—— (2007), 'Rethinking the mark three green belt', *Town and Country Planning*, 76(8), 229–31.

Hall, P., Gracey, H., Drewett, R., and Thomas, R. (1973), *The containment of urban England*, vol. Two (London: George Allen and Unwin).

Hardy, D. (1999), '1899–1999: The TCPA's first hundred years, and the next ...', Town and Country Planning Association, London.

Healey, P. (1997), *Collaborative planning: shaping places in fragmented societies* (London: Palgrave).

Herington, J. (1991), *Beyond green belts: Managing Urban Growth in the 21st Century, Report for the Regional Studies Association* (London: Jessica Kingsley).

Holmans, A. (2001), *Home Truths: Easing the Shortage of Housing* (London: TCPA).

Holmans, A. and Whitehead, C. (2006), *More households to be housed*, Tomorrow discussion paper (London: TCPA).

Howard, E. (1898), *To-morrow: a peaceful path to real reform* (London: Swann Sonnenschein).

Keeble, L. (1961a), *Principles and practice of town and country planning* (London: Estates Gazette).

—— (1961b), *Town planning at the crossroads* (London: Estates Gazette).

Kliman, A. (2007), 'Political language and the debate around the green belt', *Royal Town Planning Institute News*, [available online].

Lloyd, M.G. and Peel, D. (2007), 'Green belts in Scotland: towards the modernisation of a traditional concept?', *Journal of Environmental Planning and Management*, 50(5), 639–57.

Low Choy, D.C. and Gleeson, J. (1998), 'A Green Belt Too Far: The Abortive Green Belt Proposals of the 1944 Brisbane Draft Town Plan', 8th International Planning History Conference, Sydney 15–18th July.

Matless, D. (1998), *Landscape and Englishness* (London: Reaktion Books).

Miller, M. (1991), *Raymond Unwin: Garden Cities and Town Planning* (Leicester: Leicester University Press).

Ministry of Housing and Local Government (1955), *Green belts* (London: HMSO).

Nairn, I. (1955a), 'Outrage', *Architectural Review*, 702.

—— (1955b), 'Outrage', *Architectural Review*, 719.

Parker, G. (2006), 'The Country Code and the ordering of countryside citizenship', *Journal of Rural Studies*, 22(1), 1–16.

Reeder, D.A. (2006), 'The social construction of green space in London prior to the Second World War', in P. Clarke (ed.), 'The European City and Green Space', (Aldershot: Ashgate), pp. 41–68.

Sandercock, L. (1998), *Towards cosmopolis* (Chichester: John Wiley).

Sheail, J. (1981), *Rural conservation in inter-war Britain* (Oxford: Clarendon Press).

Tang, B.S., Wong, S.W., and Lee, A.K.W. (2007), 'Green belt in a compact city: A zone for conservation or transition?', *Landscape and Urban Planning*, 79(3–4), 358–73.

Taylor, N.M. (1998), *Urban planning theory since 1945* (Thousand Oaks, California: Sage).

Thomas, D. (1963), 'London's Green Belt: The Evolution of an Idea', *The Geographical Journal*, 129(1), 14–24.

Thorburn, A. (1970), 'A strategy for London', in 'London under stress', (TCPA), pp. 64–80.

Town and Country Planning Association (2002), *Green belt – TCPA policy statement* (London: TCPA).

Tsubaki, T. (2003), 'Anglo-Japanese exchanges in town planning: the case of Tama new town in the 1960s, and William A. Robson', *Planning History*, 25(1), 4–15.

Unwin, R. (1909), *Town Planning in practice* (London: T. Fisher Unwin).

Viljoen, A., Bohn, K., and Howe, J. (2003), *Continuous productive urban landscapes: designing urban agriculture for sustainable cities* (Oxford: Architectural Press).

Ward, S.V. (2000), 'Re-examining the international diffusion of planning', in R. Freestone (ed.), 'Urban planning in a changing world: the twentieth century experience', (London: E & FN Spon), pp. 39–60.

—— (2002), *Planning the Twentieth Century City* (New York: John Wiley & Sons).

Whittick, A. (1987), *F. J. O. – practical idealist: a biography of Sir Frederic Osborn* (London: Town and Country Planning Association).

Yokohari, M., Takeuchi, K., Watanabe, T., and Yokota, S. (2000), 'Beyond greenbelts and zoning: A new planning concept for the environment of Asian mega-cities', *Landscape and Urban Planning*, 47(3–4), 159–71.

PART I
THE COALITION OF THE
UN-WILLING: LANDOWNERS
AND THE GREEN BELT

CHAPTER 2

The Abandonement of Tokyo's Green Belt and the Search for a New Discourse of Preservation in Tokyo's Suburbs

Takashi Watanabe, Marco Amati, Kenya Endo and Makoto Yokohari

Introduction

The implementation of Tokyo's green belt is a famous case of an attempt to impose an international planning ideal on a reluctant society. A green belt for Tokyo was proposed as early as 1927 and drew its inspiration from international planning movements. Post-WWII attempts to impose the policy foundered however, first in 1946 and then again in 1956 in the face of huge urbanisation pressures and fierce opposition from landowners and most municipalities surrounding Tokyo. Of the original area that was designated for preservation only a few parks and areas of greenspace survive undeveloped, such as Mizumoto park, located about 10 kms from the centre of Tokyo (Figure 2.1).

Despite the significant amount of scholarly attention that this history has received (for example, Sorensen, 2001b, 2002, 188), its framing within a discourse of success and failure make it easy to simplify the motives and actions of the different actors. Researchers such as Hebbert (1991, 1986) and Sorensen (2001a), when describing the unequal contest between Japanese planners and post-WWII urban growth assume that the municipalities around Tokyo entirely supported landowners' protests to dismantle the green belt. A recent study of urban agriculture in Tokyo showed that these same municipalities actively support urban agriculture programs by leasing land to community groups, supporting volunteer programs and employing agricultural advisers (Yokohari et al., 2008). Since when have the municipalities' supported agriculture and how can this be reconciled with their apparent enthusiasm for abandoning the green belt?

The aim of this chapter is to look beyond the 'failure' of the Tokyo green belt to frame its abandonment as part of a re-discovery of land-use patterns that traditionally dominated Tokyo's fringes. In examining the struggle to preserve the green belt around Tokyo our objective is to recast the policy's abandonment as a continual process of evolving Japanese urban planning tools that are suited to traditional patterns of land ownership and use (Yokohari et al., 2000). While the preservation of greenspace in Japan remains a significant challenge for planners we argue that it has

水元緑地
Mizumoto

特別都市計画緑地地域
河川
鉄道
復興計画公園
復興計画緑地

Figure 2.1: The Tokyo green belt as planned in 1946 and the location of Mizumoto Park

been considerably aided by a recent discourse of urban agriculture, which was elaborated by the same municipalities that abetted the abandonment of the green belt.

We first describe the overall development of planning measures to protect greenspace around Tokyo from the inception of the Tokyo green belt in the 1920s, to the enactment of the Productive Open Spaces Act (1974). Second, we focus on the policies of the municipal government of Ichikawa city, which adjoins Tokyo to the east in the state of Chiba, between 1958 and 1968. We show that the municipality saw the weakening of the green belt as an opportunity for further development, but at the same time assiduously promoted horticulture allowing significant areas of greenspace to be preserved. Thirdly, we show how the adjacent ward of Edogawa-ku, also promoted horticulture to enable signficant areas of greenspace to be preserved close to the city. Finally, we conclude by arguing that the 'failure' of the Tokyo green belt paved the way for a revival of urban agriculture.

Tokyo's Green Belt: From Urban Restraint to Urban Agriculture

Pre-WWII Green Belt Attempts

The concept of a green belt was introduced to Japanese planners via the 1924 Amsterdam International City Planning Conference, which was characterised by an adherence to the importance of regional planning (Bosma, 1990). Regional planning was to enable the decentralisation of cities and was to be justified according to the public interest, casting the planner in the role of a harmoniser of interests. The conference had a profound impact on Japanese planners who came away with seven commitments to modern planning that were subsequently highly in uential in Japan (Ishida, 1987). These were: to stop the never-ending expansion of major cities; to employ satellite cities to decentralise the population; to surround urban areas with green belts; to carefully plan vehicle traffic to avoid congestion; to employ regional planning; to employ exibility in regional planning and finally to control land use. These principles reflected Garden City movement ideals and related ideas coming from the UK, Germany and the US.

A participant at the conference, Inuma Kazumi then introduced these seven principles to a wider audience through the book *City planning: theory and administration* published in 1927 (Inuma, 1927). This work emphasized the necessity of preserving agricultural land within a framework of open space conservation. Inuma proposed a regulatory 'regional agricultural system' for guaranteeing the preservation of open spaces in 1931, emphasising the important role of urban farmland and the need to preserve farmland in general, however the plan did not include any scheme for compensating landowners (Inuma, 1931b,a). The Tokyo Green Space Plan published in April 1939 was influenced by these ideas. The plan included the Tokyo metropolitan area, and the surrounding provinces of Saitama-ken, Chiba-ken and Kanagawa-ken. It was ambitious, aiming to purchase and preserve in addition to the 1–3 km wide green belt around Tokyo, 289,143 ha of 'Scenic parks' (*Keishōchi*); 3,882 km of parkways (*Kōraku doro*); 1,695 ha of urban parks (*Dai kōen*) and 647 ha of inner-city 'pocket parks'. Furthermore, the plan classified agricultural land in the urban area as 'productive green spaces' and 'ordinary agricultural land' aiming to preserve the former (Ishida, 1987). A purchasing scheme was clearly preferable to Inuma's earlier 'regional agriculture system' which would have severely infringed land ownership rights and was never implemented during or after the War.

The Japanese government fell under the increasing control of the military during the 1930s. This trend permeated many aspects of Japanese society including green belt planning. The Air Defence Law (1937) mandated an Air Defence Belt around Tokyo which preserved land in an open condition to enable to construction of gun emplacements and airfields (Figure 2.2). The Law was amended in 1941, with areas to be conserved subsequently designated in March 1943. Ironically, the restrictions on the private rights of landowners that this law introduced were analogous to the restrictions contained in Inuma's pre-WWII 'regional agricultural system'. However,

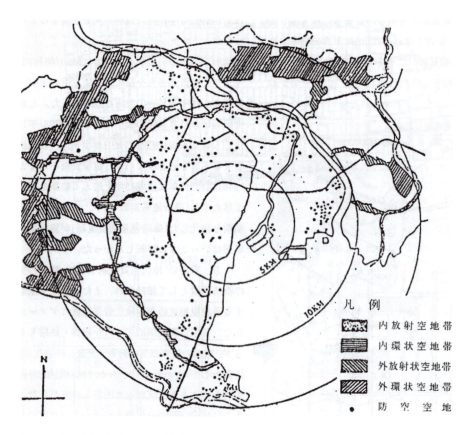

凡　例

▨	内 放 射 空 地 帯
▤	内 環 状 空 地 帯
▨	外 放 射 状 空 地 帯
▨	外 環 状 空 地 帯
●	防 空 空 地

Figure 2.2: The Tokyo Air Defence Plan (1937)

the designated areas were for military rather than agricultural use and the restrictions were based on the need to control land-use during wartime.

Post-WWII Green Belt Attempts

In the immediate post-WWII period, Article 3 of the Special City Planning Act (*Tokubetsu Toshi Keikaku Hō*) of 1946 represented the first enacted law to create a system for preserving regional green spaces in Japan. The Act was influenced by the 1939 green space plan and zoned large areas of land for green spaces, residential and industrial areas but without granting any of the necessary powers to guide development or enforce standards (Sorensen, 2002, 164). The Act left development largely at the discretion of the landowners and permitted a number of developments in the green belt (for example, shrines and hospitals), which caused this area to quickly turn into a low-density suburb.

The discussions of Tokyo's regional planning committee demonstrate that inside the city's 23 wards, the problems of planning the green belt were compounded by pressure from other powerful groups. The regional planning committee was set-up in January 1947 and met for one year and 3 months in order to designate green belt land. During this time, the committee had to contend with a group composed of mainly large landowners that did not wish to relinquish control of their land because they were developing through land re-adjustment schemes. The committee was also pressured by a group composed of smallholders and other landowners who simply wished to have their land released for development and were actively pursuing their aims through agricultural associations.

As well as suffering from weak regulations, the green belts also failed to attract support from other sections of the government. For example, despite the green belt's aim of conserving agricultural land, it was excluded from the Agriculture Ministry's plans to promote agriculture. Similarly, the green belt was not mentioned in the plans to prevent war and disaster damage in Tokyo and 10 other cities. Finally, and fundamentally, the restrictions that the 1946 Act attempted to impose were a reminder of the restrictions in the military government's 1937 Air Defence Law. Any demand that planners made to strengthen the law would have conflicted with the Allied Occupation's aims to purge the government of the pre-WWII systems of government. The law may have also fallen foul of article 27 in the Meiji constitution and the soon to be confirmed 1947 constitutional clause on private property rights (Amati and Parker, 2007).

As a result of the weakness of the Act the area of green belt was reduced by 30% from 14,015.7 ha to 9,870.8 ha between 1948 and 1955, (Ebato, 1987). In 1954 after the end of the post-WWII reconstruction period, the 1946 Act was repealed and with it the main bulwark to support regional green space planning.

The second attempt to impose a green belt around Tokyo was through the National Capital Sphere Redevelopment Act (NCSRA) (1956). Figure 2.3 shows the extensive area of green belt that the Act aimed to preserve. The purpose of the Act was to designate a series of belts around Tokyo; including one that would protect the most productive agricultural land from development. The plan also laid down provisions for permitting the location of a series of New Towns around Tokyo. The planned area occupied a 160 km circumference from the centre of Tokyo. The aspiration was for this to be enforced before 1975 (Miyamoto, 1995).

However, this plan was never realized for which a number of reasons can be cited (Narito et al., 2000). Firstly, the plan for the suburban belt did not provide any system for compensating landowners. Because of this, the suburban belt's restrictions on development met with fierce opposition from farmers and municipalities neighbouring Tokyo. Following the enforcement of the NCSRA, shortly before November 1956 the 16 towns and villages within the 3 main districts of Tama region – West of Tokyo – formed an association to oppose the creation of the suburban belt. Meeting in Hibiya park's open-air auditorium in the centre of Tokyo, they staged a number of demonstrations which they used to effectively gain publicity and prevent the suburban belt being put into place. Secondly, a number of farmers in suburban

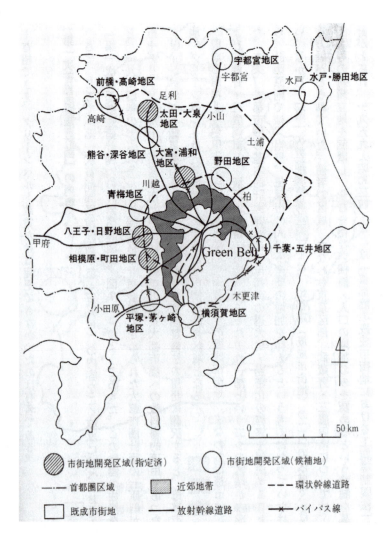

Figure 2.3: The 1956 plan that resulted from the NCSRA

areas managed to obtain terms that allowed them to develop 20–30% of their holdings, so that the suburban belt became systematically dotted with residential development. Finally, the lack of support from central government was also an important factor. At the time, the central government's policy was to obtain agglomeration economies by supporting growth in Tokyo. As Tsubaki (2003) notes, the New Residential Town Development Act (1963) sponsored by the Ministry of Construction had the explicit aim of developing New Towns. As a result of this legislation Tama New Town was built in the green belt dealing the concept a final blow. The green belt was omitted in a revision of the NCSRA in 1965 and replaced by a 'suburban infrastructure belt' that included both land for development and conservation. Although the regulations relating to the Tokyo green belt were not officially repealed until the passing of the 1968 New City Planning Law, in practice the preserved areas had been extensively, if illegally, built upon well before this.

The 1968 New City Planning Law and the Productive Open Spaces Act

As the attempts to control urban growth faltered and an increasing realisation grew of the problems associated with sprawl, the Ministry of Construction established a new way to control urban growth through a zoning system that was part of the New City Planning Law (*Shin Toshi Keikaku Hō*) of 1968. The centrepiece of this law was the definition of two zones, an Urban Promotion Area (UPA) and an Urban Control Area (UCA). In principle the system aimed to draw a line between rural and urban areas aiming to achieve complete urbanisation in the UPA within ten years and the preservation of open space in the UCA. In practice however, the system failed to meet planners' expectations. A long list of public development projects and developments of less than 1 hectare were exempt from control in the UCA. In the UPA land remained undeveloped after 10 years because of farmers' reluctance to sell land and cease farming. This reluctance was partly a result of the favourable tax rates on agricultural land, which were 1–2% of the tax rate for residential areas even in built areas of the UPA (Sorensen, 2002, 234).

As it became clear that the UPAs were not going to be urbanised because of the tax system, the government responded by introducing the Productive Open Spaces Act (*Seisan ryokuchi hō*) in 1974. In contrast to the New City Planning Law (1968) the aim of the Productive Open Spaces Act was to preserve the existing agricultural land within the UPA as long as farmers were still willing to farm it.

The Act aimed to conserve farmland plots in two classes. The first class were plots of over 10,000 square meters. The second class were those of more than 2,000 square meters. The total area of farmland designated by 1974 Act by 1977 was 358.7 ha with first class Productive Open Space comprising 264.1 ha and second class Productive Open Space comprising 94.6 ha (Hatsuhachi, 1995). While the Act allowed farmland to be taxed at the much lower agricultural rate, the owners of each plot had to agree to continue farming the land for thirty years. If they retired or died without an heir to take over, the municipality had to find a purchaser for the land. If the municipality did not succeed in finding a purchaser to farm the land then they had to purchase it themselves.

The Act was intended to be a brake on speculative investment in farmland purchases. By reducing the tax rate for active farmers only it contributed to a fairer tax rate on land that was not farmed in urban areas because this land would eventually be taxed at residential rates or owned by the municipality. The Act was also a recognition of the value of having farmland in urban areas.

At first, the Productive Open Spaces Act failed to be effective because it was ignored by farmers. The Act did not include agricultural production as an aim and a number of local municipalities already had schemes to conserve farmland that were easier to join (Nagashima, 1976). Local municipalities had already established these schemes because they wanted to promote urban agriculture and avoid the escalating costs of urban development.[1]

The minimum size for including farmland as productive open space was later dropped in a 1991 amendment to the Act to 500 square metres. From the amendment onwards, the area of land protected by the Act steadily increased. Although the Act can be regarded as a success from this point of view, it has created a number of problems. Firstly, land that has been designated as productive open space adjoins land which is not. This means that the productivity of designated plots can be negatively influenced by its proximity to non-productive land. Secondly, even though they are obliged to purchase the land by law, municipalities may not have the funds to purchase land which is likely to be expensive because many sites are located within the urban area.

Overall, this brief sketch of Japanese land use planning history around Tokyo between 1927 and 1974 has highlighted a number of trends. Firstly, while the power to implement the green belt fluctuated between the extremes of oppression under the military government and discretion given to landowners under the 1946 Special City Planning Act, a recurring theme was that of farmland preservation. Secondly, the need to restrain urban growth in Tokyo found little favour among landowners, as shown by their fierce political opposition to the green belt. Thirdly, although the NCSRA (1956) was a failure in green belt terms, it also marked a first step on a new path for Japanese planning towards the promotion of urban agriculture, which was given further support through the Productive Open Spaces Act (1974).

As we describe below, the concern for enhancing and preserving urban agriculture in the face of intense urbanisation pressure was shared by the municipalities of Edogawa-ku and Ichikawa city. As the following case studies show both of these municipalities were active in promoting urban agriculture.

The Development of an Urban Agriculture Program at the Municipal Level

Both Ichikawa city and Edogawa-ku are located to the east of Tokyo's central core (Figure 2.4). The two areas are separated by the Edogawa river and slope down towards the sea at Tokyo Bay's northern end. Open spaces in Ichikawa city were covered by the 1956 green belt, while those in Edogawa-ku were not. Both areas were selected for this study because they underwent intense urban development pressure during the 1960s, 1970s and 1980s and because they demonstrate how municipalities responded to national legislation to preserve farmland.

---

1   The Ministry of Construction formalised these local level initiatives in 1983 by establishing new institutions for ensuring the long-term continuation of agriculture, the *Chōkei nōkeizoku nōchiseido*.

Figure 2.4: Location of both study areas, Edogawa-ku and Ichikawa city

Ichigawa City and the Preservation of Pear Orchards

The following describes a recent investigation by one of this chapter's authors to examine the effect of Ichikawa city's policies on land-use and its response to the NCSRA's encouragement of urban agriculture (Endo, 2006).

Ichikawa city can be broadly divided into northern and southern halves. The land to the south adjoins Tokyo Bay, is lower lying and enjoys a higher rate of rainfall than the northern half. The area was traditionally dominated by rice paddy fields. The land to the north is drier and includes a higher proportion of dry fields and woodland. Ichikawa city's response to the NCSRA (1956) was interpreted using policy documents and the minutes of the municipal council meetings. The results from this archival research were supplemented by an analysis of the land-use in the municipality derived from 1/25,000 scale Geographical Survey Institute maps for 1960, 1970 and 1980.

The policy documents and minutes of council meetings show that apart from the reclaimed and shoreline areas to the south, the municipality on the whole encouraged the preservation of productive farmland. The council attempted to control, for example, the fragmentation of land ownership in the face of steep land price rises and implemented agricultural improvement projects. Although farmland was important for the municipality, as the attempt to enforce the green belt through the NCSRA faltered, the municipality channelled development towards the extensive areas of paddy fields to the south of the municipality. These areas also came under increasing development pressure through the 1960s, 1970s and 1980s because of their proximity to the zone of industry on the shoreline and the extension of a subway line into the area.

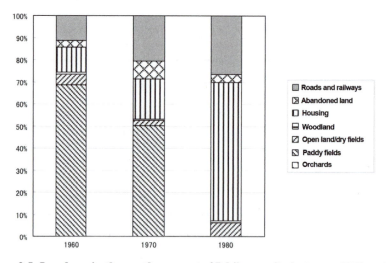

Figure 2.5: Land use in the southern part of Ichikawa city between 1960 and 1980

Source: Endo (2006)

The southern half of Ichikawa city   As Figure 2.5 shows, during the 1960s the extent of paddy fields in the southern portion of the municipality dropped by 35% as land use for roads and other infrastructure increased. By the 1980s the amount of agricultural land had almost disappeared. The reason for the shift of land use from paddy field into infrastructure during the 1960s is because of the reform of the NCSRA and the encouragement it gave to land readjustment projects. Through the 1970s, with the NCSRA removed and with it a significant bulwark to prevent the development of agricultural land, urban development increased. The results show that agriculture was comparatively weak in the face of urbanisation in the southern half of the municipality. Although some attempt was made by farmers to grow more intensive alternatives to rice such as lotus root, these were later abandoned. Clearly topology had a role to play in discouraging farmers as water-related problems, especially floods and salt water infiltration were endemic to the southern half. This picture of agricultural decline in the southern half is opposite for agriculture in the northern half.

The northern half of Ichikawa city   As Figure 2.6 shows, between 1960 and 1970 the area of orchards in the northern half of the municipality doubled. The dominant fruit grown in these orchards was nashi or Japanese pear, a crop that was actively promoted by the municipality. Nashi were grown on former dry fields and some woodland areas. Figure 2.6 also shows that between 1960 and 1970 the rate of urbanisation in the northern half of the municipality was higher than in the southern half but then stabilised during the 1970s.

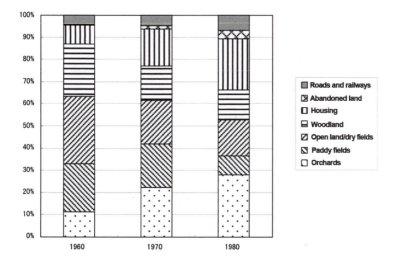

Figure 2.6: Land use in the northern part of Ichikawa city between 1960 and 1980

Source: Endo (2006)

Ichikawa city was ideally suited for growing nashi. The city is located close to Tokyo which ensures a high price for the crop. In addition, the area around the city was once famous for producing the fruit. The results show that the municipality actively funnelled development to the south while encouraging the development of nashi orchards to maintain the viability of farming in the north. The increase in the amount of nashi grown in the suburbs is unusual as most suburbs around Tokyo saw a reduction in the overall farmland use at this time.

Edogawa-ku's Promotion of Komatsuna

During the early 1970s the Agricultural section of the Edogawa-ku municipal offices struggled to prevent a collapse of agriculture in the area. Municipalities on the edge of Tokyo included *Nōgyō shinkō-ka* or Agricultural Sections that dealt with agricultural matters as well as *Toshikeikaku-ka* or Urban Planning Sections that would encourage development and the adherence to the Ministry of Construction's UPA policy. The early post-WWII period saw a steep decline in the number of farmers and the area of cultivated land in and around urban areas. In Edogawa-ku, paddy fields within the UPA were coming under increasing pressure for development, meaning that rice cultivation, always a crop with a marginal profit, was no longer viable.

Figure 2.7 shows the area of paddy field and dry fields in Edogawa-ku. While the paddy and dry field areas both declined during this time, the paddy field area dropped

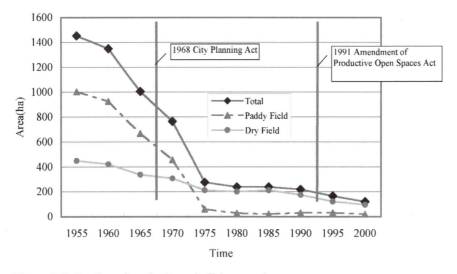

Figure 2.7: Decline of agriculture in Edogawa-ku

Source: Endo (2006)

at a higher rate than the dry field areas. Figure 2.7 also shows that the dry field area stabilised between 1975 and 1990. The reason for this stabilisation is because of the municipality's support for a particular crop that helped to maintain agricultural viability in the area as well as the shift by farmers towards more intensive forms of agriculture.

As Edo (the pre-1868 name for Tokyo) expanded in size and importance during the seventeenth century the marginal, low-lying sand dune areas near the Edogawa river came to be seen as ideal for growing a broadleaved variety of rape, which closely resembles spinach in appearance (*Brassica rapa*). The crop, which came to be known as *komatsuna* after the area of Komatsu in which it was grown, was perishable and could be easily grown and then transported to the markets in the centre of the city nearby.

By the late 1960s the cultivation of komatsuna in Edogawa-ku had all but disappeared, but by the 1970s it enjoyed a revival thanks to a combination of factors. The agricultural section of the municipality realised that the initial UPA classification was unlikely to meet its target of complete urbanisation within 10 years and began to think of ways of using the open space. During the 1970s, as rice farming was abandoned, a number of farmers converted former paddy fields into fields for growing horticultural crops such as a komatsuna and edible chrysanthemums (*shun giku*). So as to help these farmers, the municipality initiated a farmers' support project to install facilities and infrastructure. The project also gave grants to assist in controlling pests.

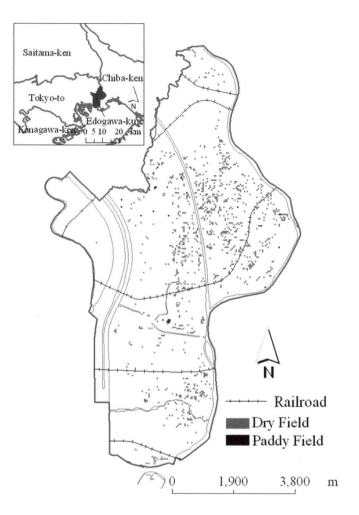

Figure 2.8: Current dry fields in Edogawa-ku

Figure 2.8 shows the result of this shift towards dry field agriculture. Very few areas of paddy field are left and the landscape of Edogawa-ku is dominated by dry fields.

The farms that were supported by the municipality were eventually protected by the Productive Open Space Act (1974). Even when the law was in place the municipality continued it efforts to preserve agricultural land by highlighting the value of komatsuna to local residents. It held festivals and fairs to promote the crop. So as to help urban residents understand farmwork and how food is produced the municipality involved the local community during harvest time.

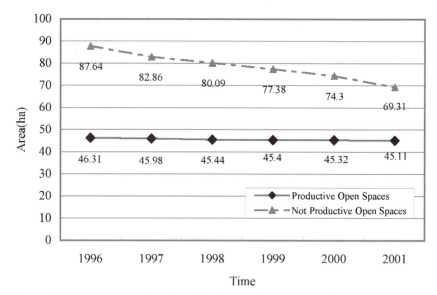

Figure 2.9: The preservation of productive and non-productive farmland as defined by the Productive Open Spaces Act (1992)

Source: Edogawa-ku Municipal Offices

Figure 2.9 shows the final result of the Productive Open Spaces Act on agriculture in Edogawa-ku. Between 1996 and 2001 the amount of land classified as productive open space hardly changed while the land farmed as non-productive land continued a decline which may be expected for agriculture in a densely urbanised area.

Conclusion

Although the Tokyo green belt is cited as a planning failure with the forces of development and preservation clearly divided this chapter has argued for a more nuanced view. In particular we show that the municipalities of Edogawa-ku and Ichikawa city resisted the green belt but also promoted the preservation of land through urban agriculture. We describe the abandonment of the green belt until the late 1960s and show that the preservation of agriculture remained a constant, although occasionally secondary, priority.

The abandonment of the green belt around Tokyo paved the way for a different approach to preserving land. Central to this, was a realisation of the value of agriculture both in an economic and a cultural sense. As the preservation of agriculture became the dominant theme during the 1970s, the type of produce became an important part of the region's identity as it was swallowed up in a wave of development. Our findings show that this realisation was acted upon at both central and local government levels.

The results also suggest that encouraging the abandonment of the green belt and supporting agriculture go hand in hand when landowners and especially farmers have a significant political voice. This would partly explain why the municipalities supported the dismantling of the green belt while then going on to support the maintenance of agriculture, although, it is tempting to suppose that the rigourous separation of farmland and urban areas as well as the permanence of a green belt made the concept appear too alien to be acceptable. Clearly a new rationale and consensus had to be found first as a way of preventing development. While the concept of the green belt may not have gained popularity in Japan, the echoing of traditional forms of agriculture through a program of urban agriculture can be seen as one way to preserve green spaces.

References

Amati, M. and Parker, G. (2007), 'Planned by farmers for farmers? Twentieth century land reform and the impact on twenty-first century Japan', in C. Miller and M.M. Roche (eds.), 'Past Matters: Heritage and Planning History Case Studies from the Pacific Rim', (London: Cambridge Scholars Press), pp. 172–94.

Bosma, K. (1990), 'Town and regional planning in the Netherlands 1920–1945', *Planning Perspectives*, 5, 125–47.

Ebato, A. (1987), *Tokyo no chiiki kenkyū* (Tokyo: Daimei dō).

Endo, K. (2006), 'The Influence of the postwar regional-scale landscape plans on the conservation and development of farmland in the National Capital Region: a case study of Ichikawa City', Graduation thesis, Faculty of Agriculture, University of Tokyo.

Hatsuhachi, K. (1995), 'The role of Productive Open Space in regional open space system', *Agricuture in Japan: toward next stage* (*Nihon no nōgyō asu he no ayumi*), 195, 120.

Hebbert, M. (1986), 'Urban sprawl and urban planning in Japan', *Town Planning Review*, 57(2), 141–58.

—— (1991), 'Drawing the line between town and country', in R. Bennett and R. Estall (eds.), 'Global change and challenge', (London: Routledge), pp. 197–216.

Īnuma, K. (1927), *Toshikeikaku no riron to hōsei* (Tokyo: Ryoshofukyūkai).

—— (1931a), 'Chihōkeikakuron to ryokuchimondai', *Toshikōron*, 14.

—— (1931b), 'Toshi ni okeru nōgyōchiiki', *Chiho gyosei*, 39.

Ishida, Y. (1987), *Nihon kindai toshi keikakushi kenkyū* (Tokyo: Kashiwa shōbō).

Miyamoto, K. (1995), 'Shuto kinkyō ni okeru ryokuchitai kōsō no tenkai ni kansuru ni, san no kōsatsu', *Landscape Research*, 58, 229–32.

Nagashima, H. (1976), 'Urban development and its influence on rural areas around cities (Toshi keikaku hō to nōgyōryokuchi)', *Geographical review of Japan*, 49(5), 314–26.

Narito, T., Yamazaki, T., and Shimoda, Y. (2000), 'Sengo no Tokyo ni okeru kadaitoshi yokuseisaku no kōtaikatei to shigaika no jittai ni kansuru kenkyū', *Collected Papers of the Japanese City Planning Association, Nihon Toshi Keikaku Gakkai Ronbun Shū*, 35, 289–98.

Sorensen, A. (2001a), 'Building suburbs in Japan', *Town Planning Review*, 72(3), 247–73.

—— (2001b), 'Subcentres and satelite cities: Tokyo's 20th century experience of planned polycentrism', *International Planning Studies*, 6(1), 9–32.

—— (2002), *The Making of Urban Japan* (London: Routledge).

Tsubaki, T. (2003), 'Anglo-Japanese exchanges in town planning: the case of Tama new town in the 1960s, and William A. Robson', *Planning History*, 25(1), 4–15.

Yokohari, M., Takeuchi, K., Watanabe, T., and Yokota, S. (2000), 'Beyond greenbelts and zoning: a new planning concept for the environment of Asian mega-cities', *Landscape and Urban Planning*, 47, 159–71.

Yokohari, M., Amati, M., and Namiki, R. (2008), 'Restoring agricultural landscapes in shrinking cities: re-inventing traditional concepts in Japanese planning', *Land Use Science*, forthcoming.

CHAPTER 3

Issues with Green Belt Reform in the Seoul Metropolitan Area

Jekook Kim and Tae-Kyung Kim

Introduction

The Seoul green belt was established in the early 1970's but has recently come under severe strain because of industrialisation and urbanisation pressures. For the last 30 years the strong central government has used the green belt as an important tool for shaping urban development. Since democratisation in 1987 however, an increasing number of calls have been made to implement a green belt reform. In particular, political crises and a *coup d'état* in 1980 led to political conditions that undermined the *raison d'être* of the green belt. Economic growth in the 1980's and accelerated urbanisation led to a rise in population and severe housing shortages. Land use regulations were relaxed in the 1990's and five new towns were constructed around the fringes of the Seoul metropolitan area to appease the unstable housing market. This gave a spur to 'leap-frog' development causing the rationale for having a green belt policy to fundamentally questioned.

In addition to urbanisation pressure the Korean green belt has come under increasing political pressure. The democratisation of Korean politics at the end of 1980's triggered a questioning of the need for restrictive land use regulations. Green belts were no longer considered appropriate in the face of landowners' demands to reassert property rights. The rampant land speculation and development beyond the green belt has caused the government to rethink whether development restrictions in green belt areas should be relaxed so as to stave off further sprawl. In 1998, the Korean constitutional court found the strict green belt regulations to be unconstitutional. Thereafter, private property rights of residents living in the green belt area could be secured under land use policies. After President Daejoong Kim's rise to power in 1998 parts of the green belt were allowed to be released. The process has played out in metropolitan areas throughout the country up until the establishment of the Wide Area Standard Urban Plan in 2006.

By the end of 2006, the green belt reforms were in their final stages in all metropolitan areas. However, green belt reform has brought on a new crisis as uncontrolled urbanisation must now be addressed. So far little research has examined the processes at play in green belt reform (significant exceptions are Bengston and Youn, 2006; Choe, 2004). At the heart of the green belt reform lies a central dilemma:

in Korea green belt regulation may no longer be politically acceptable in the light of strong property ownership sentiments and market-led reforms. For sustainable development however, Korean national urban planning policy must consider how to adequately control urban growth.

The following chapter aims to detail the process of green belt reform in Korea, highlighting how this dilemma has been addressed. We first start by describing the history of the green belt in Korea. We then go on to detail the process of reform. Finally we end by considering the future challenge of green belt reform and how it reflects on Korea's planning system more generally.

Korea's National and Urban Planning Systems

To understand the history of the Korean green belt, one needs to understand the national and urban planning systems in Korea because of their close historical relationship. Current, green belt policy is being driven by concerns about property ownership and urbanisation. The national and urban planning system however, has supported green belt regulation at various points. So although the current political climate does not favour such regulation, green belt policy has a long history in the national and urban planning system.

The Korean property ownership system was reorganized along capitalistic lines by Japanese colonial rule in 1910. A pre-modern urban planning system, which is the foundation of today's zoning-based Korean urban planning system, was introduced by Japan in 1934 to facilitate governance. The system largely remained intact after independence in 1945 and until its supplementation by the Urban Planning Law (1962). Korea was largely an agricultural country and the proportion of people living in urban areas was just 23% in 1945 and 37.2% in 1960. Between 1933 and 1962 development was concentrated mostly in urban areas. The planning system focused on managing urban areas; urban-like land use in non-urban areas was strictly prohibited by several regulations governing agricultural, mountainous and other non-developed areas. However, development in existing urban areas (e.g. residential, commercial, industrial) was unrestrained unless the area was specified as green belt, or the proposed activity would not generate sufficient revenue to pay for basic infrastructure costs and impacts.

The advent of the Third Republic by military *coup d'état* in 1961 led to a huge shift in Korea's socioeconomic situation. The national and urban planning system changed greatly, setting in motion events that would form the roots of the current system. It pushed for industrialization under its economic development plan, which induced rapid urbanisation. Since 1962, the national and urban planning systems in Korea have experienced further structural changes.

A housing crisis and land supply shortages at the end the 1980's led to pressure to relax regulations and develop new towns in non-urban areas. The zoning system was loosened by the introduction of semi-urban and semi-agricultural or forestry areas in

Table 3.1: The changing urban planning system in Korea 1993 and 2003

Classification	Urban Planning Law in 1993			National Planning Law in 2003		
	Zone	CR[1](%)	FAR[2](%)	Zone	CR (%)	FAR (%)
Urban areas	Residential	70	700	Residential	70	500
	Commercial	90	1,500	Commercial	90	1,500
	Industrial	70	400	Industrial	70	400
	Green	20	200	Green	20	100
Non-urban areas	Semi-urban	60	200	Planned management	40	100
				Production management	20	80
	Semiagricultural/Forestry	40	80	Preserved management	20	80
	Agricultural/Forestry	60	400	Agricultural/Forestry	20	80
	Preserved natural	40	80	Preserved natural	20	80

[1] Coverage Ratio
[2] Floor Area Ratio

Source: Urban Research Institute, (2003)

1994, which made development in non-urban areas easier.[1] Thus the Korean planning system was thrown into a period of ambiguity as areas assigned as semi-urban or semi-agricultural/forestry could be developed subject to a land use classification plan. Therefore, private development and suburbanisation centered on these areas. Development occurred in these areas having often 'leap-frogged' the green belt. This was environmentally unsustainable and forced workers to endure longer commutes (Jun and Bae, 2000). Such is the natural result of policies that lack a robust urban planning management scheme.

Because of the patchwork development created during the late 1990s a unified national and urban planning system was created to manage all land. Since then however, a large amount of land was still classified as developable land by the previous land use classified plan and it took a great deal of effort for the government to monitor these areas.

The History of Green belt regulation in Korea

Background of Green Belt System in Korea

Although the proportion of the population living in urban areas in 1960 was 37.2%, industrialisation and urbanisation came swiftly thereafter because of the Third Republic's economic development plan. The plan caused urbanisation to climb to over 50% by 1970. The population of Seoul increased dramatically from 1.4 million in 1949, to 5.5 million in 1970.[2] As the urbanisation process rapidly progressed, problems such as congestion, environmental degradation became key social concerns.

Population issues in Seoul stemmed not only from housing problems but also from the political and military tension between South Korea and North Korea. Presently the population in the northern and southern parts of Seoul are well-balanced, with the Han River between them. In 1970 however, Seoul had an imbalanced population because of its relatively close proximity to the Demilitarized Zone. Growth in the northern part of Seoul was a very sensitive political and military issue that had to be considered along with planning for urban expansion.

The green area scheme was initially proposed in the 1964 Seoul Metropolitan Area Plan, and its precise implementation was laid out in the Seoul Urban Basic Plan.

---

1   Non-urbanised areas can largely be divided into semi-urban areas, semi-agricultural areas, agricultural areas, and natural environment preservation areas. According to the National Planning Law of 2003, semi-urban and semi-agricultural areas were integrated, and management areas are subdivided into planned management, production management, and preservation management areas (see Table 3.1).

2   The Seoul metropolitan area consists of three 'wide area local governments' that consist of Seoul city, Incheon city, and Gyeonggi-do. Seoul city and Incheon city were separated from Gyeonggi-do as wide area local governments in 1949 and 1981 respectively.

However, the plan was suspended because the designation of green areas without compensation for landowners might raise issues of private property right infringement. Nonetheless, by 1968 President Park Chung-Hee was already pursuing a green areas plan.

The Process of Implementing the Green Belt

Initially, the green area plan was intended to be limited to locations in Seoul. By order of President Park in March 1970 an urban planning committee for Seoul city was created.[3] During the meeting, a delegation of military authorities laid down the specific location of green areas. Later that year, the green area designation plan was discussed and adopted by the Seoul urban planning committee.

However, the location of the green areas that were chosen in Seoul had a substantial problem. Since the city of Seoul intended to make a belt shaped area of green areas, it found that it did not have enough land to make a ring without compensating landowners . The president's plan could not be realised as he originally intended. For this reason, green areas installation plan of the city of Seoul, which was set in 1970, was totally cancelled. Instead, the central government's Ministry of Construction submitted an alternative green belt proposal to the National Assembly in October, which prohibited any development in designated areas. The new green belt proposal was settled through legislation from the National Assembly in December. Political and military security issues prevailed, while private property rights were pushed aside to allow the greenbelt to become a reality.

To summarize, the Korean green belt system was not devised with sufficient attention given to basic principles of law. Rather it was arbitrarily created and implemented for the sole purpose of military defence. To many, the new green belt system represented at best an administrational convenience and was certainly not based on popular support.

Designation and Management of Green Belt Areas

Green Belt Extent in Korea

Green belt areas were initially designated in the Seoul metropolitan areas in July 1971, and were expanded to over 14 urban regions throughout the country over a series of 8 rounds. The total size of the green belt system in 1998 was 5,397 km^2 which is 5.4% of the total size of Korea, with a population of approximately 740,000. The Seoul green belt is 1,567 km around, which is 29% of the total size of green belt areas in Korea (Table 3.2).

---

3   Population concentration and Seoul's rampant urbanisation was debated as a social problem in February, 1964. A plan for preventing excessive population concentrations in metropolitan areas consisting of 20 items was presented in the council of state affairs in September.

Table 3.2: Dates of green belt designations and recent (1998) green belt statistics

Urban sphere	Time of designation	Areas (km^2)	Pop. (000's)	Households (000's)
Seoul	30/07/71[1]	1,567(29%)	355	124
Busan	29/12/71	597(11%)	116	36
Daegu	25/08/72	537(10%)	41	12
Kwangju	17/01/73	555(10.3%)	56	18
Daejeon	27/06/73	441(8.2%)	30	10
Ulsan	,,	284(5.2%)	14	5
Masan-Changwon-Jinjoo	,,	14(5.8%)	27	9
Cheju	05/03/73	83(1.5%)	15	5
Chuncheon	27/06/73	294(5.4%)	16	5
Chungju	,,	180(3.3%)	24	7
Junju	,,	225(4.2%)	22	7
Jinju	,,	203(3.8%)	18	5
Tongyung	,,	30(0.6%)	4	1
Yusu	18/04/77	88(1.6%)	4	1
Total		5,397(100%)	742	245

1 Note: debated until 29/12/76

Source: Ministry of Construction and Transportation (1998)

As shown in Table 3.2, green belt areas of Seoul metropolitan region were designated in three sequences between July, 1971 to December, 1976 accounting for land occupied by approximately 360,000 people.

The extent of green belt in the Seoul metropolitan area is managed by several local governments including such as Seoul, Incheon and Gyeonggido:

Table 3.3: Extent of green belt in the Seoul metropolitan area (1998) Region

Region	Administrational areas (A) Km^2	(%)	Green belt areas (B) B/A Km^2	%	%
Seoul	605.5	5.2	166.8	10.8	27.6
Incheon	964.5	8.2	80.6	5.2	8.4
Gyeonggido	10,189.1	86.6	1,293.4	84.0	12.7
Total	11,759.1	100.0	1,540.8	100.0	13.1

Source: Ministry of Construction and Transportation (1998)

The green belt occupies 13.1% of the Seoul metropolitan area. 27.6% of Seoul, 8.4% of Incheon, and 12.7% of Gyeonggi-do are designated as green belt areas. As

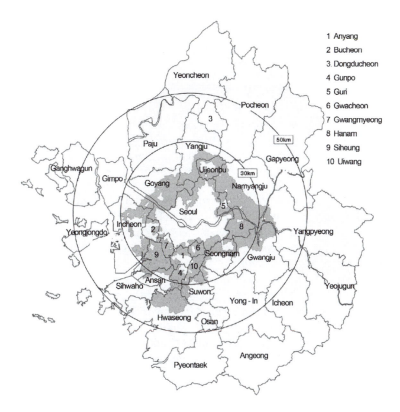

Figure 3.1: The green belt in the Seoul metropolitan area 1998

shown in Figure 3.1, Seoul is surrounded by green belt, Incheon makes up the western part of the green belt, and the rest of its area is in Gyeonggi-do. Since the area connecting Seoul and Incheon was developed in 1960 designating it as green belt was not possible. Therefore, as Figure 3.1 shows, the Seoul green belt is not perfectly ring-shaped.

Management of Green Belt Areas

Until the establishment of a special law for managing the green belt (known as the Green Belt Area Law) in 2000, control of the green belt areas was based on urban planning legislation and based on the policies that originally established the green belt. The Green Belt Area Law includes development controls, which were prescribed in the previous Urban Planning Law, but also supports basic property rights.

Basic management and development limits in green belt areas, apart from the newly introduced freedoms of land purchases and property rights, have been maintained since 1971. However, since that time the specific nature of development control has

Table 3.4: Development control in the green belt

Classification	Main contents
Banned development activities	1. new building construction 2. installation of facilities 3. alteration of land use 4. land subdivision 5. cutting trees for lumber 6. urban planning business
Permitted development activities	1. construction of buildings and facilities for public use 2. new construction or installation of NYMBY facilities[1] 3. installation of facilities for agriculture and fisheries 4. extension, reconstruction, change of use, of houses existing from the time of the area's designation as a green belt 5. reconstruction and change of use for non-residential buildings and facilities 6. transferring construction of demolished buildings and facilities by public development 7. new construction of facilities to improve residential life 8. alteration of land character that is not against its original purpose 9. land separation without new construction

[1] Also known as NIMBY or Not-in-my-back yard facilities. Development that attracts a large amount of opposition if located in a high-density area because of potential negative effects on residents.
Source: Ministry of Construction and Transportation (2000)

been continuously relaxed. For the remainder of this section, the characteristics of management and development controls in green belt areas will be explored.

As a matter of law, most kinds of new development including construction and extension, and alteration of land use are prohibited in green belt areas. Only new construction and extensions for public use, or alterations on houses predating the time of green belt designation are possible. Redevelopment of existing facilities in the green belt for public projects is also possible to a limited extent. In addition, the placement of public facilities in green belts for agricultural use or for public security and economic activity of residents is also possible.

Since the green belt system is operated on a zoning system, the floor area ratio and coverage ratio of the green belt area are prescribed at 30% and 60% respectively. However, this standard can only be applied to new construction for public purposes, but not for extension and reconstruction of an existing building, another standard based on the total base of the building is applied together as shown in Table 3.5.

Table 3.5: Regulation of building base for housing extensions

Periods	Subject of application	Main building[1]	Options Extension	Basement
1971–1973	Owner	33	–	–
1974–1976	Owner	100	–	–
1977–1985	Owner	100	33	33
1986–1989	Owner	100	33	100
1990–1992	Residents after area designation	100	33	100
	Residents before area designation	117	33	–
1993–1997	Residents who have been living on site for less than 5 years	100	66	100
	Residents who have been living on site for more than 5 years	132	66	100
	Residents before area designation	200	66	100
1998–2000	Residents who have been living on site for less than 5 years	100	66	100
	Residents who have been living on site for more than 5 years	132	66	100
	Residents before area designation	297	66	100
Since 2000	Residents who have been living on site for less than 5 years	–	–	–
	Residents who have been living on site for more than 5 years	–	–	–
	Residents before area designation	–	–	–

[1] All figures in m^2
Source: Kim (1999)

The standards on total building base have been applied since the inception of the green belt in 1971. The total building base was at most 33 m^2 in 1971 and 1973. After 1990, it was relaxed to 100 m^2, and increased depending on the house owners' years of residence in the green belt area. One of the key features was it differentiated residents who owned houses before the green belt area designation, and those who moved in after the designation. This was mainly because dissatisfaction about the green belt system stemmed from residents living there before designation.

This differential regulation policy created a new problem. Since the property of residents living in the green belt before designation became highly valued, it triggered their movement out of the green belt, collapsing the agricultural land use in these areas. At the same time, construction of new public infrastructure including buildings and various roads made the environment for agricultural management much worse. Essentially, development on private land use in the green belt was strictly limited, while development for public purposes was too widely permitted. The green belt system was being undermined by government policy and faced a crisis, including possible dissolution.

Reasons for Green Belt Reform

Backgrounds and Processes

A favorable world economy during the 1980's stimulated the Korean economy. First and foremost, the Japanese Yen was highly valued relative to Korean currency so exports of Korean merchandise had competitive power. As a result, a surplus of trade between Korea and Japan was sustained for a long time. Furthermore, the Asian Games in 1986 and the Seoul Olympics in 1988 during the great economic boom of the late 1980's were met with expanded national demand for goods and services.

A positive international trade balance did not only mean increased holdings abroad, but also the infusion of huge capital flows into the real estate market which caused a rise in prices. Large scale redevelopment projects meant to address dilapidated residential conditions around game sites at the Asian Games and Seoul Olympics led to housing shortages and rapid rent increases. Economic gaps among income groups widened, and the residential stability of the lowest-income groups were threatened. The looming housing crisis became the most important issue in the Presidential election of 1987, triggering massive new town development on the fringes of metropolitan areas.

At the end of the 1980's the Korean urbanisation process was moving in a new and disturbing direction. Urbanisation progressed into previously designated green belt areas and began to expand there quite significantly. In fact, these levels of suburbanisation were consistent with those seen in developed countries. However, despite this substantial amount of new development the housing crisis was not easily settled. Throughout the 1990's, increasing land supplies through the relaxation of land use regulations was Korea's main urban planning issue.

As previously mentioned, the second stage of the Korean national and urban planning system started in 1994. Semi-urban and semi-agricultural area classifications introduced in 1994 made land development easier. Essentially, land designated as semi-urban and semi-agricultural areas were permitted to be developed. In these areas, a large number of cooperative houses were constructed leading to tremendous development profits for property owners.

The uncohesive and patchwork pattern of land use surrounding the green belt areas made it difficult for its residents to tolerate these development regulations. A constitutional petition about how to regulate the green belt was submitted by residents. At the same time, during the Presidential election of 1997 both the Government party and the Opposition party based their election platforms on supporting the release of green belt areas with a low preservation value. Both parties asserted that these values could be determined through a series of environmental evaluations.

Adjustment Processes

In 1998, President Daejoong Kim promised a substantial settlement of the green belt system's many problems. To initiate broad reforms in national green belt policy the Ministry of Construction and Transportation organized the Committee for Green belt System Improvement. Planning specialists, representatives of environmental organizations, journalists, and other officials participated in this committee. This act marked the beginning of serious discussion (for further details on the work of this committee see Choe, 2004; Bengston and Youn, 2006).

The green belt system was not deemed to be unconstitutional in itself.[4] In fact, the court found nothing wrong with green belts *per se*. The unconstitutional aspect of Korea's green belt system was that the taking of land for inclusion in the green belt had not required compensation for landowner. However, the constitutional court did not have the mandate to set specific rules and regulations for compensation. These decisions had to be made by legislators, and thus the court allowed the green belt to stand until the legislators produced formal compensation rules.

Therefore, legislators had an obligation to end the situation by preparing legislation allowing compensation as soon as possible. During this period, the government was not allowed to designate any new green belt areas. Property owners gained the right to compensation immediately following passage of the Green Belt Area Law (2000), but disputes about the previous designation of green belts remained.

Although one problem of the green belt system might be settled by implementing compensation legislation according to the judgment of the constitutional court, the President's pledge to reform the green belt could not be withdrawn. Therefore, both the establishment of legislation for compensation and the reform of green belt areas were pursued simultaneously. First of all, the Green Belt Area Law (2000) provided a process for making compensation claims and institutionalised schemes for financial support of residents in the green belt. Meanwhile, after much discussion and some public opposition, the Committee for Green belt System Improvement produced their *Improvement plan for the green belt system*. The report failed to recommend the wholesale removal of the green belt, which angered green belt residents so much that the Ministry of Construction and Transportation asked the Town and Country Planning Association (TCPA) to comment on the plan (Town and Country Planning Association, 1999; Bengston and Youn, 2006). The principle contents were as follows: first, with the establishment of the urban basic plan, green belt areas in seven medium to small urban regions with low expansion pressures and a low probability of environmental degradation were released. Second, with the establishment of large

---

4   Case No. 97-HUNBA-78 : The discussion of constitutional court about this case was started from 19th October 1997 and ended in 24th December 1998.

areas of comprehensive urban planning, green belt areas with high expansion pressure were released in seven metropolitan areas including the Seoul region. Third, villages that were covered by the green belt must be released without further reference to the planning system.

To enable the reassignment of green belt areas, the central government prepared guidelines for both the urban basic plan and the wide area plan, and completed environmental evaluation work from July to December 1999. The environmental evaluations required by the green belt reform policy were begun at an early stage; well before the actual enactment of the improvement plan, as early analysis had been performed to support Presidential policy formulation.

Limitations of Green Belt Reform in Seoul Metropolitan Areas

Reform Stage

Co-establishment of the wide area plan for the Seoul metropolitan areas   With the 1999 announcement of the plan to reform green belts the Urban Planning Law was amended to introduce a regional plan for reform in seven metropolitan areas. Work was also begun on what was to become the Green Belt Area Law in 2000 to solve unconstitutional property right infringements. Although it was prescribed in the existing Urban Planning Law that a regional plan can be established to address a broad set of planning issues, it was necessary for the contents to be expanded further to allow for green belt reform.

In December of 1999, the Ministry of Construction and Transportation, Seoul city, Incheon city, and Gyeonggi-do, began to work on the new plan. Since the focus of their work was reforming the green belt in the Seoul metropolitan area, the Ministry of Construction and Transportation and each wide area vicinity government made an agreement to establish a plan within a year. The representatives of key institutes such as Korea Research Institute for Human Settlements (KRIHS), Seoul Development Institute (SDI), Incheon Development Institute (IDI), and Gyeonggi Research Institute (GRI) participated in drafting the plan. However, it took only a short time to realize that creating a plan in just a year would be difficult.

Conflicts between the central and regional governments over the National plan   The first part of establishing the wide area plan for the Seoul metropolitan areas was creating zones over which the plan would apply. However, this did not progress so smoothly. Although zones were defined in the 'Plan for Maintenance of the Metropolitan Area' (PMMA), the central government and each municipal government could not reach agreement on their use.

The zones in the PMMA came under the jurisdiction of Seoul City, Incheon City, and Gyeonggi-do. The controversy over the PMMA stemmed from its characteristic as a central government regulatory strategy to prevent excessive population concentration in metropolitan areas. The central government was concerned therefore to prevent the expansion of urban areas and was concerned that new regional plans set up by each of the cities would conflict with the PMMA.

Meanwhile, municipal governments in the Seoul metropolitan area, especially Gyeonggi-do, were concerned that the new regional plan might be more restrictive than the existing PMMA. For this reason, they wanted the regional plan to be limited to cities that already had green belts. Although both City and National governments wanted limits on urban growth, the spatial extent of the Gyeonggi-do regional plan is smaller than that covered by the PMMA. This implies that the municipal governments regarded the regional plan as a tool for pushing forward a green belt reform. The contents of the wide area planning in the Urban Planning Law (2000) were:

1   Spatial structure and functional sharing of wide area zones
2   Green management systems and environmental preservation of wide area zones
3   Disposition, scale, and installation of wide area facilities
4   Vista plan
5   Transportation and merchandise circulation systems of wide area zones
6   Culture, leisure space, and protections in wide area zones

While the principles of the (2000) regional plan were:

1   Objectives and strategies of planning
2   Present state and characteristics of wide area zones
3   Restructuring plan of wide area zones
4   Individual plans
5   Adjust plan of green belt areas
6   Execution and management plan

Throughout the discussion process, GRI counselled Gyeonggi-do indicating to them that the establishment of a regional plan with the same spatial extent as the Plan for Maintenance of the Metropolitan Area might be favorable to Gyeonggi-do. An agreement was made between Seoul, Incheon, Gyeonggi-do, and the central government in October, 2000. It seems that the central government eventually had to carry a political burden for delaying the regional plan establishment.

The Reform of green belt areas   Due many bureaucratic turns and twists, establishment of the regional plan for the Seoul metropolitan area could not be completed within the one year target, and the process continued into 2001. For the time being, the four research institutions charged with analyzing public policy, continuously examined various technical problems that might inhibit the reform of green belts in the Seoul metropolitan areas. They verified the results of the environmental evaluation which was conducted in 1998, and analyzed how the results could be applied to the reform criteria.

First of all, the environmental evaluation was implemented by using six criteria including altitude, slope, agricultural suitability, plant cover, forestry suitability, and water quality, to construct five classes. The maps depicting the various criteria were overlaid to create the five classes. The first and second classes define areas with a high value of preservation, the fourth and fifth classes are areas with a low value of preservation, and the third class represent areas that need additional analysis. The results of the environmental evaluation were unclear. Although the areas for preservation were in large blocks, the zones identified for development did not fit neatly into clusters that could be easily planned and instead were scattered in small areas, especially to the south-west of Seoul.

Based on this analysis, planners selected areas with concentrations of land in the fourth and fifth classes. With these criteria set, a basic direction was decided upon, although the final configurations of developable areas as they relate to other green areas was left undecided. In addition, the release of green belt was minimized by setting a 2 km buffer zone from the inner boundary of the green belt in Seoul. These areas would serve to prevent further urbanisation (see Table 3.6).

Table 3.6: Types and characteristics of green belt release in the Seoul metropolitan area

Types	Characteristics	Establishment of development restriction areas
Primarily releasable community	Grouped community with housing density over 10 units/ha, and more than 300 units (or over 1,000 persons)	Yes
Land that could be released from the green belt	Clustered areas with more than 60% of their area in the fourth and fifth classes, and larger than 10 hectares	No
National policy business area	Released for the purpose of national national policy	No
Regionally pending business area	Released for the purpose of regional policy	Yes

Source: Ministry of Construction and Transportation (2007)

Since the pledge about reforming green belt areas through environmental evaluation was announced as far back as the 1997 Presidential election, an alternative method for reforming green belt disregarding the environmental evaluation was not given to the planners who were drafting regional plans in the Seoul metropolitan areas and six other metropolitan areas. Therefore, another alternative plan for green belt reform which was commonly applicable to each of the seven metropolitan areas was established.

The total amount of adjustable land was set by the city, and the adjustment had to be made within certain limits. With the assigned ratio of green belt areas, the fourth and fifth classes of the environmental evaluation, population density, and characteristics of existing regional policies, the amount of green belt area that could be release for each city was determined, targeting 47 cities in the seven metropolitan areas. The amount of green belt area that could be released in each city was assigned a Z-score based on average ratios of the fourth and fifth classes from the environmental evaluation.

Methods of green belt adjustment   Under the basic green belt reform framework, the green belt could be released under one of four categories. First, grouped communities with more than 300 houses were released without regard to the results of the environmental evaluation, within the total amount of adjustable land in green belt areas. 300 houses were perceived as a minimum standard to demarcate locations as planned developments for maintenance. Second, releasable land of more than 10 hectares and more than 60% their land uses in the aforementioned fourth and fifth classes were classed as green belt land that could be released. In cases where the inclusion ratio of the fourth and fifth classes was lower than 60%, the total amount of land to be released was cut by 0.5% based on characteristics of each city, to reflect areas with land in the first and second classes. Third, certain lands were designated for the implementation of national policy without regard to their total amount of green belt area to be released. Fourth, depending on the needs of regional policy, certain lands could be released up to a limit of 10% of the total green belt area to be released.

Even once these classifications had been decided it did not mean that green belt land would be necessarily released unconditionally. In practice, the decision-making was made through a deliberation process conducted by the committee of central urban planning.

The designation methods for releasing green belt were subjected to political pressure by residents. The 300 house standard for release, was subsequently lowered to 20 houses. Following this change in policy, each city staged a confirmation process to determine which communities met the 20 house standard.

Next, based on a computer simulation using a Gravity Model, if the adjustable land includes more than 60% of the fourth and fifth classes, and its size is larger than 10 hectares, it could be selected in the first stage. Finally, a table of evaluation scores was drawn up to weight the decisions that had to be taken the amount of final adjustable land can be determined within the limits of the total amounts available by city (see Table 3.7).

The National Policy Business Area was intended to develop the surrounding areas of Kwangmyung station, which is a part of Seoul-Busan express railroads, largely because it is located in a green belt area of the Seoul metropolitan area. Additionally, the supply of National Rental Housing in green belt areas was set by governmental policy in response to housing market volatility in 2001. Followed by the initial area, 11 additional National Business Areas for construction of public rental housing were designated.

Table 3.7: Evaluation criteria and scores of proposed green belt area adjustment

Criteria	Detailed criteria	Evaluation scores
Environment	Inclusion ratio of classes 4 and 5 in environmental evaluation	20
	Size of proposed green belt area for adjustment	30
	Conflict with green axis	5
	Damage to scenery and ecosystem	5
Urbanity	Development axis and development induction areas	5
	Adjacency to major arterial roads and existing towns	5
	Inclusion of grouped communities	5
Opinion of municipal government	Municipal governments' preferences	25

Source: Kim (2004)

Lastly, regionally pending projects were based on demand, as long as efforts remained within 10% of the assigned amounts of adjustable lands by city. Projects favored were those with a high concentration of land in the fourth-fifth classes based on the environmental evaluation.

Hearings about the wide area plan for the Seoul metropolitan area, which includes the adjustment plan, were held on January 22nd, 2002. The adjustment plan for green belt areas in the Seoul metropolitan area are shown in Table 3.8. Approximately 8.1% of total green belt areas in the Seoul metropolitan area were to be released including 2.1% in Seoul, 10.3% in Incheon, and 8.7% in Gyeonggi-do.

Limitations

Changes in the political environment after the hearing led the green belt adjustment plan for the Seoul metropolitan area to be re-examined. The local elections in May 2002 led to all local governments in the Seoul metropolitan area being taken by the opposition party. For this reason, the wide area plan being conducted area had to be agreed upon by the incoming new executives. Work towards plan establishment was temporarily stopped, and each regional government gave briefings about their regional plan. As expected, the new officials requested changes.

The opposition party sought widespread relaxation of regulations throughout metropolitan areas to strengthen their popular support. Part of this plan would require a large scale release of green belt area. This idea was difficult to accept because it ran counter to planning policies and principles of the green belt reform to date. As such,

Table 3.8: State of the green belt adjustment in Seoul metropolitan area at time of hearing, January 2002

Classification	Seoul metropolitan region		Seoul		Incheon		Gyeonggi-do	
	No.	Area[1]	No.	Area	No.	Area	No.	Area
Primarily releasable community	655	38.3	28	2.6	37	1.5	590	34.1
Adjustable lands	130	65.5	–	–	17	6.8	113	58.7
National policy business area	12	10.2	–	–	–	–	12	10.2
Regionality pending business area	26	10.1	3	0.9	–	–	23	9.2
Total	823	124.1	31	3.5	54	8.3	738	112.2

[1] Area in km^2

Source: Ministry of Construction and Transportation (2002)

Table 3.9: Adjustment state of green belt areas in Seoul metropolitan area by city in January 2002

Classification	Green belt area (a)		Green belt adjustment (B)		B/A (%)
	Km^2	%	Km^2	%	
Seoul	166.8	10.8	3.5	2.8	2.1
Incheon	80.6	5.2	8.3	6.7	10.3
Gyeonggi-do	1,293.4	84.0	112.2	90.5	8.7
Total	1,540.8	100.0	124.1	100.0	8.1

Source: Ministry of Construction and Transportation (2002)

these ideas were scrutinized by those involved in the regional planning process, while at the same time, political deliberations among the central government and local governments in the Seoul metropolitan area progressed. The 2002 Presidential election brought the Rho Moohyun government to power on a platform of settling the Seoul Metropolitan housing crisis through green belt reform. A new political environment was fostered around the idea of green belt reform.

At the time, the persons who were in charge of the practical business of regional urban planning (including one of the authors of this chapter, Jekook Kim), attempted

Table 3.10: The final alternative for reform of green belt in Seoul metropolitan area (April 2006, cf. Table 3.8)

Classification	Seoul metropolitan region		Seoul		Incheon		Gyeonggi-do	
	No.	Area[1]	No.	Area	No.	Area	No.	Area
Primarily releasable community	680	53.5	29	6.5	52	2.6	599	44.4
Adjustable lands	79	52.1	–	–	8	5.6	71	46.5
National policy business area	25	19.7	12	6.8	–	–	12	13.0
Regionality pending business area	34	10.7	4	0.6	3	0.7	27	9.3
Total	818	136.0	45	13.9	63	8.9	709	113.2

[1] Area in km^2

Source: Ministry of Construction and Transportation (2006)

to settle the problems of green belt adjustment through utilizing changes in the political environment. That is, some attempted to modify the limitations of green belt adjustment which depended only on the results of the environmental evaluation. Various compromises were made between the local governments and the central government and the final green belt adjustment plan for the Seoul metropolitan area was completed June, 2005 (see Table 3.10). Following agreement among wide area vicinity governments, the final plan was presented to the Committee of Central Urban Planning.

Compared to the green belt adjustment plan at the time of the hearing, the final plan submitted to the Committee of Central Urban Planning has several different features. First, to prevent leap-frog development in green belt areas, the land to be released was clustered. National business policy areas were expanded from 12 to 25 to accommodate the central government's requests for additional rental houses. Third, regionally pending business areas were increased from 26 to 34 consistent with the requests of wide area local governments. Lastly, primarily releasable communities were increased from 655 to 680 to minimize departure of residents from green belt areas.

The initial objectives of the planners were not to be fully realized. As shown in Table 3.11, although they tried to accommodate the intentions of both the central government and the wide area vicinity governments through clustering of releasable lands, a larger adjustment of green belt areas was made because the government

Table 3.11: Adjustment state of green belt areas in Seoul metropolitan area (April 2006 to present, cf. Table 3.9)

Classification	Green belt area (a)		Green belt adjustment (B)		B/A (%)
	Km²	%	Km²	%	
Seoul	166.8	10.8	13.9	10.2	8.3
Incheon	80.6	5.2	8.9	6.5	11.0
Gyeonggi-do	1,293.4	84.0	113.2	83.2	8.8
Total	1,540.8	100.0	136.0	100.0	8.8

Source: Ministry of Construction and Transportation (2006)

altered the planning standard. Specifically, the development control area that was designated for stopping further urbanisation, and the principles of environmentally favorable development, which provide for low-density development in green belt areas, was removed from the plan. Moreover, the central government pushed high density public rental housing development using a special law prior to the final decision into the Seoul metropolitan area plan.

From December 2006 to the present, the Committee of Central Urban Planning has been deliberating a proposal for wide area urban planning in the Seoul metropolitan area. At the same time, a public rental housing development project in the National Policy Business Area is being implemented by central government. Initially, the wide area urban plan of the Seoul metropolitan area was established for planned management and reasonable prescribed reforms to the green belt areas. However, the Korean green belt policy reform movement was substantially limited by strong sentiments for property rights. Frequent changes of political power did nothing to assist with green belt reform.

Technical green belt adjustment methods based on the environmental evaluation, which was introduced to avoid an exodus of residents brought about new contradictions such that people who respected the law were disadvantaged. Although the plan was conceived as a technocratic exercise, in reality the central government and wide area vicinity governments abused it for short-term political gains.

Conclusions

This chapter has reviewed issues and history dealing with green belt reforms in the Seoul metropolitan area. In particular, this discussion was informed by the author's experience participating in the process since 1998.

From its birth, the Korean green belt system, rooted in principles of zoning, might be considered an inoperable system. The green belt was maintained for the last thirty years through an antidemocratic political system that supported it. Therefore, the green belt system was destined to be dismantled together with the democratisation of politics. The problems with the Korean green belt system may not be solved by any partial adjustment. Rather, rethinking property ownership itself may provide clues about possible solutions. Although residential departures could be reduced by partial adjustments to green belt areas, without a total reorganization of the property system, namely, the separation of development rights from property ownership or the consolidation of social duties involved with property ownership, the green belt system will lose its function.

The Korean urban planning system has changed continuously since the cessation of the military government in 1987, and progression of democracy thereafter. However changes seem to be rooted in short-term political motivations, which weaken the social responsibilities of property ownership while strengthening the rights of property owners. As a result, leap-frog developments continue to be built all over the country. Compared to western nations that let runaway urbanisation sweep their landscapes at the end of the nineteenth, and the beginning of the twentieth century, Korea seems to be repeating the mistakes of its predecessors.

Although the reform of the Korean green belt system was an important opportunity to deal with some critical development problems, direct solutions have been avoided in favor of passing along problems to future generations. Hereafter, to maintain the Korean green belt system, and to settle problems with leap-frog developments during the process of democratisation, a more macroscopic approach to reorganizing the extent of property ownership will be required.

References

Bengston, D.N. and Youn, Y.C. (2006), 'Urban Containment Policies and the Protection of Natural Areas: The Case of Seoul's Greenbelt', *Ecology and Society*, 11(1), [available online].

Choe, S.C. (2004), 'Reform of planning controls for an urban-rural continuum in Korea: the role of urban growth areas in achieving growth Reform of planning controls for an urban-rural continuum in Korea', in A. Sorensen, P.J. Marcotullio, and J. Grant (eds.), 'Towards sustainable cities: East Asian, North American, and European perspectives on managing urban regions', (Burlington, Vermont: Ashgate), pp. 253–66.

Jun, M.J. and Bae, C.H.C. (2000), 'Estimating the Commuting Costs of Seoul's Greenbelt', *International Regional Science Review*, 23(3), 300–315.

Kim, J.K. (1999), *A study on the Control and Preservation Effect of Korean Greenbelt as Zoning*, Ph.D. thesis, Tokyo Institute of Technology, Tokyo.

—— (2004), 'A study on the Process and Issues of the 1st Seoul Metropolitan Plan', in 'Gyeonggi Research Institute Report', (Gyeonggi Research Institute), pp. 44–6.

Ministry of Construction and Transportation (1998), *Inventory of Green Belt Areas* (Seoul: MOCT).

—— (2000), *Greenbelt Law* (Seoul: MOCT).

—— (2002), *2020 Seoul Metropolitan Plan (Draft)* (Seoul: MOCT).

—— (2006), *2020 Seoul Metropolitan Plan (Draft)* (Seoul: MOCT).

—— (2007), *2020 Seoul Metropolitan Plan* (Seoul: MOCT).

Town and Country Planning Association (1999), *Commentary on RDZ Policy Reform in Korea* (London: TCPA).

Urban Research Institute (2003), *The Understanding of New Urban Planning System in Korea* (Seoul: Bosongak), p. 107.

PART II
FALLING OUT OF FAVOUR:
DEREGULATION AND
GREEN BELTS

CHAPTER 4

Protecting Melbourne's Green Wedges – Fate of a Public Policy

Michael Buxton and Robin Goodman

Introduction

New strategic metropolitan plans have been developed recently for almost every State capital city in Australia. These plans employ similar principles. They seek to limit outer urban growth and intensify urban development in mixed use activity centres linked by improved public transport. Most identify urban growth boundaries and seek to prevent the further urbanization of countryside. The plans reflect a renewed interest in green belts and the spatial limits to cities in Australian urban planning. The loss of Sydney's green belt is the most well known Australian example of the failure of green belt planning. It originally extended over 332 square kilometres as a 'girdle of rural open space encircling the urban districts' (Cumberland County Council, 1948, 65) as part of a 'bold master plan in the Patrick Abercrombie style' for Sydney which covered over 4000 square kilometres (Freestone, 1992, 71). In contrast, Adelaide has consistently confined its urban development. Both Adelaide and the metropolitan areas of South East Queensland, particularly Brisbane, have recently introduced urban growth boundaries and reinforced the protection of non-urban areas bordering cities through strong regulatory planning controls.

This chapter will examine the development and application of green belt policy in Melbourne, Australia, the principles underlying this policy, reasons for the protection of urban green belts from development, and the lessons which can be learned from the application of the Victorian example. A number of case studies will be used to illustrate issues associated with recent developments approved in Melbourne's green belt. For almost 40 years, strategic planning for Melbourne has been based around the twin spatial principles of radial urban growth corridors serviced by heavy rail infrastructure, and green wedges between the corridors. Recently, the green wedges have been expanded into an extended green belt.

Four stages in the application of this policy now can be recognised. In the first, from 1929 until 1954, a metropolitan strategic plan was developed but never implemented. No statutory planning controls existed and market preferences determined the direction of urban growth. In the second, from 1954 until 1993, strategic plans were drawn up and implemented. In the period particularly from 1968-1990 Melbourne's green wedges were designed as non-urban areas and rigorously protected by the metropolitan planning authority, the Melbourne and Metropolitan Board of Works (MMBW), and the Victorian state government. This period demonstrated the confidence of bodies such as the MMBW and state and local government, and their belief in the importance of regulation and in the role of land use planning to define and implement a strategic direction consistently and over a long time period.

In the third period, from 1993 until 2002, state government strategic planning began to erode green wedges. A neo-liberal governance regime associated with the introduction of liberalised planning provisions and a development facilitation agenda led to the breakdown of metropolitan policy and the approval of many incremental developments in the green wedges. In the fourth, from 2002 until 2006, the state government rearmed strategic metropolitan policy but has maintained the policy of outer urban expansion and large-scale commercial developments in the expanded green belt.

Proposals for a Green Belt for Melbourne

In the nineteenth century, urban development in Melbourne followed tram and train lines radiating from the centre of the city. The central city area of Melbourne was originally encircled by an extensive ring of public land and parkland which functioned as an inner city green belt. Harris (2005, 9) argues that 'it is clear that [Governors] Gipps and later La Trobe, in consultation with Hoddle, retained crown lands to the north, east and south of Melbourne'. Royal, Princes, Carlton, Fitzroy, Flinders, Yarra, Domain, Botanic, Fawkner and Albert parks were later established in these areas, while Crown land on the western boundary was eventually used for port and industrial uses. This inner green belt has been incrementally eroded in contrast to the inner parkland belt of Adelaide. The sale of the frontages to Royal Parade and St. Kilda Road reduced and fragmented these parks. The subsequent construction of facilities for the 1956 Melbourne Olympic Games in the Swan Street area and from the 1980s of commercial entertainment and recreation facilities on Flinders Park continued this process.

Melbourne's first town plan was released by the Metropolitan Town Planning Commission (MTPC) in 1929 (MTPC, 1929). This plan did not propose a green belt but included an extensive network of public open spaces along waterways which were intended to separate urban areas. The plan was never adopted but it influenced the 1954 plan prepared by the MMBW. The open space provisions of this plan were eventually incorporated into the 1988 Metropolitan Open Space Plan (Ministry for Planning and Environment, 1988). Freestone (1989, 210) points to the early role played by the Victorian Town Planning and Parks Association in developing proposals for green belts despite the lack of official recognition. Association members proposed a ring of open spaces through outer suburbs to complement inner parklands, and a belt of agricultural land to limit the growth of the metropolitan area.

McLoughlin (1992) and others have conjectured that the sources of Melbourne's corridor-wedge model might have been Abercrombie's *Greater London Plan 1944* which proposed a green belt around London or the 1948 *Copenhagen Finger Plan* and its subsequent variants which concentrated development in urban 'fingers' outwards from the city centre (Copenhagen Municipal Corporation, 1993). However, Harris (2005) has demonstrated that the development of Melbourne's radial corridor-green wedge plan was strongly influenced by post war British planning. He examines a number of early references to the need for urban limits and green belts, such as the proposal by Melbourne planner, Frank Heath, for linear parks along streams radiating from the city centre leading to six major outer urban parks each of 2,000 acres located in a circumferential green belt (Barnett and Heath, 1944, cited in Harris 2005) (see Figure 4.1). In 1947 the MMBW related possible metropolitan boundaries to the cost of infrastructure planning (see Figure 4.2), particularly railway travel times and sewerage provision (Borrie and Cawcutt, 1947, cited in Harris 2005).

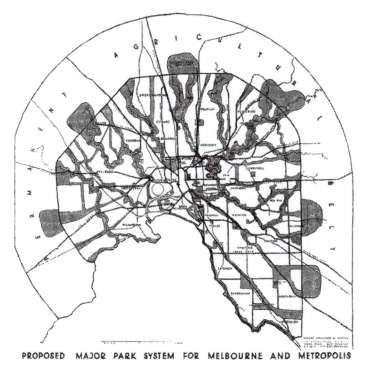

PROPOSED MAJOR PARK SYSTEM FOR MELBOURNE AND METROPOLIS

Figure 4.1: Proposed park system for metropolitan Melbourne, 1944

Source: Barnett and Heath (1944)

The Development of Melbourne's Green Belt

Melbourne's second town plan, and its first planning scheme, was developed in 1954 (MMBW, 1954). The plan showed existing residential zones following rail lines and

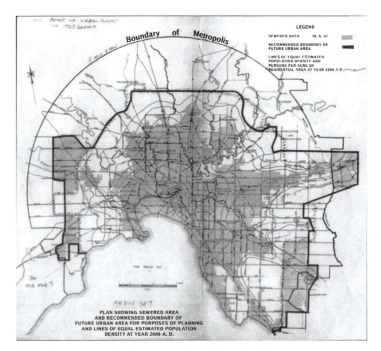

Figure 4.2: Infrastructure basis to corridor boundaries

Source: Borrie and Cawcutt (1947)

provided for more linear development. This plan extended over an area of 1,800 square kilometres and was intended to accommodate a population of two and a half million people through outer urban growth in accordance with demand. A non-urban area surrounded the specified urban zones, but this was regarded as a holding zone for urban development required in future years. The plan raised the notion of limits to an urban area arguing that 'a line must be drawn somewhere, or the city will continue sprawling over a wider and wider area … The method proposed for controlling the uneconomic spread of the city is the provision of a rural zone surrounding the urban area and extending to the metropolitan boundaries' (MMBW, 1954, 22). Linear open space reservations were introduced over many waterways.

The first published government mention of green wedges was in a 1959 MMBW report by planners Keith Rasmussen, Alistair Hepburn and E.F. Borrie (MMBW, 1959). The MMBW then incorporated the corridor-wedge strategic principle in Amending Planning Scheme No 1 in 1962. This planning amendment outlined the option of 'controlled outward expansion of a number of continuous centres along main lines of communication but with each line of development separated by substantial wedges or buffers of rural land' (MMBW, 1962, 16). The shape of Melbourne was decided finally between 1965 and 1971. The then Victorian Minister for Local Government, R.J. Hamer, played a pivotal role in this process. Hamer later reinforced his protection of Melbourne's non-urban areas as the Liberal (Conservative) State Premier. Harris (2005, 27) claims that although Hamer's views were an 'absorption, distillation and re-statement' of the evolving views of the MMBW senior planners, he was an innovator who significantly advanced the concept of green wedge protection. In 1965, Hamer raised the need for regulatory planning to require a 'starfish' shape for Melbourne (Hamer, 1965). In 1966, he wrote to the MMBW and to the Town and Country Planning Board (TCPB) requesting a report on the future shape of Melbourne arguing that 'nobody could happily contemplate a future metropolis of seemingly endless suburbia spreading outwards indefinitely. It must be strongly emphasised that future planning should take full account of the surrounding countryside as a vital part of the metropolitan environment' (MMBW, 1967, 29). Hamer's principles were the need for green belts, the containment of urban growth and the need for an interventionist government role to achieve these outcomes. He drew explicitly on the British planning tradition as the source of these principles. The MMBW (1967, 14-16) considered three outward growth scenarios and adopted the corridor-wedge model to define the outer limits of urban development and 'provide relief from continuous building development ... [and preserve] ... countryside near to established population'. In this sense, the MMBW and the government believed that green wedges or green belts needed no further justification than their function in preventing continuous urban development.

They also argued that metropolitan planning must be integrated with the protection of the non-urban areas of a city's hinterland. This led them to adopt the British regional planning tradition. A ministerial statement in 1968 formed a context to the MMBW planning. The TCPB also produced a report advocating the corridor-green wedge model (Town and Country Planning Board, 1967).

The views held by MMBW planners, Hamer and other emerging members of the government at the time, such as future planning minister Alan Hunt, were remarkably similar to those of the American planning historian, Lewis Mumford, and other influential supporters of green belts. Mumford (1961, 587–95) attacked 'the boundless expansion and random diffusion of the conurbation'. He criticised as 'anti-city' the 'extension of vast masses of suburban ... housing ... into open country' because such growth would lead to the loss of the values of both city and country. Limiting the area of a city could only be achieved through appropriate zoning and land-use legislation, he argued.

The Victorian state government and its planning agencies in these years put in place Victoria's long standing green wedge protection policy. This was finally adopted in Melbourne's third strategic plan, the 1971 *Planning Policies for the Melbourne Metropolitan Region* (MMBW, 1971), and its statutory implementation through Amending Planning Schemes 3 and 21 which modified the Melbourne Metropolitan Planning Scheme (MMPS) and included non-urban statutory zones. The 1971 plan was Melbourne's first regional plan. The area affected was revised from 1,800 to 5,029 square kilometres and extended to the Dandenong Ranges in the east and far to the north, south and west of Melbourne. The non-urban areas, including nine green wedges, covered 2400 square kilometres or about half the

MMBW planning area. The plan proposed seven urban growth corridors separated by permanent green wedges. All future urban development was to be confined to the growth corridors which would not be wider than 4–6 miles.

The purposes of these green wedges were to contain metropolitan growth and provide breaks to continuous urban development, enable the continuation of agriculture close to the city, protect areas of high natural value including landscapes, protect deposits of minerals and other resources, provide locations for infrastructure and major public utility installations or large institutions, and locations for recreation and the reservation of public open space (MMBW, 1967, 14–16).

Wale (2003) argued that the 1971 plan tried for the first time in Victoria to change landowner expectations and eliminate land speculation in rural areas. Four statutory non-urban zones were put in place. These prevented the introduction of any urban related uses. These zones 'removed urban expectations from major portions of the Metropolitan planning area' (MMBW, 1977, 12). Over 4,000 objections were received to the exhibited plan. As in the case of the Sydney green belt, most opposition came from landowners within the proposed green wedge areas. Many people believed that the proposed standards were too inflexible and restrictive compared to the more permissive nature of previous zoning provisions. Numerous individual objectors argued against the effect of zoning provisions on individual properties (MMBW, 1974, 12). However, unlike the situation in Sydney, the MMBW and the state government held firm and rejected almost all of the objections to green wedge zonings. The 1971 plan remained substantially in place for over 20 years. Its principles were later endorsed in the 1980 Metropolitan Strategy (MMBW, 1980) and the *Metropolitan Strategy Implementation* report (MMBW, 1981). Its directions for green wedges were rearmed by a revised metropolitan strategy released by the Cain state Labor government in 1987 (Government of Victoria, 1987), and are still clearly discernible in the 2002 metropolitan strategy, Melbourne 2030 (see Figure 4.3). Bi-partisan political agreement was a feature of planning for the protection of Melbourne's non-urban areas during these decades.

A notable aspect of the planning from the late 1960s to the early 1990s was the undertaking of studies to identify environmentally significant areas around Melbourne and inside the growth corridors. Floodways, wetlands, water quality, landscape values, native vegetation, terrain characteristics, and other physical and economic constraints on development were identified. These helped to define the features to be protected in the green wedges. The Conservation Council of Victoria made an important contribution to identifying environmental values and boundaries to the green wedges (Champion, 1971). The MMBW recognised areas of special interest including the Dandenong Ranges, Upper Yarra Valley and the Dingley area, and proposed the public purchase of large regional parklands in green wedge areas. The state Liberal government released a series of statements of planning policies during the 1970s and established regional planning authorities designed to protect the environmentally significant Mornington Peninsula, and the Dandenong Ranges and Upper Yarra Valley. A similar statement was prepared for the Macedon Ranges. In the late 1980s, detailed assessments of habitat were included in the plans eventually

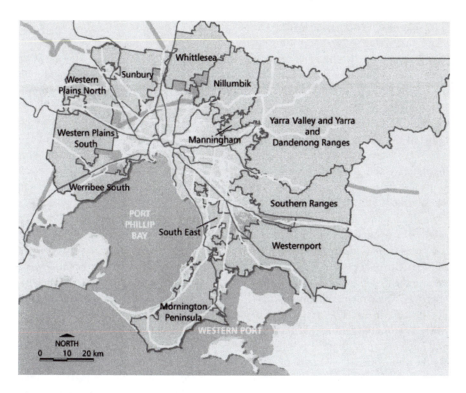

Figure 4.3: Projected metropolitan countryside, 2002

Source: Department of Infrastructure (2002)

developed for the three nominated growth corridors, that is, the Plenty Valley to the north of Melbourne, Berwick-Pakenham-Cranbourne to the south-east, and the Werribee corridor to the west. These assessments were used to exclude some important areas of habitat inside the corridors from development. For example, only about one third of the Plenty Valley corridor was to be developed, and large areas containing significant redgum eucalypts and stream sides were protected in non-urban zones there. Regional parklands were developed in all corridors. However, recently, it has become clear that these environmental assessments were not comprehensive, particularly in the western corridors. Significant areas of habitat remain unprotected inside corridors and in the broader green belt. Data on environmental values remain inadequate. Corridor boundaries have been determined before comprehensive data on habitat values have been gathered.

A Weakening of Strategic Policy

The third stage in Melbourne's green belt planning involved a weakening of State government strategic planning from 1990-2002. Much of this period coincided with the period of office of the Kennett Liberal-National Party coalition government. Planning for Melbourne ceased to be bi-partisan from this time. Kennett and his Planning Minister Robert Maclellan introduced a neo-liberal planning regime which reduced the role of government, limited regulation and regarded the role of the planning system as development facilitation (Maclellan, 1993). This government saw no place for the traditional regulatory planning policy and statutory system which emphasised the importance of interventionist strategic planning. As a result, although Melbourne's 1971 policy of protecting green wedges and the green belt was never formally repealed, many planning panels and local councils ceased to regard it as binding or even as important. These bodies interpreted policy differently and their decisions varied. A substantial number of a new generation of planners were unaware of the traditional policy. Local councils were able to instigate processes to rezone land in the green wedges. Once commenced, these processes applied pressure for approval. The land use planning process therefore was used to develop green wedges, not protect them. The dismemberment of the independent planning body (the MMBW) and the removal of its planning functions to a state government ministry and local councils in the 1980s had removed the champion of green belt protection. By the end of the 1990s, incremental, ad hoc decisions about development in non-urban areas had become the norm and strategic metropolitan policy had, in effect, ceased to exist. This had clearly been the intention of the Kennett government.

However, Labor governments which immediately preceded and succeeded the Kennett government damaged Melbourne's green wedges more extensively than did the Kennett neo-liberal regime. The Victorian Cain Labor government began this process in 1990 when it released structure plans for two urban growth corridors. A comparison of the 1981 MMBW strategic plan, and the 1990 corridor structure plans shows that the Cain government added 7,600 hectares of green wedge land to the Werribee urban corridor, and 3,300 hectares to the south-eastern urban corridor. Most of this land was excised contrary to publicly exhibited structure plans so denying the public the opportunity to object to the excisions. Between 1996–2002, over 4,000 hectares of additional non-urban land in green wedges was approved for residential subdivision or related urban uses (Buxton and Goodman, 2002). About two thirds of this was approved by the Labor government from 1999 despite promising to protect green wedges. Table 4.1 shows approved rezonings, and Table 4.2 shows proposed rezonings, at 2002. In addition to its non-urban land rezonings, the former Kennett government created 1,369 residential and rural residential lots in the Upper Yarra and Dandenong Ranges region contrary to the Regional Strategy Plan and planning schemes. Rural rezonings by the Kennett government and its predecessor, the Kirner Labor government, caused 800 hectares of land to be excised from the green wedge in this region (Buxton and Staindl, 1999).

During the fourth stage in planning for green belt protection, from 2002, the

Table 4.1: Residential rezonings 1996–2002

Name	Municipality – (previous if different)	Amendment	Approval date	Location	Size (ha)	No of house lots
Eynesbury Station	Melton and Wyndham	C20	May 2002	Melton South	1,350	2,100
Adrenaline Sports Complex	Brimbank	C23	January 2002	Derrimut	359	N/A
Epping North	Whittlesea	C12	September 2002	Epping North	1,337	8,000
Kingston Waterways Estate	Kingston	L33	February 1999	Braeside	157	700
Boat Sales and Repair	Kingston	Permit only required	March 2000	Springvale Road, Kingsborough	N/A	
The Keysborough Concept	Greater Dandenong	C2	August 2001	Keysborough	227	900–1,100
Sandhurst Golf Estate	Frankston	RL174	August 1996	Skye	300	1,950
Flora Park Estate	Frankston	L98	July 1997	Carrum Downs	15	124
Castlebrook Estate/Pindara	Frankston (Cranbourne)	L188	April 2000	Langwarring	74	320
Acacia Ridge	Frankston (Cranbourne)	L242	April 2000	Langwarring	43	
Botanic Ridge Stage 1	Casey (Cranbourne)	L218	January 1999	Cranbourne South	280	1,450
Moonah Links	Mornington Peninsula	C2	June 1999	Rye	185	250

Source: Buxton and Goodman (2002)

Table 4.2: Proposed further green wedge residential rezonings as at October 2003

Name	Munici-pality	Amend-ment	Status	Location	UGB status	Size (ha)	No of house lots
Cooper St Industrial Precinct	Whittlesea	None as yet	Not exhibited at time of writing	Cooper St, Epping	Inside UGB	407	750
Pitrones – retirement village	Kingston	C22	On exhibition to July 2002, no panel at time of writing	Dingley	Outside UGB	2.4	110 elderly units
Keysborough Golf Club	Greater Dandenong	C27	On exhibition to May 2002, no panel at time of writing	Hutton and Springvale Roads, Kingsborough	Outside UGB	160	480
Stotts Lane	Frankston	C1	Panel report submitted March 2001	Stotts Lane Frankston South	Outside	42	
Burdetts Quarry	Frankston	C7	Panel report submitted March 2002	Potts Road Langwarrin	Outside UGB	101	390
Botanic Ridge Stage 2	Casey	C39	On exhibition at time of writing	Cranbourne South	Outside UGB	115	515
Botanic Ridge Stage 3	Casey	None as yet	Not exhibited at time of writing	Cranbourne South	Outside UGB	220	1,200
Hume freeway extension	Hume/ Whittlesea	N/A		Craigieburn to Thomastown	N/A		N/A
Scoresby Freeway	Frankston	N/A		Keysborough to Frankston	N/A		N/A

Source: Buxton and Goodman (2002)

Victorian government reasserted an interventionist and controlling role for the state in metropolitan strategic planning for Melbourne's non-urban areas through its new metropolitan policy, *Melbourne 2030* (Department of Infrastructure, 2002). In releasing this new metropolitan plan, the Premier, Steve Bracks (2002, 1), stated that 'Development pressures on the fringe of Melbourne and ad-hoc changes to local planning controls have undermined the protection of ... [green wedges] ...we are acting to protect these areas of great significance ...They are the premium open spaces for our city-dwellers and a home for those who enjoy living in a more open landscape'. The government passed the Planning and Environment (Metropolitan Green Wedge Protection) Act in May, 2003. This defined an Urban Growth Boundary (UGB) and green wedges, required prior ministerial approval before councils could initiate planning scheme amendments, and parliamentary ratification for any change to the UGB and subdivision controls protecting 12 green wedges in a total of 17 fringe area planning schemes. These measures followed the publication in 2002 of proposals in Melbourne 2030 to protect the green wedges.

The government also extended the concept of green wedges to form a true green belt which extends from the inner metropolitan boundary defined by the UGB to the outer boundaries of the rural fringe area councils (see Figure 4.4). It did this by adopting the boundaries of the Melbourne Statistical Division (plus the entire rural area of Yarra Ranges Shire) which includes 31 local government authorities. The area

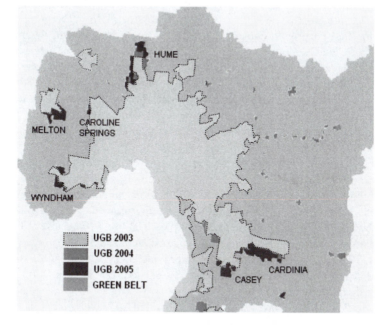

Figure 4.4: Excisions from Melbournes green wedges, 2003–2005

Source: Department of Sustainability and Environment (2006)

affected by this new strategic plan rose from the 5,029 square kilometres of the 1971 plan to 8,829 square kilometres. The outer non-urban areas extend far beyond the green wedges and the outer boundaries of most urban corridors.

These measures appeared to indicate a return to a strong role for the state after the market facilitation period of the Kennett government. The introduction of Melbourne 2030 prevented most of the proposed rezonings shown in Table 4.2 above from proceeding. The government reliance on legislation recognised that the strongest regulatory protection was needed to protect the UGB and the green belt, and that land use planning and policy tools alone are unlikely to be effective in protecting non-urban metropolitan areas in the long term. UGBs define inner metropolitan boundaries to protect non-urban land beyond them. They influence the operation of land markets by limiting or managing the rate and direction of urban expansion and by controlling speculative land price increases in the green belt. A UGB attempts to differentiate between urban and non-urban land by distinguishing between allowable uses for different land categories. The clearer the demarcation between urban and rural land, and between allowable and prohibited land uses, the more successful a UGB is likely to be in preventing the conversion of rural land to urban purposes. Green belts extend from the UGB to a defined outer boundary.

Both managed and inflexible green belts are now in place in Melbourne. A managed UGB on the Portland, Oregon, model ensures orderly, sequential development and infrastructure provision in defined areas (Daniels, 1999). In Melbourne, a managed UGB will apply to land releases from the green wedges adjoining the four growth corridors subject to demonstrated need. An inflexible boundary, on the UK model, seeks to provide permanent protection to the green belt by prohibiting or strongly regulating development (Morris, 1997). This approach will be applied to all other parts of the UGB, such as the environmentally sensitive areas of the Dandenong Ranges, Upper Yarra Valley and Mornington Peninsula, where the boundary 'is settled ... Future growth will be directed into designated areas, to better safeguard our green wedge land and deliver greater efficiency in the delivery of infrastructure and services' (Delahunty, 2003, 1).

Over 500 submissions were received by the government on the proposals for a UGB and green belt making these the most contentious issues among the more than 1,500 submissions made on Melbourne 2030. Most supported the government's proposals (Department of Sustainability and Environment, 2003). However, in December 2003, the government extended the UGB by 1610 hectares to provide more industrial land in Dandenong South and residential land in the northern Hume corridor. The government also undertook to provide 'a guaranteed 15-year supply of land for development that will be released as needed' (Delahunty, 2003, 1). The Minister therefore sent a clear signal to developers that the UGB would be expanded around the nominated urban corridors. This led to development companies purchasing land or development options over large areas in the green belt round the UGB adjoining urban corridors. The government also required councils to select one or both of the two new zones, the Green Wedge Zone and the Rural Conservation Zone, for their green wedge areas and prohibited small lot excisions. These new 2003 zones allow large scale accommodation, tourist and commercial development and are considerably weaker than the zones which were published in the 2002 *Melbourne 2030* documentation. They represent a substantial shift away from strong regulation embodied in the 2002 proposed zones which would have prohibited most urban related uses throughout the extended green belt and fundamentally changed the Kennett government's permissive non-urban zones. These boundary and zone changes reflected the influence of industry and economic ministers in the state Cabinet.

The government also appointed five 'Smart Growth Committees' to advise on corridor boundaries and development planning. These committees comprised representatives of local councils, the development industry and government. These are the bodies primarily responsible for inadequate land use planning in corridors and who largely have attempted to expand corridor boundaries into green wedges. This approach contrasts with a metropolitan wide planning approach through a state or metropolitan agency, such as the former MMBW. Such institutional fragmentation has led to fragmented strategic planning. The composition of these committees ensured that recommendations would be made to expand corridor boundaries. Each committee examined only the corridor allocated to it and avoided a metropolitan wide approach to land supply or the examination of alternative options to increasing the area of corridors. In November 2005, the government released the Smart Growth Committee reports and expanded the UGB by increasing the size of corridors by 11,132 hectares or 34 per cent, increasing the number of residential lots inside corridors from 180,500 to 225,000 (see Figure 4.4). This raised the supply of greenfield land from 18 to 25 years at one of the world's lowest densities, 10 dwellings per hectare gross residential density. The government could have achieved the same land supply by increasing residential density inside the corridors to 15 dwellings per hectare gross residential density, as promised in *Melbourne 2030*, and not extending the boundaries into the green belt (Buxton and Scheurer, 2005). These extensions of the UGB rewarded speculative behaviour by development companies and contradicted the government's stated intention to transfer development from the urban fringe to the city by limiting the supply of greenfield land. In total, 28,442 hectares was excised from green wedges during these third and fourth planning stages.

Case Studies

Independent panels are appointed in Victoria to consider submissions and make recommendations to the planning authority on proposals to rezone land. An analysis of all panel reports into rezoning applications seeking development in the green wedges between 1996 and 2002 showed that some panels sought to make policy on an incremental basis (Buxton and Goodman, 2002). Some panels ignored long standing government policy and relied on their interpretations of a new narrow statutory planning policy which, they argued, no longer clearly supported the protection of green wedges. Some key cases will be examined here.

Figure 4.5: Eynesbury Station incursion into the green wedge

Source: Buxton and Goodman (2002)

Eynesbury Station is a 7,414 hectare grazing and cropping property located in the green wedge on Melbourne's western plains midway between the Melton and Wyndham growth areas (Figure 4.5). An application was made to rezone 1,350 hectares to allow 2,100 residential lots, two 18 hole golf courses, a golf clubhouse and pro shop, a 200 room four star hotel with conference and accommodation facilities, and horse agistment and equestrian facilities. The panel report stated that at first sight the amendment 'appears to be an audacious attempt to create a substantial new urban settlement with a potential population of 3000–4000 people in the middle of the non-urban "green wedge" …This appears to conflict with what is commonly understood to be green wedge policy' (Melton C20 Panel, 2000, 13). However, it argued that as there is 'no longer any clear statement endorsing the retention of green wedges *per se* in … [state statutory policy] … It is left to the … [local statutory policies] … of individual municipalities to make clear policy statements about the green wedges within their municipalities', (Melton C20 Panel, 2000, 22). The state government supported the panel's recommendation for approval.

This view was supported by the panel report into 'the largest urban development yet proposed outside the traditionally designated urban growth areas' on 13 square kilometres north of Epping in Melbourne's north (Whittlesea C12 Panel, 2001, 52). The report commented that state government policy towards green wedges was no longer clear and that a decline in state government direction about spatial planning occurred during the 1990s. In 1988, the state government rejected the development of this land, maintaining the nearby Plenty corridor as its northern development area. In supporting the recommendations for development by Whittlesea council and the panel in 2002, the state government allowed its own strategic planning over a thirty year period to be radically altered in response to a local council initiative. A continuation of this approach would have meant an end to state sponsored metropolitan strategic planning.

In contrast, other panels opposed developments in green wedges. A panel argued that the council had failed to establish need, a large area of the nearby growth corridor remained undeveloped, and there was no strategic basis for approval (Cranbourne L218 Panel, 1998, 7). The council and government ignored the panel recommendation and the amendment was approved in January 1999. The Frankston C3 2001 and C7 2002 panel reports argued for the ongoing relevance of the concept of green wedges in Melbourne's planning. Kingston Amendment L33 in Braeside proposed an 'environmental trade-off' between a residential development of 700 housing lots on 65 hectares in the green wedge in return for promised environmental improvements including a 'major wetlands system' (City of Kingston, 1998, 3). The panel rejected the proposal arguing that approval 'would undermine the very clear direction set in ... [state] ... policy' (Cranbourne L218 Panel, 1998, 50). However the government approved the amendment in February 1999.

This approval was then used as a precedent for rezoning 227 hectares of land in nearby Keysborough from Rural to Residential 1. The Panel assessing this proposal acknowledged that previous rezoning decisions, in particular L33 in Kingston, had created a precedent it could not ignore. 'It would be fair to say that approval of this development at state level has opened the door for other similar proposals in the green wedge area', it argued (Dandenong C2 & C5 Panel, 2000, 48). Yet other panels have rejected the possibility of their decisions acting as precedents. The panel considering the Eynesbury Station development argued that 'the values of the Werribee/Melton green wedge will not be eroded by Amendment C20' and that it would not create an undesirable precedent (Dandenong C2 & C5 Panel, 2000, 33). The panel believed that approval would lead to the retention of the property in single ownership, maintain productive agriculture, allow environmental management problems to be overcome, and protect environmental assets. In contrast, the Frankston C7 panel report into the Burdetts Quarry development rejected the concept of offsetting environmental values.

These and other case studies demonstrate that by 2002, Melbourne's green wedge policy, in place for over 30 years, was on the brink of collapse. Melbourne's green wedges and broader green belt were rapidly being developed, as Sydney's green belt had been, through incremental, ad hoc decisions which built on the power of precedent. Freestone 1992, for example, showed that public confidence in Sydney's green belt was progressively undermined by incremental rezoning. In Melbourne, the abolition of the metropolitan planning authority, and a state government uninterested in metropolitan strategic planning allowed local councils, planning panels and developers to use the land use planning system to destroy, instead of to protect, green wedges by adopting a local, development facilitation approach to planning on the urban fringe. In November 2005, the Victorian government announced that it would establish a Growth Areas Authority to coordinate and manage develop in outer urban corridors.

Lessons from Melbourne's Experience

The first lesson to be drawn from Melbourne's strategic planning experience is that a metropolitan wide focus which includes non-urban areas in a regional plan is necessary for the ongoing protection of green belts. Institutional fragmentation, including local decision making, is fatal for green belts. The United States provides the most well-known example of the impact of institutional fragmentation. Many commentators, such as Mattingly (1999), Daniels (1999), and Carrion-Flores and Irwin (2004) have shown how the lack of coordination between local government bodies in the US has led to continuous outward expansion of American cities. The lack of institutional integration inevitably leads to spatial fragmentation.

Planning for metropolitan areas should be integrated with planning for the protection of nearby green belts. Non-urban areas are unlikely to be protected if urban growth is not contained or accommodated elsewhere. A regional approach therefore needs to connect the values of a green belt with the intensification of development in established metropolitan areas or in existing or new townships outside the green belt. Alterman (1997) concludes that the best way to protect the countryside is not by protecting farmland but by constraining urban growth. Regional planning can be achieved through a metropolitan planning authority, or by a state agency applying clear legally enforced policy.

Table 4.3 shows how the Melbourne strategic land use plan seeks to shift a substantial amount of development from nominated urban growth corridors to mixed use activity centres in the established city. The plan also seeks to increase outer urban densities. However, this shift and outer urban intensification is not occurring because of the operation of different land markets and because the government is making available a continuous supply of land for outer urban development. In Australia, different types of development companies generally build different housing types in either outer urban or established urban areas catering to different market segments.

Table 4.3: Melbourne metropolitan housing starts

Average annual housing starts 1996–2001		Proposed starts 2001–30	
	%	%	Number
Greenfields (corridors)	38	31	195,000
Activity centres	24	41	255,000
Dispersed (existing metropolis)	38	28	170,000

Source: Department of infrastructure (2002)

While the government continually extends the UGB and provides a continuous supply of outer urban land for housing, companies specialising in outer urban development will continue to build detached houses on the expanding urban fringe instead of being forced to redirect their construction activities to higher density housing in established areas.

Secondly, the reliance on multiple values for green belts will provide stronger protection than limited or sectoral approaches. Integrated, cross-sectoral policy is essential. For example, peri-urban regions in Australia contribute at least 25 per cent of the gross value of agricultural production although comprising less than 3 per cent of the land used for agriculture (Houston, 2005). The Melbourne non-urban areas are the second most productive agricultural productive region in the state of Victoria. However, green wedges contribute differentially to this total, some hardly at all. Reliance on their value solely for agriculture would result in their loss.

New purposes for green belts internationally have emerged in recent years. The coincidence of the impending oil peak and the end of the oil economy, climate change, and the issue of food security will increase the importance of green belts and broader peri-urban areas for their agricultural and other resources. It is likely that, this century, cities which preserve their hinterlands will be the most productive and liveable. The amount of food shipped between countries has increased four times in the last 40 years, but far reaching changes in the highly centralised supermarket food production and distribution system are likely in the coming decades as transport costs rise (Box and Smith, 2005). James Lovelock (2006, 13) integrates these concerns by arguing that

Our future food and energy supplies can no longer be taken as secure from a world that is devastated by climate change ... climate change will surely disrupt the political and trading world, imports of food, fuels and raw materials will increasingly become inadequate as the suppliers in other regions are overwhelmed by droughts and floods.

Folke et al. (2002) have pointed to the complex non-linear consequences likely from periods of rapid change. These consequences may include sudden catastrophic and perhaps irreversible impacts. This uncertainty also increases the potential importance of non-urban areas near cities, particularly as other areas important for food production, water harvesting and resources come under stress. It would therefore be prudent to retain the possibility of a range of flexible futures for green belts by adopting effective measures to protect their resources and environmental values.

Thirdly, a clear demarcation between urban and non-urban land uses, and inflexibility in applying this distinction over time is likely to lead to clarity, consistency and certainty in the application of policy. Policy vagueness is also fatal for green wedges. The MMBW Metropolitan Strategy Implementation report (MMBW, 1981, 85) summarised this position, arguing that by removing urban expectations from rural areas a 'clear demarcation between urban and non-urban areas ... helps eliminate land speculation ...'

Introducing a green belt and not controlling land uses in the broader peri-urban belt surrounding a city may lead to unintended consequences. Audirac (1999) points to two: an increase in subdivision of countryside in the green belt, particularly for hobby farms; and the 'leap-frogging' of development leading to uncontrolled land speculation beyond the green belt. For example, Robinson and Marzluff (2005), in a study on the eastern fringe of Seattle, US, found a high proportion of new development occurred outside the UGB after its introduction. Without strict controls on rural land uses and rural subdivision, land in green belts and in broader peri-urban areas may continue to be developed even while governments are pursuing consolidation and urban limitation policies. Melbourne illustrates this conclusion. Extensive new low income housing, higher income integrated residential/ tourist/commercial developments and subdivision for hobby farms is continuing in and beyond the Melbourne green belt because the government in 2003 liberalised the proposed restrictions on urban related uses in the original *Melbourne 2030* planning zones.

Different techniques have been used internationally to achieve this demarcation, including the application of policy, regulatory land use planning tools and legislation in the UK, Europe and Australia, and the purchase or transfer of development rights in the US. Voluntary, community based and market based tools have been less successful. Generally accepted time periods for the operation of green belts need to be extended. After over 50 years, some UK green belts are being threatened with development. In contrast, the purchase of development rights is intended to protect green belts in perpetuity.

Fourthly, maintaining a UGB, and protecting green wedges and green belts requires ongoing commitment by communities and governments. Maintaining this commitment will prove increasingly difficult. Unprecedented urbanisation is placing increasing development pressure on green belts and broader peri-urban areas globally. Massive urban conurbations will develop internationally over the next generation at incalculable environmental, economic and social costs. This apparently inexorable crisis of urbanism is the realization of Mumford's nightmare. Australia, with one of the lowest continental populations but the least efficient land uses, illustrates the difficulties of maintaining the values of land on the urban fringe. If Australians cannot protect their urban fringes and broader peri-urban areas there is little hope that most other countries can. Melbourne lost its inner parkland green belt because successive governments regarded open space as commercially expendable and as a free input to public and private projects. The same fate appears certain for much of Melbourne's new outer urban green belt.

Finally, the most effective mix of protective tools needs to be put in place for long term protection. Folke et al. (2002) argue that control mechanisms such as regulation cannot respond adequately to uncertainty and rapid change and that only adaptive management which builds adaptive capacity can respond adequately to a dynamic world. However, regulation may respond rapidly to trends. Flexibility may close off long term options so lessening the possibility of long term adaptability and survival. If green belts fulfil increasingly crucial functions for cities, their protection may require a more rigorous form of strategic land use planning which identifies clear long term end points and rigorously selects methods to achieve these objectives, excluding all others. In contrast, strategic planning usually seeks to achieve broad, flexible aims through a variety of allowable methods. Regulation has also been criticised as ineffective and causing undesirable effects. For example, development groups such as the Urban Development Institute of Australia, and some other commentators claimed that the 2002 Melbourne UGB caused a 30 per cent rise in the price of land on the urban fringe in 2002 (Underwood, 2003; Baillieu, 2004). However Valuer-General figures and government research disproved this claim (Valuer General, 2003; Department of Sustainability and Environment, 2003). The application in the UK and some European countries of regulatory tools has demonstrated their greater effectiveness in protecting green belts than reliance on market or voluntary measures practiced widely in the US.

Regulation may take many forms. Of the Australian states, only Queensland pays a form of compensation for financial losses through zoning changes. As a result, the Victorian state government has traditionally relied on policy and land use planning measures to protect its non-urban areas, but has also used the techniques of government land purchase and legislation. Only land purchase has worked as a long term protective tool. Daniels (1999) has advocated the use of the purchase or transfer of property rights to protect green belts and has described their effectiveness in the US. The South Australian government used this technique in the 1980s to protect large areas of remnant native vegetation. In Melbourne, for example, these tools could be used to require landowners within the urban growth corridors to purchase development rights from landowners in the green belt, preventing windfall gains and protecting the green belt from development permanently. Australian governments have consistently rejected the use of transferable property rights or betterment taxes, although the national capital, Canberra, has been developed by preventing private land betterment.

Governments may attempt to promote land management to help protect countryside from inappropriate uses and development. Land use planning can assist protective land management by allowing or preventing certain uses of land, for example, by preventing degrading land practices, or promoting agriculture through agricultural zoning, prohibiting incompatible land uses and intensive subdivision and controlling land speculation to limit rural land price increases and assist farm viability. However planning cannot require the adoption of uses. Governments can provide land management subsidies and reduce land holding costs but these can never outweigh the returns from subdivision and development and so are predicated on effective land use controls. The Victorian government is requiring all councils in Melbourne's green belt to prepare 'Green Wedge Management Plans' in order to assist the protection of the non-urban areas. These are expected to address the management of environmental values such as soils, water and remnant vegetation and to assist in the control of inappropriate uses.

Conclusion

In conclusion, Melbourne's strategic planning draws from British and European traditions but has much in common with more recent American trends. Australian state governments are using common techniques in renewed attempts to limit outer urban growth and protect green belts, with varying results. The Victorian state government has reinforced in principle the forty year long attempt to protect Melbourne's green wedges and a green belt in the non-urban zones on the urban fringe. However, if long term protection of these areas is to be achieved, the rigorous application of a stronger long term vision will be needed.

References

Alterman, R. (1997), 'The Challenge of Farmland Preservation: lessons from a six-nation comparison', *Journal of the American Planning Association*, 63(2), 220–44.

Audirac, I. (1999), 'Unsettled views about the fringe: rural-urban or urban-rural frontiers?', in O.J. Furuseth and M.B. Lapping (eds.), 'Contested Countryside: The Rural Urban Fringe in North America', (Aldershot: Ashgate), pp. 7–32.

Baillieu, T. (2004), The Age Newspaper 20 August.

Barnett, F., Burt, W.O. and Heath, F. (1944), *'We Must Go On': A Study in Planned Reconstruction and Housing* (Melbourne: Wilkie and Co).

Borrie, E. and Cawcutt, F. (1947), *The Future Urban Boundaries of Melbourne and the Distribution of Population Therein* (Melbourne: Melbourne and Metropolitan Board of Works).

Box, D. Wakeman, T. and Smith, J. (2005), 'The end of cheap oil: the consequences', *The Ecologist*, 35:8, 44–52.

Bracks, S. (2002), *Press Release: Bracks Government Protects Green Wedges* (Melbourne: Oce of the Premier).

Buxton, M. and Goodman, R. (2002), *Maintaining Melbourne's Green Wedges – planning policy and the future of Melbourne's green belt*, RMIT University School of Social Science and Planning, Melbourne.

Buxton, M. and Scheurer, J. (2005), *Urban Form in Melbourne's Growth Corridors* (Melbourne: RMIT University Publishing).

Buxton, M. and Staindl, P. (1999), *Planning on the Run. A Review of Victorian State Government Planning Practice in the Upper Yarra Valley and Dandenong Ranges*, Tech. rep., Upper Yarra Valley and Dandenongs Environmental Council, Lilydale.

Carrion-Flores, C. and Irwin, E. (2004), 'Determinants of Residential Land-Use Conversion and Sprawl at the Urban-Rural Fringe', *American Journal of Agricultural Economics*, 86(4), 889–904.

Champion, R. (1971), *Melbourne Region Conservation Report*, Conservation Council of Victoria, Melbourne.

City of Kingston (1998), *Amendment L 33 Explanatory Report*, City of Kingston, Kingston.

Copenhagen Municipal Corporation (1993), *Copenhagen Municipal Plan* (Copenhagen: The Municipal Corporation of Copenhagen).

Cranbourne L218 Panel (1998), *Cranbourne Planning Scheme Amendment L218 Report of the Independent Panel*, Department of Infrastructure, Melbourne.

Cumberland County Council (1948), *The Planning Scheme for the County of Cumberland, New South Wales* (Sydney: Cumberland City Council).

Dandenong C2 & C5 Panel (2000), *Amendments C2 and C5 Greater Dandenong Planning Scheme – The Keysborough Policy and Proposal*, Department of Infrastructure, Melbourne.

Daniels, T. (1999), *When City and Country Collide: Managing Growth in the Metropolitan Fringe* (Washington: Island Press).

Delahunty, M. (2003), *Melbourne's Urban Growth Boundary Settled* (Melbourne: Ministerial Press Release).

Department of Infrastructure (2002), *Melbourne 2030: Planning for Sustainable Growth, Melbourne*, Department of Infrastructure, Melbourne.

Department of Sustainability and Environment (2003), *Urban Development Program Report 2003*, DSE, Melbourne.

—— (2006), 'Metropolitan Melbourne 2003–2005', Personal Communication.

Folke, C., Carpenter, S., Elmqvist, T., Gunderson, L., Holling, C., Walker, B., Bengtsson, J., Berkes, F., Colding, J., Danell, K., Falkenmark, M., Gordon, L., Kasperson, R., Kautsky, N., Kinzig, A., Levin, S., Mäler, K.G., Moberg, F., Ohlsson, L., Olsson, P., Ostrom, E., Reid, W., Rockström, J., Savenije, H., and Svedin, U. (2002), *Resilience and Sustainable Development: Building Adaptive Capacity in a World of Transformation* (Stockholm: The Environmental Advisory Council to the Swedish Government).

Frankston C3 Panel (2001), *Frankston Planning Scheme Amendment C3 – Report of Panel*, Department of Infrastructure, Melbourne.

Frankston C7 Panel (2002), *Frankston Planning Scheme Amendment C7 – Panel Report*, Department of Infrastructure, Melbourne.

Freestone, R. (1989), *Model Communities – The Garden City Movement in Australia* (Melbourne: Thomas Nelson).

—— (1992), 'Sydney's Green Belt 1945/1960', *Australian Planner*, 30(2), 70–77.

Government of Victoria (1987), *Shaping Melbourne's Future – The Government's Metropolitan Policy* (Melbourne: Government of Victoria).

Hamer, R. (1965), 'Town and Country Planning in Victoria', *Australian Planning Institute Journal*, 3(4), 130–33.

Harris, G. (2005), *Melbourne's Green Belts and Wedges. A short history of open places and spaces in the city and their strategic context* (Melbourne: RMIT University Publishing).

Houston, P. (2005), 'Revaluing the Fringe: Some Findings on the Value of Agricultural Production in Australia's Peri-Urban Regions', *Geographical Research*, 42(2), 209–23.

Lovelock, J. (2006), *The Revenge of Gaia, Why the Earth is Fighting Back – and How We Can Still Save Humanity* (London: Allen Lane).

Maclellan, R. (1993), *Planning a Better Future for Victorians: New Directions Development and Economic Growth* (Victoria: Department of Planning and Development).

Mattingly, M. (1999), *Institutional Structures and Processes for Environmental Planning and Management of the Peri-urban Interface* (Strategic Environmental Planning and Management for the Peri-urban Interface Research Project).

McLoughlin, J. (1992), *Shaping Melbourne's Future?* (Melbourne: Cambridge University Press).

Melton C20 Panel (2000), *Eynesbury Station, Wyndham and Melton Planning Schemes Amendment C20 Panel Report*, Department of Infrastructure, Melbourne.

Ministry for Planning and Environment (1988), *Melbourne's Open Space – The Metropolitan Open Space Plan*, Ministry for Planning and Environment, Melbourne.

MMBW (1954), *Melbourne Metropolitan Planning Scheme 1954 – Report*, MMBW, Melbourne.

——(1959), *The Problem of Urban Expansion in the Melbourne Metropolitan Area*, MMBW, Melbourne.

—— (1962), *Amending Planning Scheme No 1*, MMBW, Melbourne.

—— (1967), *The Future Growth of Melbourne: A report to the Minister for Local Government on Melbourne's future growth and its planning administration*, MMBW, Melbourne.

—— (1971), *Planning Policies for the Melbourne Metropolitan Region*, MMBW, Melbourne.

—— (1974), *Report on General Concept Objections, 1974*, MMBW, Melbourne.

—— (1977), *Review of Planning Policies for the Non-Urban Zones*, MMBW, Melbourne.

—— (1980), *Metropolitan Strategy*, MMBW, Melbourne.

—— (1981), *Metropolitan Strategy Implementation*, MMBW, Melbourne.

Morris, E.S. (1997), *British Town Planning and Urban Design – Principles and Policies* (Edinburgh Gate: Addison Wesley Longman).

MTPC (1929), *Plan of General Development Melbourne* (Melbourne: Government Printer).

Mumford, L. (1961), *The City in History: its origins, its transformations and its prospects* (London: Secker and Warburg).

Robinson, L. Newell, J. and Marzluff, J. (2005), 'Twenty-five years of sprawl in the Seattle region: growth management responses and implications for conservation', *Landscape and Urban Planning*, 71, 51–72.

Town and Country Planning Board (1967), *Organisation for Strategic Planning*, TCPB, Melbourne.

Underwood, G. (2003), 'Wedge Politics', The Age Newspaper 3 May.

Valuer General (2003), *Guide to Property Values* (Melbourne: Department of Sustainability).

Wale, N. (2003), 'Green Wedges and Metropolitan Strategies', *Planning News*, 29:3, 17–18.

Whittlesea C12 Panel (2001), *Epping North – Whittlesea Amendment C12*, Department of Infrastructure, Melbourne.

CHAPTER 5

The Green Belt that Wasn't: The Case of New Zealand from 1910 to the 1990s

Carole Miller and Marco Amati

Introduction

It is almost an automatic assumption that planning ideas and concepts will generally achieve some international currency and use, given the twentieth century nature of the profession and discipline. This assumption is stronger where the transmission path for those ideas is a colonial pathway. New Zealand was one of Britain's later colonies where systematic colonisation dated from the 1840s. It nurtured strong ties with Britain through to the post-World War II period, and thus seems a prime candidate to be an open and willing recipient for such ideas. The process of the transmission of planning ideas and concepts has been addressed by a number of writers including King (1976), Home (1997) and Ward (1999), with the latter dealing with it in the most comprehensive manner. He suggested that the diffusion of ideas ranged from uncritical borrowing to more complex forms of borrowing that involved the ideas becoming adapted and alterations in response to local conditions and concerns. From this Ward develops a simple typology of diffusional episodes that are essentially predicated on the relative power of the country exporting the idea and the country importing them (Ward, 1999, 58). In directly administered colonial societies such as India, as Home (1997) so clearly demonstrates, direct imposition was both expected and accepted but that was not the case in New Zealand. While an intensely loyal member of the British Empire that was somewhat reluctant to, until 1947 (through the Statute of Westminster), to take on full independence, the reality is that New Zealand was self ruling from the late 1860s. It merely placed its defence and foreign relations, minor concerns for such a small and isolated nation, in the hands of Great Britain. Thus it was free to take up or reject any town planning concepts that were presented by the often zealous proponents of town planning. These varied from Reade and Davidge from the Garden City and Town Planning Association who demonstrated, in their work, 'an evangelical zeal to spread the message' (Hardy, 1991, 94) to home grown enthusiasts such as Samuel Hurst Seager. Given the potential for the transmission of planning ideas, then what was the process of transmission of the green belt as a method to control and shape urban growth to New Zealand and how far was it transformed or adapted to meet local needs?

In the following sections we trace the history of the reception and use of the green belt, as a planning tool in New Zealand. The receptiveness of New Zealand's planning system to the green belt ideas is examined from the early development of town belts and beautifying societies, to its ultimate use in regional planning plans. We argue that the need for green belt was not obvious to New Zealand planners and in most New Zealand cities it struggled to gain acceptance as a planning tool. The exception to this trend was Christchurch where a green belt was used to shape development from the 1940s to the 1990s. We end by describing how the re-organisation of New Zealand's planning system at the end of the 1980s has finally seen the demise of the green belt as a viable tool for limiting and guiding urban and regional growth patterns.

Green Belt Precursors – Town Belts and Beautifying Societies

The acceptance of any planning idea or concept is made easier if the recipient population are able to associate it with some aspect of their existing urban environment. As already noted New Zealand was one of Britain's later colonies and in the earliest period of organised settlement much of the work of laying out new towns fell to the grandly conceived but ultimately unsuccessful New Zealand Company and church based developers such as the Canterbury Association, rather than any government organisation. Equally, all the early town developers benefited from the advancement in surveying practice which allowed the use of trigometric surveying to produce relatively fast and accurate surveys, which ultimately allowed the early marketing of the sections created. The role of the surveyor in the development of New Zealand towns cannot be underestimated and to this day they are a strong presence within the town planning system in a way which is not evident elsewhere. The New Zealand Company under the erratic but inspired leadership of Edward Gibbon Wakefield, was the most ambitious of the early town developers, and planned settlements at Wellington, Wanganui and New Plymouth in the North Island and Nelson in the South Island. The Canterbury Association confined itself to the laying out of Christchurch which they envisaged as a capital city with 'land designated for a cathedral and city churches, a marketplace, civic buildings, and reserves earmarked for later expansion' (McIntyre, 2000, 89). The reference to reserves for later expansion created in effect a town belt on which Christchurch's Hagley Park would be established on the fringe of the central city, though much of the rest was lost, sold to meet the ever increasing debts incurred in trying to develop a rather grandiose city on a swamp. However, the town belt also made an appearance in the New Zealand Company city plans – 'the Company had wanted a broad belt of open space left for public use as at Adelaide between the town and the farm allotments' (Hamer, 1990, 237). It survived relatively intact inWellington, despite parts of them being lost to everything from the Governor General's residence to Wellington Hospital, to provide a green backdrop to the central city. Reporting on his trip to New Zealand in 1914, William Davidge called the town belts in Wellington and Dunedin 'a singularly attractive feature, and from the natural and undulating character of the ground, superior even to the attractions of the famous 'parklands' surrounding Adelaide' (Davidge, 1915, 173). In 1871 management of the Wellington town belt passed to the Wellington City Council through the *Wellington City Reserves Act* 1871 and in other cities, including Dunedin whose Presbyterian founders had also provided for a town belt, concentrated on the management, or rather benign neglect of these town belts. The Dunedin Amenities Society, founded in 1887 which began as the Dunedin and Suburbs Reserves Conservation Society before it became the Dunedin Amenities and Town Planning Society in 1915. With the Christchurch Beautifying Association founded in 1897, it had among its practical projects work on beautifying and developing the town belts. As such, much of the New Zealand urban population had been exposed to the notion of open space in the form of belts girding the developed urban areas, and being used to define the boundary between the city and the country. This town and country split, even where specific town belts did not exist, was an integral part of the development of New Zealand's urban areas. It partly arose from the perceived need to ensure that the new settlers would have urban facilities and markets close at hand and later as towns grew, that there would be sufficient land to feed urban dwellers. There was, however, little concern with restraining urban growth – as Hamer (1995) points out when the government became involved in town development 'the often desperate needs of governments for revenue impelled them both into the business of town creation and into selling land that could then be used by others for this purpose' (Hamer, 1995, 15). This tension between the demands of growth which was invariably seen as progress, and a responsibility for ensuring orderly development would become underlying theme to much of New Zealand's planning history.

A Solution Seeking a Problem

An essential aspect of the up take of any planning idea such as green belts, is the existence or at least the perception of existence of a planning problem for which green belts provided a logical and useable solution. The development of town planning and in particular the creation of town planning legislation had been bedevilled by this from its earliest years. The mania of town planning had quickly reached New Zealand as Miller (2002) demonstrates, with the potential for the development of slums the most obvious and potent symbol of urban dysfunctionality, being used to advocate for the creation of town planning legislation.[1]

Slums were however in short supply. Isaac and Olssen point out that in 1921 the Board of Health rejected the British measure of overcrowding of 1.5 people to a

---

1   This fear of slums and other urban ills, offering as they did both a physical and moral threat to a young society, was enforced by a number of events from articles on the slums of Auckland that Charles Reade had produced for the Weekly Graphic, to his solo lecture series in 1911, which culminated in the 1914 Australasian Town Planning Tour of Reade and William Davidge in which lantern slides of slums played a major role.

room, replacing it with a standard of 1 per room to reflect the 'healthier conditions' that should be expected in New Zealand. Even that standard revealed that only 12.6% of the population could be considered to be living in overcrowded conditions (Isaac and Olssen, 2001, 113). Given the paucity of support for the development of the urban ills typified by the slum, the need to town planning legislation was easy to ignore. Thus, despite the efforts of the town planning enthusiasts such as Hurst Seager and E. Leigh Hunt, the interested professions including the architects and surveyors and the support of a varied band of politicians, no town planning legislation was forthcoming with bills failing in 1911 and 1917–19. In 1917 Seager was sent to the second Australian Planning Conference to report on the conference's impact on planning in New Zealand. Seager invoked Australia's, and particularly Sydney's, experience as being a warning sign for New Zealand towns. He reported that

> Not only must care be taken to carry out all possible improvements within the city, but it is extremely important that it should be at once determined how far the main city area is to extend and to form around that area a broad tree-lined avenue, with reserves for park and dairying lands (Hurst Seager, 1918, 13).

Despite some interest in urban growth in New Zealand there was no equivalent to the propaganda and attention that the issue was receiving in the UK which is best exemplified by Clough William-Ellis' vituperative attack in *England and the Octopus*. William-Ellis heaped scorn on the tragic loss of countryside that urban growth inevitably entailed. As he sarcastically remarked of those who might benefit from the destruction of the countryside:

> You may ravish and defile the most divine landscape in the world, and your children (being your children) will rise up and call you progressive. You are a lucky 'prospector' or a 'successful real-estate operator' a 'live wire' and what local newspapers call 'a prominent and respected citizen.' By your exploitation of the land you have enriched yourself and your heirs. You have done very well. (William-Ellis, 1928, 19)

The reality was that New Zealand's cities were hardly old enough or big enough, as the figures in Table 5.1 suggest, to have the population that made slums or uncontrolled urban growth either a possibility or a threat. Urban growth was universally accepted and welcomed.

Table 5.1: Population of selected cities 1926

City	Population
Auckland	193,385
Wellington	121,961
Christchurch	118,644
Dunedin	85,197
Wanganui	26,388

Source: New Zealand Yearbook, 1926

Although there was recognition of the 'problem of overgrowth' (Hurst Seager, 1918, 13), the need for green belts and town planning in general was a solution to ensure that urban growth was shaped in an orderly manner.

In many respects, local government remained unconvinced that town planning legislation was necessary or useful, even after it was unexpectedly achieved in 1926. This lead them to commence work on town planning schemes with what can only be called glacial speed. The *Town-planning Act* 1926 required boroughs with a population of 1,000 or greater to produce a town plan the purpose of which was 'the development of the City or Borough to which it relates in such a way as will most effectively tend to promote its healthfulness, amenity, convenience and advancement' (S3(2), *Town-planning Act* 1926). It also included provisions for the reservation of areas as open space and identification of areas to be used exclusively or principally for specific purposes, for which zoning provided the most likely implementation tool. There was no specific provision for any larger scale regional or metropolitan beyond a rather modest provision for extra-urban schemes which dealt with land on the urban periphery, but these were voluntary and were rarely completed. Given that local authorities were reluctant to institute the compulsory town planning the new act instituted – originally the town plans were to be completed by the end of 1930, this is not unexpected.

The problems with getting town planning implemented were compounded by the lack of government support for the venture. Reginald Hammond, was appointed the first Director of Town Planning. He was an architect turned town planner who had trained at the London University course, and had been the author of the legislation. He was given negligible resources and within 2 years of his appointment he resigned to enter private practice to be replaced by John Mawson. The talented and often mercurial Mawson was the son of Thomas Mawson and could boast of experience in Britain, Canada and Greece as a member of his father's well known firm. Mawson moved quickly to secure an amendment to the legislation in 1929 which provided for regional planning. Regional plans would promote economic and social development within a framework of regulation that achieved the best use of natural, social and economic resources. While the regional plans would establish basic standards for density and amenity, much of this detail would be in the town planning schemes that would form a complementary part of the regional plans. Mawson had used a speech to the Municipal Association Conference in Wanganui in February 1929 to expound a definition of regional planning. Regional planning, he said, was 'the co-ordination and correlation of all matters of interest common to the separate local authorities within the region in order to secure the economic use and development of the land for the purpose for which it is best suited' (Mawson, 1929, 5). This was an ambitious definition which would have simultaneously overcome many of the problems created by the fragmented nature of local government and would have created the opportunity to introduce a wide variety of planning tools including green belts. Regional planning, despite Mawson's strongest efforts, was never to develop in the manner he envisaged when he secured the 1929 Amendment (see Miller, 1998).

Nevertheless, despite this there is evidence that there was a growing awareness of the issue of uncontrolled urban expansion. An editorial in the *New Zealand Journal of Commerce* called it 'subdivision mania' and suggested that much of subdivision on Auckland's fringes rather than being 'the normal expansion of a progressive town' was the creation of speculators and that it is 'doubtful whether the conversion of these estates into building sections was a necessary step in overcoming the shortage of houses' (Anonymous, 1923, 1). The study by Rogerson (1976) of the Auckland property market prior to World War II, suggests that 'suburban subdivision was less the result of arcadian idealism and a desire to neutralise the effects of urban growth, than of a desire to share the financial rewards of that growth'. Given the propensity of New Zealand towns to effectively sprawl, as Hamer (1995) observes, there appeared to be the makings of a town planning problem to which the green belts might be an answer. In 1938 a whole copy of the planning journal *Planning*, the official bulletin of the Town Planning Institute of New Zealand,[2] was devoted to 'the future in relation to town planning' (Hammond, 1938, 1). An article by the Hon. T. Bloodworth, a member of the Legislative Council, New Zealand's appointed upper house that was abolished in 1951, quite baldly stated that 'this is a land still in the making, still in the process of growth, and that growth should be planned so far as it is humanly possible to do so' (Bloodworth, 1938, 4). In the same edition another writer, F.B. Stephens identified both the existence of urban drift from rural areas, the impact of the car on urban areas and the need for planning to replace 'the present system of haphazard growth' (Stephens, 1938, 13). These were not the only concerns. In a country that then and now largely depends on exporting agricultural products as the mainstay of its economy, there were by the late 1930s concerns about the encroachment of towns and cities onto agricultural land. Writing in 1937 Charles Putt, town planner for Auckland,[3] the country's largest city, and an endless worker for the profession, observed that 'in the absence of a master plan, this has inevitably led to haphazard growth, and in many cases, the premature intrusion of urban development into agricultural land' (Putt, 1937, 6). In the same article he was also concerned about the effects of speculative development of fringe urban land. Many of the articles also identified a concern with the development of what were called 'decadent areas' of slum or substandard housing that they saw developing in the larger and older cities. Putt suggested in 1937 that there were 'nearly 100 acres' (Putt, 1937, 9) of such decadent housing in Auckland.

This suggests that the small town planning community in New Zealand was increasingly becoming aware of the conditions which encouraged urban sprawl and which would require some town planning response if the problem was not to become

---

2   The New Zealand Planning Institute was set up to encourage an interest in town planning and was not a professional body, given the paucity of town planners. This resulted in it being dominated by lay members.

3   In this and later periods local government was severely fractionated with Auckland city being made up of the Auckland City Council which covered the main part of the isthmus that the city occupied, but the city proper included a myriad of boroughs such as Mt Eden Borough Council. This was particularly a problem in Auckland but also characterised other New Zealand cities.

widespread. To some extent the New Zealand town planning community's perceptions of town planning problems would have been influenced by their knowledge of overseas town planning literature. There was a dearth of qualified town planners in New Zealand. In 1926 'there were only seven Town Planning Institute (TPI) members in the country, and only two had any formal qualification in town planning' (Miller, 2007, 2) which had only risen to '13 Academically qualified Town Planners in New Zealand, seven within the Government, two in the service of Local Authorities, and the balance engaged in the practice of Architecture and Town Planning' (Basire, 1945), by 1945. All of these town planners had qualified through the Town Planning Institute (later RTPI), a challenging process as students sitting the exams had to study the British syllabus including British town planning legislation. This was a situation that continued until 1958 when the first town planning diploma was established at the University of Auckland. Town planning literature was also widely distributed primarily through the journal *Community Planning* and its successor *Planning*, which the ever energetic John Mawson established as the journal of the Town Planning Institute of New Zealand. That Institute was essentially a collection of those with an interest in town planning rather than a professional body, but its magazine provided a wide variety of town planning material. This information included 'Items of Interest' which in 1931 included a report from the National Town-Planning Conference held at Blackpool in 1930. That included a discussion of the use of town planning powers 'for the reservation from use for building purposes' (Mawson, 1931, 107). Later editions of *Community Planning* featured both reading list of new and established town planning literature, ensuring that those who practiced or had an interest in town planning issues were kept up to date with new practices and polices, including the emergence of green belt methods.

Overall, therefore the adoption of the green belt in New Zealand was likely to follow in the steps of another planning concept that had been introduced through colonisation: garden cities and suburbs (see Miller, 2002). At the point that the New Zealand planning system was being established it is clear that the green belt was known as a planning tool. Nevertheless, the concern of the public and politicians about urban growth was insufficient to inspire the widespread implementation of the green belt. Decisions were made to not designate green belt because they were not thought on the whole to be necessary.

Christchurch – Trialing the Green Belt

In Christchurch however, despite the reluctance of the New Zealand planning system to identify urban growth as a problem, the green belt was enthusiastically adopted as a planning tool after the Second World War. The following charts the history the green belt in Christchurch, comparing its reception there with that in Auckland. Christchurch's adoption of the greenbelt as an urban growth tool, contrasts strongly with its lack of use elsewhere, particularly in Auckland where it appeared to be a very appropriate tool and the reasons for this are complex.

Mawson's regional planning aspirations never came to fruition, partly due to the lack of staff combined with the onset of the Depression but also due to his deteriorating relationship with the government of the day which saw him leave government service in 1933 to return to a lesser position in 1937. While the reduction in Mawson's status from Director of Town Planning to Town Planning Officer brought a corresponding reduction in his powers he remained convinced that regional planning offered the potential to produce better planning while overcoming the fragmented nature of local government. He found a ready audience for his ideas in Christchurch which had always been concerned about the potential for fragmented planning that would result from the urban area of Christchurch being controlled by the Christchurch City Council and six other local authorities. As a result, in 1941, the local authorities concerned were persuaded to co-operate and commenced a comprehensive survey of the Christchurch Metropolitan area to provide the foundation of a 'comprehensive and co-ordained town planning scheme for Greater Christchurch as a single social and economic unit' (McGibbon, 1948, 9). It was a community based effort which used everything from high school students to the Canterbury Geographical Society, to collect the vast amounts of information needed. The eventual town planning scheme would provide a common set of controls for all Christchurch local authorities and a logical plan for the social, economic and growth of Christchurch.

The Christchurch Metropolitan Planning Committee produced an interim report in 1945 which was announced in *The Press*, the main Christchurch newspaper. In the introductory paragraph in the newspaper report there was a mention of 'general recommendations on greenbelt [sic], residential, industrial and other zones [...]' (*The Press*, 1945). The newspaper report went on to explain that 'the rural district is the most restricted, the intention being to preserve it as a green belt for farming and market gardening serving the needs of the urban population and for public grounds' (*The Press*, 1945), though there is no specific reference to this green belt providing a restraint on urban growth. This is clearly the first specific example of the green belt, albeit in a limited form being used in New Zealand and confirms that the concept of green belts had been quickly transmitted to New Zealand where it had been adapted to the specific conditions that existed in Christchurch.

Unfortunately, despite all the work and the relatively high profile of the Christchurch Metropolitan Plan it had no statutory power or authority. With the deepening of World War II the work of the Committee seemed to grind to a halt. Equally, as Mawson who was the driving force behind the Metropolitan Plan, having been 'lent' to the Committee by the government, had done in the past, he moved on to what he believed were more pressing concerns. As it became clearer by 1944 that World War II would end in the near future, the government became concerned with the reintegration of returned soldiers into the work force and the issues that surrounded the return of the economy to a non-war footing. As a result in 1944 the Organisation for National Development (OND) was formed as a small group within the Prime Ministers Department. Mawson quickly advocated for the inclusion of regional planning as an integral part of the OND's work and with immense enthusiasm quickly organised a range of Regional Councils. These broadly based bodies with representatives from organisations as diverse as the Chamber of Commerce and the Labour Councils were set up around the country. They, however, concentrated on the economic aspects of growth and there is nothing to suggest any direct advocacy of urban growth controls. However, the OND's importance lay in the vast literature that it made available to regional council's from the *County of London* plan to the work of the Tennessee Valley Authority. While much of the material that was circulated has not survived, the OND was a powerful transmitter of planning information and ideas. Unfortunately it had a short existence. It was abruptly terminated in November 1945 with its planning functions passing to the newly formed Town and Country Planning Division of the Ministry of Works.

Christchurch, however, had by 1948 managed to issue its final report that included green belts, 'the intention being to preserve it substantially as a green belt in which various forms of farming and market gardening will be carried on to serve the needs of the urban population for dairy produce and fresh fruit and vegetables' (Christchurch Metropolitan Planning Committee, 1948, 32). It was also clear what the green belts were there for

The preservation of the green belt as proposed by the Committee is recognized as the most practical method of limiting the size of a town and of compelling a compact and economic type of development. Once the pre-determined limit of growth has been reached, new satellite towns are established outside of the rural District linked with the parent city by rapid transit facilities.' (Christchurch Metropolitan Planning Committee, 1948, 32)

While the function of a green belt to allow the development of satellite towns echoes the British ideas for the green belt at the time, the emphasis on the need for a green belt to provide the city with fresh market produce, however, is peculiar to New Zealand. In Britain the link between agriculture and the green belt had been famously made by Ebenezer Howard in his plans for the Garden City. Despite this endorsement the agricultural function for the green belt in the UK was mainly invoked during the pre-War period. It appeared for example in the London Society's proposal for preserving a green belt that could be paid for through agricultural rents (see Amati and Yokohari, 2007). While rural preservation and agricultural productivity underpinned some of the momentous changes that British planning underwent in 1942,[4] the problem that the green belt was intended to solve in the UK was much more than that of sprawl and a lack of land for recreation. The green belt was to serve a strategic role permanently safeguarding land from development. Forshaw and Abercrombie's highly influential *County of London Plan* (1943) envisaged the green belt as part of a larger open space system, existing for the recreation of Londoners and important in separating the central urban area from its surrounding satellite towns (Forshaw and Abercrombie, 1943, 37). In 1955 Duncan Sandys, the then Minister of Housing and Local Government re-emphasised the green belts' strategic role issuing

---

4   In particular the report of the Scott Committee on Land Utilisation in Rural Areas. This ushered in a planning reform that effectively gave a subsidy to rural areas, (see Sheail, 1997).

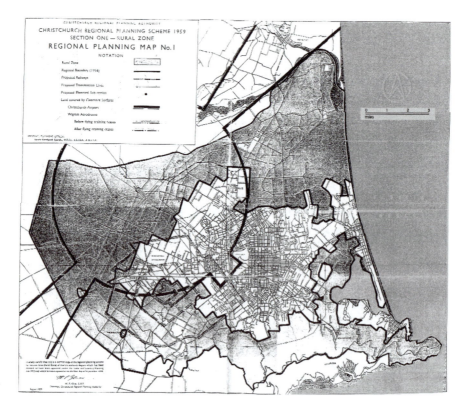

Note: Green belt is the area between bold lines. It covered an approximate ring around the city forming a belt of up to 4 miles (6.4 km) in width. Source: Christchurch Regional Planning Scheme (1959) with thanks to Malcolm Douglass.

Figure 5.1: Christchurch green belt 1959

a circular that led to the implementation of green belts nationally. The green belts had three purposes, which Collins (1957) remarked on as being 'townsman's' [*sic*] (i.e. urban and non-agricultural). Green belts should be considered:

● in order to check the further growth of a large built-up area;
● in order to prevent neighbouring towns from merging into one another;
● to preserve the special character of a town (Collins, 1957).

Already by the post-war period therefore, a substantial variation can be seen between the implementation of the green belt in New Zealand and Britain. While the post-War British green belt became linked with the prevention of urban sprawl and the development of new towns, in New Zealand the green belt was partly seen as an area for forestry or agriculture that might also define the edge of the urban area. Indeed, such was the concern for the loss of market gardening land that it became something of a clarion call for green belt enthusiasts in New Zealand during the 1950s. Even Wellington, a city whose growth was in any case limited by steep hills was concerned to implement a green belt to protect market gardens and the availability of fresh produce nearby (Amati, 2006). Elsewhere in New Zealand interest in and concern with urban expansion continued, powered it would seem by the uncontrolled expansion of urban areas, often into the areas controlled by rurally based County Councils. These were until 1953, exempt from any plan writing requirements while a quirk of the various Counties Acts allowed subdivisions of less than 10 acres in these areas to proceed without any effective controls. The result was that small urban style developments popped up on urban boundaries, usually with the minimum of services but at a significantly discounted price from that of the adjoining urban area. Equally, the State Housing Division (later Corporation) which was responsible for instituting the huge State Housing programme was not above creating urban expansion, particularly on the boundaries of the major cities. The government excluded itself from any planning controls until 1991 which made its activities beyond any town planning schemes that they forced all local authorities to produce.

Auckland, the country's largest city provided the most pressing need for some form of control over its urban growth and provides an excellent counterpoint to the approaches used in Christchurch. Its population had grown from 226,309 in 1936 to 399,224 in 1956, a massive 74% population increase (Regional Growth Forum, ND, 4–5), with much of the growth including sprawling State Housing suburbs on the city's periphery. New Zealand planners, such as F. W. O. Jones, an engineer turned town planner, the Chief Planning Officer of the Auckland Metropolitan Planning Organisation, another voluntary planning organisation with no statutory power, were deeply concerned with the effects of urban growth. He also demonstrated a clear understanding of the growth issues that faced Auckland. Writing in 1949 he stressed the New Zealand nature of urban planning which 'involves no decanting of population, no reduction of density, with new towns serving as receptacles of the resultant "overspill" as the English call it. Rather it does involve compaction, filling up and the attainment of an urban entity out of the all too loosely sprawling structure' (Jones, 1949, 78). His solution was 'the use of and urban fence or rural zoning (greenbelts [sic]) to prevent sprawl and the positive encouragement to redevelopment and urban rehabilitation' (Jones, 1949, 78). This linking of urban containment with the need for urban renewal became a linked theme in New Zealand planning particularly in the 1950s when there was almost a panic about the effects of accelerated population increase. In 1953 John Cox, the head of the new Town and Country Planning Division of the Ministry of Works, quoted Dr Kenneth Cumberland, an Auckland University geographer, that 'New Zealand's population [is] growing faster than ever before' (Cox, 1953a, 39). Cox went on to suggest that 'the policy of expanding our towns endlessly outwards is causing them to become rotten at the core' (Cox, 1953b, 60). His answer was however to promote urban intensification rather than to rely on urban containment. This material is however indicative of the level of understanding of town planning issues and techniques that existed in New Zealand in the post-War period. John Mawson[5] had a large collection of British town planning documents and given his extensive communications with the few town planners in New Zealand, it is not unreasonable to suggest that these would have been made available to those planners. It also meant that there were a number of planning ideas and tools to provide an alternative to the use of green belts. Regional planning was statutorily established, under the new *Town and Country Planning Act* 1953, allowing the Christchurch Regional Council, under the guidance of its Regional Planning Officer, Nancy Northcroft, featured green belts as a method in the first Christchurch Regional Planning Scheme. Nancy Northcroft had taken up a British Council scholarship in 1942 to study local-body housing in Britain, gaining her diploma in town planning with distinction before returning to New Zealand in 1947. Given that she had been involved in planning projects in Britain prior to her return she was well placed to transmit a number of planning ideas to New Zealand, or, as in the case of green belts, to recognise their utility. She joined the new Christchurch Regional Planning Authority in 1954. Thus the first Christchurch Regional Planning Scheme produced in 1959 included as one of its Principles: '(1) To define the inner boundaries of the Rural Zone, or urban fences, in such a position as to allow for enough additional land within the future built-up, or urban areas of the Region, to accommodate the estimated increase in urban population up to 1976' (Christchurch Regional Planning Authority, 1959, 1), see Figure 5.1.

The green belt had become an urban fence, a name it would retain in the Christchurch situation and which was interchangeable with the term green belt.[6] The four principles in the scheme specifies why land should be excluded from development. It identifies land with poor drainage and areas where sewerage will not be available. Land to which the State is already committed to build housing. Finally, the scheme identifies the areas that were regarded which might be 'of particular value to farming or of significance in supplying the Christchurch market' (Christchurch Regional Planning Authority, 1959, 2) as part of the urban fence. The green belt could thus be established in a utilitarian manner which reflected local concerns that good land was not wasted. It was equally a policy that was combined with encouragement of urban consolidation and 'orderly development', 'to mitigate the problems that arise as a result of very low density and scattered development throughout the rural lands of the Region' (Christchurch Regional Planning Authority, 1959, 1).

This use of an urban fence/green belt by the Christchurch Regional Planning Authority, however remained good advice as the *Town and Country Planning Act* 1953, while providing for regional planning, made sure any such plans produced had no teeth, '[…] being a guide only for the consideration in the development of District

---

5   This is based on the material contained in the Mawson Files held by the University of Auckland.

6   The London University geographer Dr Dudley Stamp is credited with coining the terms urban fence. His Land Utilisation Survey of Great Britain (1936–1945) was highly influential on UK planning through the Scott Report (Matless, 1998, 220)

Planning Schemes' (Robinson, 1981, 12), schemes which in contrast had the force of regulations. In Auckland where there was a long tradition of little local body cooperation, this would have ensured that any such plan would be ignored. Thus in 1963 the *Auckland Regional Authority Act* was passed in which 'Regional planning was referred to in the new structure as "the keystone of the arch"' (Coulam, 1975, 15) in an attempt to develop a solution to Auckland's burgeoning growth problems. Essentially, the 1953 legislation provided the opportunity to use green belts, now a potential solution to a well recognised problem, to address the issue of uncontained urban growth.

Spreading the Word

If the green belt was to become better used in New Zealand, then it would have to be actively disseminated through a variety of channels. The 1953 legislation promoted the growth of planning as a profession in New Zealand and this was encouraged by the establishment in 1958 of a town planning diploma course at the University of Auckland (see Miller, 2007). In terms of the transmission of ideas the Auckland diploma course was, with the New Zealand Planning Institute's journal *Town Planning Quarterly* (TPQ, from June 1965), major conduits for planning ideas and methods. Jim Dart one of the earliest lecturers in the Auckland diploma course, has clear memories of himself and Professor Robert Kennedy, the foundation Professor of Town Planning, lecturing on the green belt and its use (Dart, 2007). In 1970 as part of the National Development Conference, New Zealand ran a land use focused sub-conference – The Physical Environment Conference, which addressed all aspects of the development issues that faced the country over the next three decades.

Using a series of working parties to address specific topics such as Urban Development and Urban Expansion, the Conference involved a wide range of 'experts', and given the size of the country, probably means the outcomes were produced a comprehensive picture of current knowledge and opinions. Perhaps unexpectedly urban containment got negligible comment and the recommendations of the various working parties while emphasising the need for better planning for urban areas through regional plans, concentrated more on the need for better social planning combined with a clear concern for environmental issues. The term green belt is significant in its absence from the large volume which emerged from the Conference (Organising Committee, Physical Environment Conference, 1972). In an article in TPQ by Ivan Boileau, the second Professor of Town Planning at Auckland University specifically offered an alternative when he wrote 'the current fashion in England, Australia, and in the United States is for "corridor" plans. Green belts and satellites are no longer favourites' (Boileau, 1970, 10). On a similar dismissive note, Montgolfier, one of TPQ's unnamed columnist, when discussing urban expansion noted 'clearly the failure of the green belts was but the routing of outposts in a battle already lost (Montgolfier, 1972, 6).

This negative view appears to be the product of the Auckland experience and the failure to establish New Zealand's first planned satellite town of Rolleston, 25 kms southwest of Christchurch. In March 1974 the Ministry of Works and Development commissioned a multidisciplinary group, the Rolleston Planning Group, to prepare a plan for a new town, beyond the Christchurch urban fence, to cater for an eventual population of 30–40,000 people. This was a revolutionary step for New Zealand with Christchurch not the most pressing candidate for such a response to urban growth and an unmet demand land for housing. Rolleston was the pet project of the Labour government of Kirk and Rowling, a government with a strong South Island and Christchurch bias in its cabinet. It was also expected that the development of Rolleston would counter the shift of economic development to the North Island. The project was always controversial and despite a large area of land having been bought for the new town, the project did not survive the defeat of the Labour government in late 1975. The abandonment of Rolleston refocused the attention of both the Christchurch City Council and the Canterbury Regional Planning Authority, on the issue of how to address Christchurch's growth. The now Canterbury Regional Council was actively addressing the issue of urban growth partly because, as Barcley Millar, the Regional Council's Director of Planning put it in a newspaper report, 'there was a great deal of pressure for urban peripheral development of Christchurch, and there had been "unfortunate results" with the Town and Country Planning Appeal Board in the authority's effort to control the speculators' (The Press, 1976b).

The Regional Council responded with a regional report which addressed the issue of urban growth and recommended that 'principal growth points must be separated from Christchurch by a green belt of some 25 km' (*The Press*, 1976a). This approach did not meet universal approval, and *The Press* ran a number of stories which questioned this logic of the approach and its likely outcomes. This rearmation of the green belt was contained in the Canterbury Region Indicative Plan: Long Term Urban Development Alternatives for a Regional Plan, which was put out for public comment in mid-1976.

That plan comprehensively analysed national objectives, employment patterns and socio-economic conditions within the region. It concluded by exploring four potential patterns of urban growth to consider when preparing the Regional Scheme –

- A duplicated pattern, which was to decant the growth of Christchurch into another similar urban centre.
- An independent pattern which was to establish three stand alone towns beyond the green belt.
- A linear pattern in which Christchurch grew to the North and South along transport axes and
- A hierarchic development which was to allow growth into town and villages. (Douglass et al., 1976, 10)

The plan considered the possibilities of each of these whilst reaffirming the 'containment of the Christchurch urban area and further concentration of development by infilling and redevelopment' (Douglass et al., 1976, 10)

The public response was wide, varied but generally of a thoughtful nature. The Real Estate Institute of New Zealand wanted a 'rationalisation of the existing urban fence to natural and economic boundaries' (Douglass et al., 1976, 12) while one of the adjoining local authorities, Paparua County, was concerned that 'research is needed on how these 'green belts' are to be maintained' (Douglass et al., 1976, 15). Generally while there was understanding of the need for the green belt approach there was concern as to how they could be maintained in some form of productive use.

While the indicative plan did not have any legislative teeth it was highly influential because it was an immediate expression of support for the green belt following the debacle of Rolleston New Town. In November 1977 the Regional Council produced a comprehensive report on Regional Policy No.5: Control of Urban Form which 'examined some of the fundamental concepts underlying Policy No.5' (Canterbury Regional Planning Authority, 1977, 1). It includes an extensive discussion of green belts which reveals a clear knowledge of overseas use of the technique. Consequently, in 1978 the Canterbury Regional Plan's Objectives included the following:

> To define the non-settlement area (green belt) for the purpose of conserving land and capital resources by securing the most efficient use of land both inside and outside a defined settlement area having regard to accessibility and interconnectedness between land uses. (Canterbury Regional Planning Authority, 1978, 7)

The impact of the *Canterbury Region Indicative Plan* can be seen in the second review of the *Canterbury Regional Planning Scheme* (Canterbury Regional Planning Authority, 1979). While identifying the containment of Christchurch as one of its main objectives, the plan aimed for an 'Equable Distribution'. It was hoped by doing this to balance out the traditional dominance of Christchurch in the region. The plan used a matrix to evaluate the method that would involve the least conflict in planning. This method pointed to a 'Structured settlement growth' of satellite new towns as being the most viable option. It identified six existing settlements to accommodate medium to long-term growth. The plan contained a mixture of the elements in the Canterbury Region Indicative Plan. There is a clear hierarchy in the type of growth envisaged that depends on the size of the town and its location. There is also evidence of a linear strategy being used. Growth was favoured at Kaiapoi, Rangiora, Woodend and Amberley to the North of Christchurch. It was also favoured in Rolleston and Ashburton to the South-West.

Another important trend that concerned planners during the 1960s and 1970 were the discussions surrounding the size of a viable farm unit. In New Zealand the primary method for controlling growth is by preventing the subdivision of land into smaller blocks, which can then be sold for development. The *Town and Country Planning Act* 1977, introduced another associated concern in its identification of 'Matters of National Importance' (S3, TCPA 1977), which included both the preservation of productive land and the avoidance of sporadic subdivision. These concerns were powered by an influential farming lobby which perceived a need to contain urban areas and to avoid them sprawling onto adjoining rural areas. This containment approach also applied to the growing areas of rural-residential lifestyle blocks that were viewed as urban sprawl by stealth. Such developments had the potential to fragment rural and green belt land and planners responded with various tests of what represented a viable or economic farming unit. To prevent development and preserve the green belt, planners in Christchurch had developed sophisticated techniques for calculating the economically viable unit for farming. While it was assumed that that extensive farming e.g. raising stock is not viable on small rural blocks, orcharding and horticultural were (Douglass, 2006). To gain approval to subdivide and use a small rural blocks, potential owners were commonly required to produce a plan for economic land use, usually some form of horticultural crop or specialised stock such as angora goats. In the midst of these debates developers would exploit confusion and uncertainty by proposing the planting, of then unproven crops, such as chestnut trees. They would employ a consultant to argue that such a crop was viable on a small block of land (Thomson, 2006). Subsequent to gaining a subdivision consent the crop would 'fail' and the developer would be able to reap the benefits of selling-on or developing a smaller block of land, partly because there was no effective planning mechanism to require subsequent owners to re-establish the failed enterprise. This type of development gave rise to a multitude of small (around 4 ha in size), unviable farms that could be marketed to ex-urbanites as 'lifestyle blocks'.[7]

If the green belt found acceptance in Christchurch the same could not be said for other areas. The Auckland Regional Authority addressed the issue of regional growth in a number of discussion documents such as *Growth Alternatives: A Progress Report*. That report looked at a number of approaches that could be used to control urban growth from land use controls to administrative and fiscal incentives (Auckland Regional Planning Authority, 1974, Appendix IV) but did not give any definite consideration to green belts. As Arnold Turner, a Town and Country Planning Appeal Court Judge, observed 'after 13 years the Auckland Regional Authority, as the regional planning authority, is now beginning to have some effect on the urban form ... although it's doing that mainly by providing or withholding water and sewage services' (Turner, 1977, 5). In the face of the intransigence of Auckland local authorities and the lack of planning powers, the ARA had found an effective way of trying to rein in Auckland's growth.

The regional councils achieved enhanced powers in 1977 with the arrival of the *Town and Country Planning Act* which replaced the former voluntary regional councils with the newly created regional councils in the main centres and united councils elsewhere. These strengthened powers however seem to have had little effect on the up take of green belts outside Christchurch. When the ARA eventually produced Section One of the Proposed Auckland Regional Plan, after a rather torturous process, its policies on urban containment and growth were surprisingly

---

7   Post-1991 the minimum subdivision areas were based on the area required to support efficient disposal beds and the creation of specific rural-residential zones. In a sense therefore the green belt could also have been more strongly enforced as a result (Thomson, 2006).

limited. Objective 3B encapsulated the approach, stating 'To contain the growth of the metropolitan area by defining the metropolitan limits, and managing urban expansion within these limits' (Auckland Regional Planning Authority, 1978, 34).

These metropolitan limits merely established the outer limits of urban growth and effectively allowed the city to grow, relatively unconstrained towards them, which would have done little to either limit urban growth or avoid land speculation. A similar approach was adopted in Wellington, though the relatively dissected nature of the greater Wellington region provided some natural barriers to development particularly as that city's growth never reached the levels predicted in early studies. This rejection, or perhaps ignoring, of the green belt concept also needs to be seen within the context of New Zealand planning legislation and practice. As an economy that was dependent on agriculture, New Zealand has always been protective of productive or fertile land and this is reflected in its planning legislation. The 1960 regulations which accompanied the *Town and Country Planning Act* 1953, and which guided the formulation of District Schemes, identified the 'preservation of productive land and the concentration of urban development' (Regulation 16(2), *Town and Country Planning Act* 1953), as a matter to be incorporated in those Schemes. This approach was upheld through various Town and Country Planning Appeal Board decisions, which called such preservation 'a fundamental principle of town and country planning' (Robinson, 1981, 21). In safeguarding rural land, District Schemes could effectively place a limit on urban growth particularly when the 1977 legislation established 'Matters of National Importance' in Section 3 that included:

- The avoidance of encroachment of urban development on, and the protection of, land having high actual or potential value for the production of food;
- The prevention of sporadic subdivision and urban development in rural areas; and
- The avoidance of unnecessary expansion of urban areas into rural areas in or adjoining cities (S3(d, e, f) TCPA 1977)

This provided a solid rural focused approach to planning that in many ways made the creation of green belts an unnecessary technique. Equally the response to the Christchurch green belt often focused on the potential for those green belts to become wasted land that would lose its productive purposes, something that was inconceivable in the New Zealand context particularly as open space was never in short supply in any city.

Green Belts Under the *Resource Management Act*

One of the ironies of UK planning is that during the 1980s the Thatcher government, characteristically following its neo-liberal agenda, dismantled large parts of the planning system but largely left the green belt intact. In New Zealand as the following describes, the neo-liberal wave of reforms caused the green belt to collapse.

In 1984 the election of a Labour government at a time when the New Zealand economy was heavily indebted, was functioning on a devalued currency and ravaged by inflation, set off a process of extensive economic and social reform. Based on a Neo-Liberalist agenda the reforms, by the late 1980s, transformed both local and central government and the environmental management system. State assets such as the Post Office, rail system and telephone service were sold or turned into profit orientated State Owned Enterprises (SOEs). Local government was reformed through amalgamations and new requirements for transparency and accountability. On a positive note regional councils were established on a sound footing with their boundaries being based on river catchment areas. For the first time New Zealand had a comprehensive system of regional councils. A new bureaucracy responsible for environmental management came into being as a result of the Environment Act 1986 (Ministry for the Environment) and the Conservation Act 1987 (Department of Conservation). Finally, the *Resource Management Act* 1991(RMA) ushered in a new basis for planning, the peculiarly construed (sustainable management), which attempted to use only the environmental aspects of the more comprehensive sustainable development concept. Under the RMA regional planning was strengthened but almost exclusively environmentally focused and both regions and cities and districts had to produce plans. Planning was now to be 'effects based' with the main focus being to avoid, remedy or mitigate adverse effects on the environment. Of central impact to planning was a major reform of local government. In November 1989 The Canterbury United Council that was charged with the task of planning the green belt and regional land use planning generally, was merged with Aorangi United Council, three catchment boards, seven pest destruction boards, fourteen noxious plant authorities and one Nassella Tussock board to form Canterbury Regional Council (now known as Environment Canterbury) (Douglass, 2004). The area that the regional council covered was drastically extended from the hinterlands of Christchurch, pre-1989 to an area that went almost to the top of the South Island beyond Kaikoura and South beyond Timaru.

The effect of these changes was to make a sub-regional scheme like the green belt unviable. The newly created Canterbury Regional Council was faced with establishing its existence while meeting the RMA's requirement to produce the first level regional planning document, which it did by 1995 although it was not approved until after much argument and drawing of teeth by 1998. While existing planning documents were 'saved' by the RMA, many were now out of step with the new planning approaches. As Laurie McCallum the Energy, Transport and Built Environment Policy Manager of the Canterbury Regional Council explained:

> That was a huge job, to churn out, to do all the consultation, look at whole of Canterbury and produce under this [...] effects-based legislation [policies]. All the time we were being thumped by the Ministry for Environment on what this act *meant* (McCallum, 2006) [emphasis in original]

Malcolm Douglass, the first Chief Executive of the Canterbury Regional Council highlighted two main reasons why the green belt collapsed during this time. The first was that in the space of two years the concern of the regional council extended to a much larger rural area and had to emphasise rural political interests. The regional council no longer had the stomach for taking urban decisions. Second the pressing matters of river catchment management, river pollution, water allocation, flood protection measures plus the pest eradication programme with an explosion in the pest rabbit population, commanded the attention of the newly formed Regional Council. As a result while $20 million was being spent on rabbit control less than $2 million was spent on regional planning and only a small part of that on the protection of the green belt and the metropolitan growth strategy.

The final demise of the green belt as a planning tool in Christchurch was a product of the dominant ideology of the time and the new focus of the RMA (Memon, 2003). The reform of the economy along market lines brought pressure to break the selling monopoly that saw most of New Zealand's primary producer sold by a single desk seller. In the case of pip fruit that selling monopoly, developed from the mid-1930s onwards in generally successful attempt to ensure stable grower incomes, was exercised by the New Zealand Apple and Pear Marketing Board. Inspired by the new market reforms, a publicly listed company, Apple Fields Ltd, was established in 1986. By 1997 it owned nearly 7,000 hectares on the periphery of Christchurch (Roche, 2001, 149), much of it on green belt land. Apple Fields Ltd became the largest single apple producer in New Zealand and moved to attempt to break the Apple and Pear Marketing Board's selling monopoly. In making its export consent application 'Apple Fields signalled that, if unsuccessful, it would rip up the trees and convert the orchards to residential properties' (Roche, 2001, 149). The export consent was denied and Apple Fields moved quickly to put its threat into action, resulting in a series of Environment and High Court cases which inevitably brought the existence of the green belt into question.

The timing could not have been worse. This challenge to the green belt was brought within the context of the replacement of the TCPA's 'Matters of National Importance' with its focus on rural land preservation, with the RMA's 'Matters of National Importance' (S6) which focused solely on preserving and protecting the natural environment. This refocusing of direction of planning to the natural environment effectively withdrew the de facto support for the green belt that the preservation of rural land had so effectively provided. Faced with expensive legal challenges on a number of fronts and a council preoccupied with emerging issues such as water allocation and quality the Canterbury Regional Council, abandoned any real attempt to set urban limits for Christchurch and with that abandonment the green belt faded from use. The green belt had largely served Christchurch well and many practitioners regarded its demise with some concern. However, planning as a discipline so frequently shaped and directed by political concerns was powerless to resist and the limited up-take of the green belt as a planning technique beyond Christchurch, did little to support its use in the face of change.

Conclusions

For New Zealand the green belt never represented a planning tool that was adapatable to local conditions. While its existence and use were well understood, in Ward's terms the diffusion of the concept was successful, it was often viewed as a tool seeking a problem. At the point at which New Zealand cities were beginning to recognise that urban growth and urban containment were planning issues that needed to be addressed there was a range of planning tools, including the green belt, that they could have elected to use. However, the green belt approach was one that was in the New Zealand context best suited to a regional level of governance, something which existed only in the most ad hoc manner until 1991. Thus urban containment fell to be addressed at the local level. City and district councils used S3 of the *Town and Country Planning Acts* 1953 and 1977 as a de facto urban containment instruments – protecting rural land became a means of excluding urban uses. Equally, New Zealand, while often adopting and then adapting British planning concepts, was also capable of developing its own planning instruments that better suited the particular New Zealand planning environment. While Christchurch made use of green belts in its planning, its use there never appeared to present a compelling example that others were willing to follow. In such a climate the establishment of the green belt as a major planning tool was never likely and it has quietly faded into New Zealand's planning history.

References

Amati, M. (2006), 'Ascribing changing values to suburban greenspaces: the inception of Wellington's green belt', in C. Garnaut and K. Round (eds.), 'The Adelaide Parklands Symposium. A Balancing Act: Past-Present-Future', Centre for Settlement Studies and the Bob Hawke Prime Ministerial Centre (Adelaide: University of South Australia), pp. 1–12.

Amati, M. and Yokohari, M. (2007), 'The establishment of the London green belt: reaching consensus over purchasing land', *Journal of Planning History*, 6(4), 311–37.

Anonymous (1923), 'Editorial: The Subdivision Mania', *The New Zealand Journal of Commerce*, 9(64), 1–2.

Auckland Regional Planning Authority (1974), *Growth Alternatives: A Progress Report* (Auckland: Auckland Regional Authority).

—— (1978), *Proposed Auckland Regional Planning Scheme: Section One, Volume One Policies* (Auckland: Auckland Regional Authority).

Basire, F. (1945), 'Letter F Basire to Consultative Committee, 7 May 1945.', PM Series 12 File 1/5/2, National Archives, Wellington.

Bloodworth, T. (1938), 'What of the Future?', *Planning*, 12(2), 3–5.

Boileau, I. (1970), 'Regional Scheme – Auckland Regional Authority, 1969', *Town Planning Quarterly*, 19, 9–11.

Canterbury Regional Planning Authority (1977), *Regional Policy No.5: Control of Urban Form, 'The Non-Settlement Areas'* (Christchurch: Canterbury Regional Planning Authority).

—— (1978), *Canterbury Region: Regional Planning Objectives* (Christchurch: Canterbury Regional Planning Authority).

—— (1979), *Canterbury Regional Planning Scheme Draft second review* (Christchurch: CRPA).

Christchurch Metropolitan Planning Committee (1948), *Final Report: Christchurch Metropolitan Planning Scheme* (Christchurch: Christchurch Metropolitan Planning Authority).

Christchurch Regional Planning Authority (1959), *Christchurch Regional Planning Scheme 1959: Section One – Rural Zone: Scheme Statement, Code of Ordinances* (Christchurch: Christchurch Regional Planning Authority).

Collins, B.J. (1957), 'A talk on green belts', *Town Planning Review*, 219–30.

Coulam, J.H. (1975), *Auckland Regional Authority: Evolution, Organisation and Jurisdiction* (Auckland: ARA).

Cox, J. (1953a), 'The Next Million', *Design Review*, 5(2), 39.

—— (1953b), 'Rotten At The Core', *Design Review*, 5(3), 60–62.

Dart, J. (2007), 'Interview with James Dart', by C.L.Miller, Auckland.

Davidge, W. (1915), 'Town Planning in Australia and New Zealand (II)', *Garden Cities and Town Planning Magazine*, 5(8), 173–9.

Douglass, M. (2004), *History of Regional Institutions 1944 to 2004 Canterbury Regional Symposium* (Christchurch: Environment Canterbury).

—— (2006), 'Interview conducted on the 29th of November', by M. Amati, Christchurch.

Douglass, M., Barber, M., and Sheppard, D. (1976), *Canterbury Region Indicative Plan: Long Term Urban Development Alternatives for a Regional Plan* (Christchurch: Canterbury Regional Planning Authority).

Forshaw, J.H. and Abercrombie, L.P. (1943), *County of London Plan* (London: HMSO).

Hamer, D. (1990), 'Wellington on the Urban Frontier', in D. Hamer and R. Nicholls (eds.), 'The Making of Wellington 1800–1914', (Wellington: Victoria University Press), pp. 227–54.

—— (1995), 'The Making of Urban New Zealand', *Journal of Urban History*, 22(1), 6–39.

Hammond, R.B. (1938), 'Editorial', *Planning*, 12(2), 1–2.

Hardy, D. (1991), *From Garden Cities to New Towns: Campaigning for Town and Country Planning, 1899–1946* (London: E & FN Spon).

Home, R. (1997), *Of Planning and Planting: The Making of British Colonial Cities* (London: E & FN Spon).

Hurst Seager, S. (1918), *Report to the Hon. Minister of Internal Affairs on the Brisbane Town-Planning Conference and Exhibition and their bearing on town-planning in the Dominion* (Wellington: Government Printer).

Isaac, P. and Olssen, E. (2001), 'The Justification for Labour's Housing Scheme', in B. Brookes (ed.), 'At Home in New Zealand: History, Houses, People', (Wellington: Bridget Williams Books), pp. 107–25.

Jones, F.W.O. (1949), 'Urban Development', *Design Review*, 2(4), 76–81.

King, A.D. (1976), *Colonial Urban Development: Culture, Power and Environment* (London: Routledge).

Matless, D. (1998), *Landscape and Englishness* (London: Reaktion Books).

Mawson, J. (1929), 'Speech to the Municipal Conference, 6th March 1929', on IA S1 F34/202 Pt.1, National Archives, Wellington.

—— (1931), 'Items of Interest', *Community Planning*, 1(3), 104–7.

McCallum, L. (2006), 'Interview with Laurie McCallum', by M. Amati, Environment Canterbury 30th November.

McGibbon, W.S. (1948), *Report of the Christchurch Metropolitan Planning Committee* (Christchurch: Christchurch City Council), chap. Foreword.

McIntyre, W.D. (2000), 'Outwards and Upwards – Building the City', in J. Cookson and G. Dunstall (eds.), 'Southern Capital Christchurch: Towards a City Biography, 1850–2000', (Christchurch: Canterbury University Press).

Memon, P.A. (2003), 'Urban growth management in Christchurch', *New Zealand Geographer*, 59(1), 27–39.

Miller, C.L. (1998), 'Regional Planning in New Zealand 1929-1946: An Exercise in Frustration', in R. Freestone (ed.), '8th International Planning History Conference on the Twentieth Century Urban Planning Experience', (Sydney, Australia: University of New South Wales), pp. 627–32.

—— (2002), 'The Origins of Town Planning in New Zealand: A Divergent Path?', *Planning Perspectives*, 17(3), 209–26.

—— (2007), *The Unsung Profession: The History of the New Zealand Planning Institute, 1947–2002* (Wellington: Dunmore Books/NZPI).

Montgolfier (1972), 'Swine Before Pearls', *Town Planning Quarterly*, (27), 6.

Organising Committee, Physical Environment Conference (1972), *The Physical Environment Conference 1970: Reports, Papers and Proceedings* (Wellington: Government Printer).

Putt, C.E.H. (1937), 'Housing in Relation to Civic Development: Part I', *Planning*, 9(2), 4–11.

Regional Growth Forum (ND), *A Place Sought By Many: A Brief History of Regional Planning for Auckland's Growth* (Regional Growth Forum).

Robinson, K. (1981), *The Law of Town and Country Planning* (Wellington: Butterworths), third edn.

Roche, M.M. (2001), 'Rural Canterbury in the Global Economy', in G. Cant and R. Kirkpatrick (eds.), 'Rural Canterbury: Celebrating Its History', (Christchurch: Daphne Brasell Press/Lincoln University Press), p. 149.

Rogerson, E. (1976), *Cosy Homes Multiply: A Study of Suburban Expansion in Western Auckland*, Master's thesis, University of Auckland, Auckland.

Sheail, J. (1997), 'Scott revisited; post-war agriculture, planning and the British countryside', *Journal of Rural Studies*, 13(4), 387–98.

Stephens, F.B. (1938), 'What of the Future? III', *Planning*, 12(2), 10–14.

The Press (1945), 'Planning Proposals for Christchurch', 4th October.

—— (1976a), 'City Spread Problems Outlined in Report', *The Press*, 10th July.

—— (1976b), 'Hasten Slowly on Rolleston,', *The Press*, 22 July.

Thomson, I. (2006), 'Interview', by M. Amati, Christchurch City Council Offices.

Turner, A.R. (1977), 'Conference Critique: Observations on the 1977 NZ Planning Institute Conference', *Town Planning Quarterly*, (47), 5–8.

Ward, S.V. (1999), 'The International Diffusion of Planning: A review and Canadian Case Study', *International Planning Studies*, 44(2), 53–77.

William-Ellis, C. (1928), England and the Octopus (London: Geoffrey Bles).

PART III
RE-FORMING GREENERY: FROM GREEN BELTS TO GREEN NETS

CHAPTER 6

The Adelaide Parklands and the Endurance of the Green Belt Idea in South Australia

Christine Garnaut

Introduction

In 1911 the Lord Mayor of Adelaide, Lewis Cohen, declared that 'the parks are the pride and glory of this city – the best and greatest asset it has or ever can have. To every generation they are becoming more valuable' (Cohen in Reade, 1912, 5). Cohen was referring to the city's extensive belt of parkland that had been deliberately reserved in the City of Adelaide plan of 1837 and maintained over the years 'for the use and re-creation of the citizens' (Rees, 1948). The Parklands were integral to the Adelaide plan and have survived as a swathe of open space that distinguishes the South Australian capital from its national equivalents and sets it apart internationally. However, as their history attests, in the absence of specific instructions at the time of settlement about their purpose and potential function, they have been variously used and abused. At times a contentious space, even today they spark local discord and debate.

The Adelaide Parklands have pre-nineteenth century precursors but also hold a significant place within the modern and larger idea of the green belt that emerged with Ebenezer Howard's late nineteenth century garden city idea. Howard proposed the green belt as a means of containing urban growth and of separating town and country. In fact, as will be revealed, he identified the City of Adelaide plan (1837) as an exemplar of his desired model of urban growth. While, in the case of Adelaide, parklands did encircle the city and act as a containment device, ultimately they did not fulfil the function of separating urban and rural areas. In the earliest plans they divided the city from what were laid out and titled 'country sections'. But, in reality, the 'country sections' became suburban settlements, usurping the purpose of the parklands as a separating green belt.

As Freestone (2002, 67–98) demonstrates, the green belt has taken a range of forms in response to diverse circumstances and conditions. He categorises the Adelaide Parklands as a colonial 'Parkland Town', the forerunner of numerous parkland towns across rural South Australia. Amongst the other green belt forms in his typology are several that surfaced in twentieth century open space schemes for metropolitan Adelaide: parkways, green corridors and greenways.

This chapter examines the Adelaide Parklands and several other forms of the green belt as identified by Freestone and applied in South Australia. The discussion is divided into two parts. The first surveys the background to, and the establishment and evolution of, the Parklands and introduces themes and issues that have affected their progress. It refers to their multifarious functions and to their changing circumstances over time. The second examines the rise of schemes to carry over the initial planning idea of reserving an unbuilt-upon zone of open space into the expanded metropolis and to reinstate the riverine portion of the Parklands. The conclusion reflects on the endurance of the green belt idea in South Australia.

Background to the Adelaide Parklands

Several generations of scholars have described and analysed the City of Adelaide plan and explored a range of potential precedents for, and influences on, its layout (for example, Cheesman, 1986; Bunker, 1986; Johnson and Langmead, 1986; Dutton, 1960; Walkley, 1952; Price, 1924). Military camps, Classical, Medieval, Hispanic and New World town layouts have been examined and exemplars proposed. The conventional wisdom is that there is no specific inspirational source (for example, Daly, 1987, 11–16; Dutton, 1960, 215–16; Price, 1924, 109–10) although speculation continues on possible foundations for the parklands (Johnson, 2006, 115–27 and Henderson, 2006, 73–89).

The notion of incorporating open space for various purposes – community gathering places, markets, defence, agriculture, animal grazing or recreation – in towns and cities has a long historical lineage (Morris, 1994). In industrialised Britain, public urban land previously used for active and passive recreation and for agriculture, horticulture and animal pasture was frequently overtaken in the drive to build factories, house workers and install new means of transportation. As urban populations swelled and the attendant problems of poverty, inadequate housing and sanitation emerged side-by-side with pollution and degraded living and workplace environments, reformers promoted the need for open space on health, social, environmental and civic grounds (Creese, 1967).

The physical means of introducing urban open space has varied from discrete sites such as public piazzas, squares and gardens, and private parks and estates (Thorsheim, 2006, 24–37) within towns, to perimeter agricultural or grazing lands. Encircling open public land emerged in the design of towns based on the sixteenth century Spanish Laws of the Indies in which 'commons', 'where the people may go for recreation and take their cattle to pasture' (quoted in Hutchings, 2006, 109), were prescribed around the central urban core. In the British colonial planning tradition, reserved land separating town and country was designated for a range of purposes including defence, agricultural gardens, and animal pasturing, as well as to frame the town to achieve a 'fine prospect on drawing near it' (Mountgomery in Reps, 1992, 185). Montgomery (2006, 141) suggests that reserved encircling land could be regarded as a psychological framing device delineating a 'civilising buffer between nature and urban life' and representing the town as a safe haven from the unsettled lands beyond.

In Britain, in the period when the foundation of the colony of South Australia was under consideration, Madras-born barrister John Arthur Roebuck, a follower of the Utilitarian Jeremy Bentham, was one of a circle of advocates of public open space both within and on the edge of cities. Roebuck urged parliament to purchase land for public parks and walks and included encircling common lands (Henderson, 2006, 74) in his suggestions. In 1833 a House of Commons Select Committee enquired into the most appropriate means of acquiring public open spaces for the 'health and comfort' of the 'middle and humble classes'. Recommendations and legislation for public walks and other urban spaces ensued and were in the air during the time when the British parliament was debating and ultimately passed (in 1834) the South Australian Colonization Bill.

The Colonization Commissioners for South Australia (1839, 34–35) issued instructions to Surveyor-General William Light (1786-1839) in March 1836 to 'make the necessary reserves for squares, public walks and quays' in the South Australian capital, suggesting that their directive was influenced by contemporary thought about the need for public space in urban environments. Light is also considered likely to have been familiar with the book *The Friend of Australia* written by a retired officer of the British East India Company, Thomas John Maslen. Maslen (1830, 263) proposed a rationale for, and means of, incorporating urban open space that was strikingly similar to that applied in Adelaide:

> All the entrances to every town should be through a park, that is to say, a belt of park of about half a mile in width, should entirely surround every town, excepting such parts or sides as are washed by a river or lake. This would greatly contribute to the health and pleasure of the inhabitants; it would render the surrounding prospects beautiful, and give a magnificent appearance to a town, from whatever quarter viewed.

Whether or not he had read Maslen, Light's decision to include an encircling belt of parklands, and one of such vast proportion, was novel for Australia (Brown and Sherrard, 1951, 27; Reade, 1927, 62).

'Systematic Colonization' and the City of Adelaide Plan (1837)

Adelaide was founded in December 1836 as the capital city of South Australia. The colony (or province as it was known) was envisaged as an experiment in 'Systematic Colonization', a theory of settlement devised by London-born Edward Gibbon Wakefield (1796–1862) which, uniquely, depended on a balance between land, labour and capital. Conceived at a time when liberalism and laissez-faire capitalism were on the rise, South Australia was proposed to be a self-supporting place, independent of Britain, where there would be political and religious freedom in a 'Paradise of Dissent' (Pike, 1957).

The City of Adelaide plan is usually attributed to retired British military officer Surveyor-General William Light, although in more recent times, a case has been made for accrediting Light's deputy, George Strickland Kingston (1807–1880), with its authorship (Johnson, 2004; Johnson and Langmead, 1986). The plan has been described as 'textbook' (Proudfoot, 2000, 16), the layout exemplifying the key characteristics of Lord Shaftesbury's seventeenth century 'Grand Modell' of colonial planning:

> wide streets laid out in geometric, usually grid-iron form, usually on an area of one square mile; public squares; standard sized rectangular plots …; some plots reserved for public purposes; and a physical distinction between town and country, usually by common land or an encircling green belt (Home, 1997, 9).

Like the theory underpinning the colony's foundation, the Adelaide plan was 'systematic' (Garnaut, forthcoming; Bunker, 1998, 15–16). It comprised three parts, a central urban core, a periphery of suburbs and a buffer of parklands that visually and physically separated the built areas (Figure 6.1). Collectively these elements contributed to the capital city's distinctive urban morphology (Williams, 1974, 389).

The central core was divided by the River Torrens into two parts known as South and North Adelaide. South Adelaide was promoted as the administrative and commercial hub but in effect took on mixed uses (Collins et al., 2006, 32), whilst North Adelaide was conceived as purely residential. In both sections the regularly-gridded and generously-wide streets were interrupted only by squares, five in the south and one in the north. The perimeter terraces all adjoined parkland, their regular line broken occasionally as the topography intervened. North Adelaide, on the higher ground, comprised three rectangles of uneven size each set to take advantage of the landscape. Key connector roads were marked indicating that, from the outset, road incursions would break the continuity of the ring (Daly, 1987, 116–19).

The encircling parklands also extended into the intervening valley to encompass the river and its reaches, their overall form suggestive of a figure-of-eight (Stretton, 1970, 142). The river and the parklands along its edges formed a natural break between the southern and northern sectors and created a space of respite, once praised for its 'succession of cool walks, opening up vistas of trees and flower strewn gardens from the waterside edge' (Reade, 1912, 5). The decision to incorporate the river valley, set in parkland, created Australia's first greenway, the full potential of which was only recognised in the last third of the twentieth century (Mugavin, 2004, 223).

The City of Adelaide plan was the model for the layout of the government-founded towns that emerged in rural South Australia in the decades following the capital's settlement. The key elements of town core, encircling parklands, perimeter suburban allotments and radial streets emanating from the centre, described by Meinig (1962, 175) as 'the mark of Adelaide', were indelibly stamped across the South Australian countryside (Figure 6.2). The 'Parkland Town' paradigm was not challenged until the 1910s when South Australian Government Town Planner, Charles Reade (1880–1933), questioned the efficacy of 'locking up' country towns with rings of

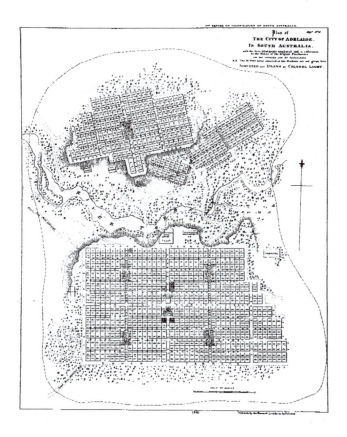

Figure 6.1: Plan of the City of Adelaide 1837

Source: *2nd Report of Colonization of South Australia* (London)

parklands and proposed an alternative arrangement of parkland wedges (Garnaut, 2003, 73–4 and Reade, 1919, 18).

Implementing the Adelaide Plan: Establishing the Parklands

The first colonists arrived in Adelaide in December 1836, in advance of the site for the capital being fixed. It was several months before they could select town lots and more than two years before country sections were available, upsetting the intentions behind the founding theory. A dual system of governance, which saw authority divided between Adelaide and London, political and personal tensions and economic mismanagement affected the colony's early progress and threatened its survival. It was against this background that the task of laying out the city streets, squares and parklands was carried out.

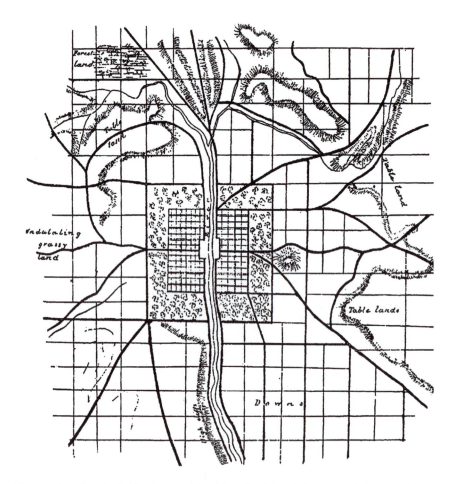

Figure 6.2: Goyder's ideal township, 1864. Parkland Town model applied by Surveyor-General G.W. Goyder in the laying out of South Australian country towns

Source: Williams (1974)

The cocoon of parkland surrounding Adelaide originally comprised 2,300 acres (930 hectares) of lightly wooded forest. Sheoaks and eucalyptus trees provided habitats for a substantial bird life (Lock-Weir, 2005, 24). Early artists captured the 'cultivated' appearance of the vegetation, the result of thousands of years of 'fire-stick farming' by the Kaurna people who occupied the land prior to European settlement and used it for camping, gathering food, initiation ceremonies and other special cultural activities (Amery and Rigney, 2006, 14). Following the arrival of the British, the Kaurna were allocated an area of the Parklands that became known as the

'Aboriginal Location'; as Harris (2006, 56–72) explains, it was the first of several spaces allotted to the Indigenous Adelaide Plains community.

The 'ownership' of the Parklands was initially uncertain due to vagaries in the colony's legislative framework and administrative structure (Price, 1924, 109–10 and Daly, 1987, 19–23). The Colonization Act required that all land, other than that designated for roads, be purchased. Consequently, in 1839, Governor Gawler bought the Parklands for the use of the people. In 1852, following a period of responsibility by various groups and individuals, the non-alienated parts were placed under the custodial 'care, control and management' of the Corporation of the City of Adelaide (later the Adelaide City Council) which has administered and tended them ever since (Morton, 1996, 147–54).

Using and Improving the Parklands

In the initial years of settlement there were no plans or principles to guide how the Parklands should be used or laid out. It took time to delineate them as a distinctive space, separate from the central administrative and business area, and to restore and improve them in order to realise their potential and benefits as a public space.

Due to the delay in the town and country section surveys, settlers were permitted to live on the Parklands for the first three years. The government assigned Emigration Square in the West Parklands as an official residential area but many squatted elsewhere, particularly along the River Torrens. The Parklands provided natural resources in the form of fresh water in the River Torrens, firewood, and building and road making materials, particularly limestone, sand and gravel. Quarries and brickyards were set up along the river. Sheep and cattle markets as well as a slaughterhouse were opened in the West Parklands and animal grazing permits were issued for sheep, cattle and horses. Olive plantations were established (Hill, 2006, 90–95). Highly odious uses included waste disposal in the form of nightsoil pits and rubbish dumps. The Torrens became an open sewer.

Diverse and environmentally inappropriate uses of the Parklands led to their despoliation. Within the first decade the original trees had been removed and the fauna lost. Although later revegetated, the sweeping panoramas captured by photographer Townsend Duryea in 1865 graphically illustrate the then still largely barren open spaces (Figure 6.3). In the wake of public outcry, the City Corporation took action, firstly to raise revenue for improvements and subsequently to instigate various programs of works (Morton, 1996, 157–77).

Over a number of decades, the Corporation introduced native and ornamental tree planting schemes (Jones, 2000, 233–44; Morton, 1996, 165–71; Daly, 1987, 124–8). In the 1880s it established a botanical and a zoological garden, and commissioned the building of a weir to create the River Torrens Lake. From the 1920s, in response to concerns about public health and inner city overcrowding, it opened children's playgrounds as dedicated play areas for the city's young (Gatley, 2001, 34–5). Later it created discrete, formally landscaped parks and gardens, many inspired by Town

Photographed by Townsend Duryea in 1865. Courtesy History Trust of South Australia

**Figure 6.3: View from the Adelaide town hall looking south across Victoria
Square to the denuded South Parklands. The village of Unley is in
the far distance**

Clerk W.C.D. Veale's overseas study trip of 1957 (Veale, 1958). The increasing
availability of various formal and informal spaces in the Parklands encouraged a
broad range of community activity (Sumerling, 2006, 210–23).

An early, and ultimately a chief, use of the Parklands was as a sporting venue. Leases
were granted for cricket, football, tennis, golf, lacrosse, lawn bowls, croquet, athletics,
swimming, cycling, archery, and horse riding (Morton, 1996, 173–5 and Daly, 1987,
137–64). Clubs developed grounds and erected buildings and other structures
appropriate to the individual sports. Generally these sporting areas needed to be fenced
off, raising the perennial issue of public access to the parklands, discussed below.

Original and Subsequent Alienation of the Parklands

The City of Adelaide plan of 1837 showed areas in dark green reserved as 'Park
Grounds' within which nine blocks were set aside for particular purposes: government
house and its associated domain, military barracks, guard-house, hospital, cemetery,
market place, botanic gardens, stores, and school. Although the location of several of
the reserved sites was altered for practical reasons, apart from the school designated in
the North Adelaide Parklands, all of the originally intended functions were fulfilled.

The reservation of such sites in parkland suggests that Light regarded the Parklands as a public space and foresaw and foreshadowed their use for government and institutional purposes in conjunction with citizens' activities. However, in the absence of any instructions, it is not clear whether he envisaged further alienation. But that has occurred, as several authors have documented (Daly, 1987; Rees, 1948; Morton, 1996, 147–54), mostly on the northern side of North Terrace and in the north-west and north-east parklands.

The Municipal Corporations Act (1849) and its successor legislation guided decisions over excision of sections of parklands for government and other ends. The earliest alienation was a band of land extending from the north-west corner of the city where settlement was first focused to the north-east corner. Bounded by North Terrace and the River Torrens, the loss of such an expansive area and its conversion for prominent cultural and institutional buildings including Parliament House, the Art Gallery and University of Adelaide, destroyed 'the open prospect down to the river' (Morton, 1996, 148). The expunging of this significant strip marked as 'Park Lands' in the original plan provided a precedent for later severances that progressively further masked and eroded the intended purpose of the river valley.

Other alienated sections of the Parklands were turned over to roads, bridges, railway yards, tracks and sheds, a major tramcar depot, and water and sewerage works. Some housed facilities like the Adelaide Gaol and Police Barracks, both built in the north-western Parklands, and an Astronomical Observatory and the Bureau of Meteorology constructed in the West Parklands. After World War 2 the observatory and weather bureau were replaced by the Adelaide High School. The Adelaide Railway Station and Environs Redevelopment (ASER) on North Terrace in the 1980s comprised a multi-storey hotel, casino and convention centre and heralded the first major commercial development on the parklands.

'Hands Off the Parklands!'

A portion of the East Parklands was alienated in 1863 by a parliamentary Act that specified it for exclusive use as a horse racecourse. The passage of the Act invoked protests over the separation of a portion of the Parklands for the use of a limited sector of the population and over the private developer's stated intention to charge an entry fee to the course. Consequently the entire site, known as Victoria Park, was left unfenced for public access at all times, apart from race days (Daly, 1987, 137–40, 143–4).

Since the 1980s the Victoria Park racecourse and its East Parklands environs have been used for motor sport races, firstly the Formula One Grand Prix and, latterly, a V8 Supercars race, the Clipsal 500. In the four months leading up to and following such races the area is progressively taken over by temporary facilities and infrastructure reducing and, eventually preventing, free public access to the Parklands. The long saga of protest against this use of the Parklands entered a new chapter in December 2006 when the state government released the Victoria Park

Masterplan (www.dtei.sa.gov.au/vicpark). It proposed a permanent three-storey, linear building for the north-east corner of the parklands between the horse and motor racing tracks (Reed and Bildstien, 2006, 4). This highly controversial structure was vigorously opposed by the Adelaide Parklands Preservation Association (APPA), a watchdog group formed in 1987, as well as by local residents' associations and other pressure groups, and by numerous individuals communicating through the daily press and other fora. At the time of writing an alternative proposal was being formulated.

Issues of contemporary concern relate to the purpose of the Parklands – what and who are they for? – and the right of public access to them; to their physical characteristics and amenity; and to the matters of the public interest and of balancing development on and conservation of, the Parklands (Moscaritolo, 2006, 19). These have been recurring themes in previous debates over the construction of other proposed permanent buildings on the Parklands (Daly, 1987, 154–6 and Morton, 1996, 152–4). The Park Lands Preservation League, the forerunner of APPA, formed in 1903 in an effort to block the Corporation of Adelaide's move to construct a refuse incinerator within the precinct occupied by the slaughterhouse in the West Parklands. In the 1910s, Mayor Cohen fought long and hard to prevent a Commonwealth government takeover of a sizeable portion of the West Parklands for military administration buildings and barracks.

The decision to provide a major concert hall in Adelaide in the 1960s led to the construction of the Adelaide Festival Centre that opened in 1973. This multi-purpose complex with theatres, plaza, amphitheatre and carparks is nestled between Parliament House and the River Torrens and the Adelaide Railway Station and King William Street. Initially recommended for a site in North Adelaide, the City Council subsequently considered several inner city locations, mostly on parkland. Adelaide City Council Alderman James C. Irwin voiced a popular concern over the choice of sites:

> The parklands are very accessible and look awfully easy to use for such a purpose as a Festival Hall. If we do we shall not have any parklands eventually. I am entirely opposed to using any part of Adelaide's open space and that includes Government House and the Torrens bank for this type of use. We need the parklands and in hundreds of years we will need them more desperately than now (Miles, n.d.).

Ultimately, an already alienated section of parklands, the present day location, was selected for the Festival Centre. However, amongst other changes, it meant the demolition and relocation of the City Baths. Consequently, a swimming centre was built in the North Parklands. Originally outdoor, it was converted to a covered complex in 1985, creating the Adelaide Aquatic Centre, and raising local ire over what was regarded as a visual intrusion into the Parklands (Daly, 1987, 81).

Since the 1980s, other executed developments on the Parklands – the ASER project, previously mentioned, the National Wine Centre in the East Parklands and the redevelopment of the Memorial Drive tennis complex adjacent to Adelaide Oval

– have all met with strong opposition. The underlying issues – what are the Parklands for and who should use them – and the tensions that these raise have not changed: 'the real threat has never been wholesale alienation [of the Parklands], but there has always been the risk … of slow, piecemeal allocation of parts … for inappropriate, intrusive and sometimes tasteless 'development', often in the name of adding to the public amenities' (Morton, 1996, 154).

The Future of the Adelaide Parklands

Despite the alienations, today the total area of the Adelaide Parklands is a generous 1730 acres (700 hectares) (see Figure 6.4). 'There is no typical landscape but many landscapes held together within a statutory boundary' (Hayter, 2006). The Parklands

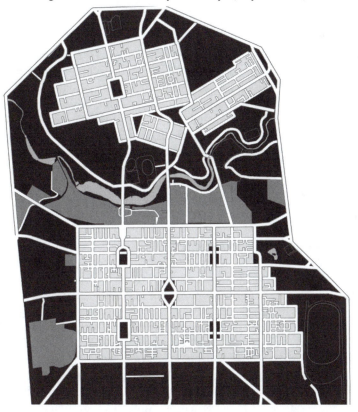

Courtesy I.T. Applications (GIS), Information Management Department Adelaide City Council, October 2006. (No reproduction without permission)

Figure 6.4: Plan of the City of Adelaide 2006 showing the encircling Parklands (dark grey) and alienated sections (light grey)

are used for active and passive recreation as well as for events such as festivals, concerts, public meetings, and circuses. The City Council's administration and management of the Parklands is guided by Community Land Management Plans prepared under provisions of the Local Government Act 1999. Devised in consultation with the community, they record the physical features and Indigenous and European cultural significance of the individual parks and define guiding principles for their future use and management. Under the Adelaide Park Lands Act 2005, the state government has established the Adelaide Park Lands Authority as a strategic body to advise on policy in relation to the Parklands' management and protection and related matters. The City Council is represented on the Authority through the Chair and will not relinquish its day-to-day responsibility for the Parklands. The passage of the 2005 Act places the Adelaide Parklands on the brink of a new era.

The Adelaide Parklands and the Larger Green Belt Idea

In 1902 Britain's Ebenezer Howard (1850–1928) referred to the City of Adelaide plan in his book *Garden Cities of Tomorrow*, the revised version of his earlier *Tomorrow: a peaceful path to real reform* (1898). Howard described Adelaide's parklands as an agricultural belt and mistakenly explained that when the central area had reached its population ceiling it had 'jumped across' the river and established a satellite settlement to the north. He regarded Adelaide as a real-life example of his own proposition for the correct model of a city's growth. Just how Howard came to know about the 1837 plan remains a mystery (Freestone, 2006, 38) but his garden city idea and the green belt concept were to have demonstrable impact in twentieth century Adelaide.

A Second Ring of Parklands for Adelaide

Victor Ryan, Director of the South Australian Intelligence and Tourist Bureau, mooted the idea of an outer belt or circle of parks for Adelaide in 1913. He was cognisant with the literature on civic improvement overseas and familiar specifically with the British Town Planning Act of 1909. Ryan proposed that the government lead a process to acquire land beyond a designated suburban limit in order to secure 'adequate open spaces where vegetation can flourish and purify the air' (Ryan to Young, 1913), protect against overcrowding and regulate future expansion. Although his proposal was not taken up, in 1916 Ryan successfully petitioned the government to secure the services of Charles Reade, a visiting lecturer from the London-based Garden Cities and Town Planning Association (GCTPA), as an Adviser on Town Planning in South Australia (Garnaut, 2006, 24). The following year Reade teamed with Ryan to organise Australia's First Town Planning and Housing Conference and Exhibition at which a plan was exhibited showing a proposed outer belt of parklands for Adelaide.

Reade was an advocate of comprehensive, strategic planning. Fresh from several intensive years of voluntary work with the GCTPA, he repeatedly called for city and suburban growth to be 'scientifically organized in conformity with a prearranged

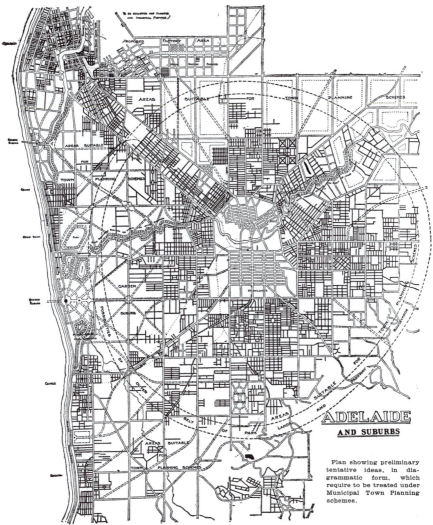

Figure 6.5: Charles Reade's 1917 Plan for Adelaide showing the original city and parklands and his proposed outer ring of parklands

Source: Reade (1919)

plan anticipating normal requirements in traffic, convenience, industry, production, public health, amenity or welfare generally' (Reade, 1919, 12). He praised the original plan for Adelaide and, drawing on his international perspective, emphasised the uniqueness of the parklands and their role as the 'lungs of the city', but lamented the subsequent ad hoc, laissez-faire development that had led to what he described as a city in a state of 'muddlement' (Freestone, 1986, 75).

For the 1917 conference, Reade produced a plan that illustrated how the garden city idea could be applied at metropolitan scale to contain urban growth and to reinstate a sense of order (Figure 6.5). Mindful that similar proposals had been made for London by Lord Heath (Garden Cities and Town Planning, 1906, 59), and by George Pepler (Cherry, 1981, 133), he suggested a second ring of parklands and a parkway boulevard (or parkway) at the fringe of the then metropolitan area. Parkways featured in American cities. They were roads of generous width used to connect parks. Typically formally landscaped with lawns, trees and shrubs they were considered an instrument of 'beautification and recreation ... enabl[ing] many citizens, who would otherwise rarely see the beauties of nature, to come into daily contact with parklike surroundings' (Bold, 1918, 154). As a further means of connecting people and nature, Reade proposed a linear park along the River Torrens from the hills in the north-east to the coast at Henley Beach (Garnaut, 2000, 56). Such a park would reinstate the riverine parkland space identified in the original plan for Adelaide.

Reade's metropolitan plan was well ahead of its time – the concept of the master plan was not taken up nationally until the postwar decades (Alexander, 2000, 100–101) – and was largely ignored. Despite the significant political and community support for town planning in South Australia in the second half of the 1910s, by 1920 political will had waned. Reade left Adelaide later that year for a secondment in the Federated Malay States. However the concepts of a second generation of parklands and of a River Torrens linear park remained as latent ideas; both re-emerged in the era of postwar expansion when considerable emphasis was placed on the growing metropolis' need for open space (Anonymous, 1948a) and later through heightened consciousness of environmental issues.

Visiting British planner Patrick Abercrombie revived the outer parklands idea in a public lecture in Adelaide in November 1948. Praising the capital's 'classic town plan' and remarking specifically on 'the amazing circle of parks around Adelaide', he opined that 'wedges of open space radiating outwards from the ... park lands, linking the inner green belt with an outer one, and separating the suburbs into a number of self-contained communities would have been a 'lovely idea' (Anonymous, 1948b). As metropolitan Adelaide continued to expand north and south of the capital, opinion pieces and letters to the editor in the local press not only kept the idea of an outer parkbelt, now usually referred to as a 'green belt', alive, but also regularly called for a master plan to guide the city's future growth and development (for example, Cheesman, 1952). Frequently, correspondents drew attention to Adelaide's 'rich heritage' as a planned city and emphasised the need to follow the example of the original Parklands by including public open space in the newly developing suburbs (for example, Anonymous, 1953; Walkley, 1953).

In 1955 the state government established a Town Planning Committee to prepare a development plan for metropolitan Adelaide. Chaired by Stuart Hart, a British planner appointed as South Australia's Government Town Planner in 1956, it produced its comprehensive Report on the Metropolitan Area of South Australia in 1962. Amongst its many recommendations, the Report proposed the identification of a hierarchy of open spaces and the creation of a system of discrete regional parks and district open spaces through metropolitan Adelaide (Town Planning Committee

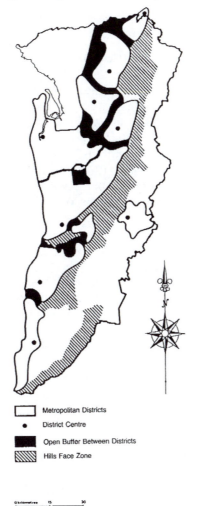

Based on recommendations in *Report on the Metropolitan Area of Adelaide* (Town Planning Committee South Australia, 1962; Hutchings, 1988)

Figure 6.6: Schematic plan for metropolitan Adelaide, 1962

South Australia, 1962, 292–3). Significantly, as part of its proposal for a green corridor, the Report also recommended limiting development on the visually prominent Hills Face Zone of the Mount Lofty Ranges that bounded Adelaide to the east (see Figure 6.6). The state government implemented both recommendations following the passage of the Planning and Development Act of 1967. In so doing it revived the parkway idea mooted earlier by Charles Reade and paved the way for the implementation of a second generation of parklands in Adelaide (Hutchings, 1988, 136).

The Metropolitan Open Space System (MOSS)

In the early 1980s Minister for Environment and Planning Don Hopgood proposed a scheme to preserve the surviving natural environment of the Mount Lofty Ranges and the Adelaide Plains, as well as to protect watercourses and the coastline. He suggested a linked system of public and privately owned land that would inject a strong visual component into the built environment and be available for active and passive leisure pursuits (Hopgood, 1986, 12). This holistic vision captured the environmental and planning concerns of the time as well as the health and aesthetic benefits of open space. Like Hart and the Town Planning Committee and Reade before them, Hopgood was looking forward as well as back, seeking to 'define those open spaces which will be such an important structural element in twenty-first century Adelaide and which will come to be regarded as equal … with Colonel Light's parklands' (Hopgood, 1986, 112).

Hopgood's vision was realised in 1994 in the Metropolitan Open Space System (MOSS) and implemented under the Parklands 21 Strategy (Planning SA, 2001, 11). MOSS includes the Adelaide Parklands; the Hills Face Zone which incorporates national and conservation parks; major watercourses crossing the metropolitan area; 70 kilometres of metropolitan coastline known as Coast Park; ten linear parks along various major creeks and rivers; and privately owned land that is not normally accessible to the public but has been incorporated for its 'amenity value' (see Figure 6.7). Land has continued to be added to MOSS and the quality of the system's open space progressively improved through state and local government initiatives.

The River Torrens Greenway

Adelaide's first linear park was created along the River Torrens and, as Mugavin (2004) reveals, it became the exemplar for subsequent greenways locally and nationally. Although the 1962 Report on Metropolitan Adelaide recommended that the 'principal rivers and creeks should be incorporated in parks and gardens, and … [that allowance be made] for a continuous road and public reserves along each bank' (Town Planning Committee South Australia, 1962, 283), that advice was not taken up fully until the late 1970s. Then a number of factors combined to bring it to fruition:

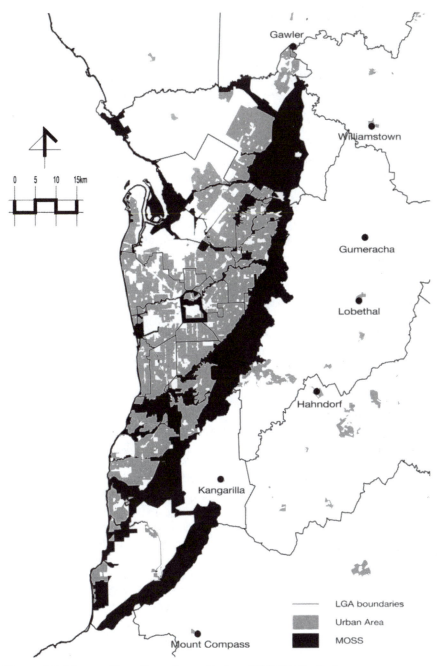

Figure 6.7: Metropolitan Open Space System (MOSS) Study Area

Source: Planning SA (2001)

concern for the detrimental effects of intensive suburban settlement along the River Torrens east of the city on the natural habitat, on Adelaide's drinking water and on river flooding; a rising community interest in recreation; and the government's decision to introduce a guided busway to the north-eastern suburbs (Mugavin, 2004, 225–33). Following the passage of the River Torrens Acquisition Act (1970) which allowed for the transfer of privately owned land into public ownership and the formulation of a development plan for the 50 kilometre greenway, a staged process of implementation occurred between 1982 and 1998.

The Torrens Linear Park incorporates formal and informal landscapes including revegetated sites, cultural heritage places, pedestrian and cycle paths, and active and passive recreation spaces. It restores public access to the river and to its tributaries, previously denied because the original survey of country sections designated the Torrens as the boundary for allotments adjoining the water (Mugavin, 2004; Bunker, 1986, 225; 17). Additionally, it realises the concept of a riverine park along the River Torrens embodied in the original plan for Adelaide and in Charles Reade's 1917 metropolitan master plan.

Conclusion

This chapter has introduced the City of Adelaide plan with its encircling belt of parklands and briefly considered aspects of their translation from two- to three-dimensional form. Issues associated with their management, use, improvement, alienation and protection have been raised, as has their role as a catalyst for the development of an outer belt of parklands to address a variety of needs in the postwar city. Although not painted in detail, the picture is of a richly-textured, multi-layered site strongly connected to Adelaide's cultural, social, political and planning history.

The Adelaide Parklands are defined as 'the prime open space focal point for the whole metropolitan area' (Planning SA, 2001, 17) and are intimately connected to the achievement of open space on green belt lines in South Australia. Their sustainability and endurance as a physical planning model is demonstrated in MOSS, Adelaide's second generation of parklands. In aiming to provide a visual and a scenic contrast to Adelaide's built environment, as well as a buffer between developed and undeveloped land, MOSS reflects the Adelaide Parklands' role in demarcating firstly the built from the unbuilt parts of the city and then in cushioning urban and suburban development. MOSS also creates recreation areas, reinforcing the idea of the recreational potential and benefits of open space and taking opportunities for community engagement in recreation out into the suburbs. By aiming to 'enhance' and 'add value' to the foundational concept of encircling parklands (Laidlaw, 2001, 1), MOSS achieves what Dennis Winston, Professor of Town and Country Planning at the University of Sydney, encouraged in supporting an outer parklands belt for Adelaide: a 'way ... [in which] the present [can] repay the past and leave a worthy inheritance for the future' (Winston, 1961).

While twentieth century visions for open space in metropolitan Adelaide were shaped by professional and popular appreciation of the contribution, benefits and enduring legacy of the Adelaide Parklands, they looked to forms of the green belt other than the original all-encompassing concept. Their propositions were models more responsive to contemporary needs and circumstances – the actual physical (linear) form of the growing metropolis, broader appreciation and recognition of environmental concepts and values, the rise of the nature conservation movement, and acceptance of a greater diversity of recreational pursuits, notably bicycle riding and walking. This local shift in view and application mirrors Freestone's observations on the green belt form as 'an evolving, adaptable and functional concept; … the importance of planning for specific places rather than imposing generic solutions; and the … shift toward a genuine ecological rationale for greenbelts *sic*' (Freestone, 2002).

In proposing the Adelaide Park Lands Bill, Minister Hill argued for it as 'a major step in an ongoing process to protect and enhance the Adelaide Park Lands as a major identifying cultural icon and community asset' (Hill, 2006). The Parklands' 'iconic' status stems from their unique encircling form and its intactness, while their value as a community asset arises from their public accessibility and their social, recreational and environmental benefits. Their physical planning influence lies in the government-sponsored towns of rural South Australia and in the postwar open spaces of metropolitan Adelaide. Collectively, these features have contributed to the enduring idea and open space legacy of the Parklands. Crucially though, while their prospect as a unique and iconic form of open space is not explicitly under question, the tension over their purpose, evident from the first years of settlement, lives on. A challenge of the past remains alive for the future to not leave forthcoming generations of South Australians disinherited from the green belt idea as expressed in the 'Parkland Town' of Adelaide, and in its progeny.

References

Alexander, I. (2000), 'The Post-war City', in S. Hamnett and R. Freestone (eds.), 'The Australian Metropolis: A Planning History', (Sydney: Allen and Unwin).

Amery, R. and Rigney, L.I. (2006), 'Recognition of Kaurna Cultural Heritage in the Adelaide Parklands: A Linguist's and Kaurna Academic's Perspective', in C. Garnaut and K. Round (eds.), 'The Adelaide Parklands Symposium. A Balancing Act: Past-Present-Future', Centre for Settlement Studies and the Bob Hawke Prime Ministerial Centre (Adelaide: University of South Australia), pp. 12–26.

Anonymous (1948a), 'City Area Needs More Recreation Space', Newspaper Clippings book. S293/16, p. 8, LLSAM.

—— (1948b), 'World Expert Views Light's City', Newspaper Clippings book. S293/16, p.11, LLSAM.

—— (1953), 'It's Time for a Master Plan', Newspaper Clippings book. S293/16, p. 55, LLSAM.

Bold, W. (1918), 'The Distribution of Parks, Playgrounds and other Open Spaces', in 'The Second Australian Town Planning and Housing Conference and Exhibition', (Brisbane: Government Printer), pp. 153–9.

Brown, A. and Sherrard, H. (1951), *Town and Country Planning* (Melbourne: Melbourne University Press).

Bunker, R. (1986), 'Town Planning at the Frontier of Settlement', in A. Hutchings and R. Bunker (eds.), 'With Conscious Purpose: A History of Town Planning in South Australia', (Adelaide: Wakefield Press), pp. 7–20.

—— (1998), 'Process and Product in the Foundation and Laying out of Adelaide', *Planning Perspectives*, 13, 247–9.

Cheesman, J. (1952), 'Adelaide Need of a Master Plan', Newspaper Clippings book related to Planning 1947–1967. S293/16, p. 47, Louis Laybourne Smith School of Architecture and Design, University of South Australia, Architecture Museum (LLSAM).

Cheesman, R. (1986), *Patterns in Perpetuity* (Adelaide: Thornton House).

Cherry, G. (1981), 'George Pepler (1882–1959)', in G. Cherry (ed.), 'Pioneers in British Planning', (London: Architectural Press).

Collins, J., Ibels, A., Collins, S., and Garnaut, C. (2006), 'Adelaide Rises from the Plain: Perspectives on the Emergence of Tall Buildings in South Australia's Capital City', *Australian Planner*, 43(3), 24–33.

Colonization Commissioners for South Australia (1839), *Third Report*, Colonization Commissioners for South Australia, London.

Creese, W. (1967), *The Search for Environment: the Garden City Before and After* (Yale: Yale University).

Daly, J. (1987), *Decisions and Disasters: Alienation of the Adelaide Parklands* (Adelaide: Bland House).

Dutton, G. (1960), *Founder of a City* (Melbourne: F.W. Cheshire).

Freestone, R. (1986), 'Exporting the Garden City Idea: Metropolitan Images in Australia, 1900–1930', *Planning Perspectives*, 1, 61–84.

—— (2002), 'Greenbelts in City and Regional Planning', in K. Parsons and D. Schuyler (eds.), 'From Garden City to Green City: The Legacy of Ebenezer Howard', (Baltimore: John Hopkins), pp. 67–98.

—— (2006), 'Contribution of the Plan of Adelaide to Modern Town Planning Theory', in C. Garnaut and K. Round (eds.), 'The Adelaide Parklands Symposium. A Balancing Act: Past-Present-Future', Centre for Settlement Studies and the Bob Hawke Prime Ministerial Centre (Adelaide: University of South Australia), pages 38–55.

Garden Cities and Town Planning (1906), 'A Green Girdle Round London', pp. 59–60.

Garnaut, C. (2000), 'Towards Metropolitan Organisation: Town Planning and the Garden City Idea', in S. Hamnett and R. Freestone (eds.), 'The Australian Metropolis: a planning history', (Sydney: Allen and Unwin), pp. 46–64.

—— (2003), 'Making Modern (River) Towns: Town planning and the Expansion of the Upper Murray Irrigation Area', *Journal of the Historical Society of South Australia*, 31, 69–84.

—— (2006), *Colonel Light Gardens: Model Garden Suburb* (Sydney: Crossing Press, first published 1999).

—— (forthcoming), *Adelaide Snapshots 1837–1975* (Adelaide: Wakefield Press), chap. A Capital City in the Making: the Implementation of the City of Adelaide Plan (1837).

Gatley, J. (2001), 'Giant Strides: the Formation of Supervised Playgrounds in Adelaide and Brisbane', *Journal of the Historical Society of South Australia*, 29, 34–46.

Harris, R. (2006), 'The "Aboriginal Location" in the Adelaide Parklands (1837-1851)', in C. Garnaut and K. Round (eds.), 'The Adelaide Parklands Symposium. A Balancing Act: Past-Present-Future', Centre for Settlement Studies and the Bob Hawke Prime Ministerial Centre (Adelaide: University of South Australia), pp. 56–72.

Hayter, J. (2006), 'Adelaide Parklands Symposium: Program Summing up', available online, http://www.unisa.edu.au/hawkecentre-/events/2006events/Parklands Symp.asp, accessed 28 December 2006.

Henderson, K. (2006), 'History and Myth: The Origin of Colonel William Light's 'Park Grounds' and their Universal Significance', in C. Garnaut and K. Round (eds.), 'The Adelaide Parklands Symposium. A Balancing Act: Past-Present-Future', Centre for Settlement Studies and the Bob Hawke Prime Ministerial Centre (Adelaide: University of South Australia), pp. 73–89.

Hill, C. (2006), 'The Past and Future of the Adelaide Parkland Olives', in C. Garnaut and K. Round (eds.), 'The Adelaide Parklands Symposium. A Balancing Act: Past-Present-Future', Centre for Settlement Studies and the Bob Hawke Prime Ministerial Centre (Adelaide: University of South Australia), pp. 90–105.

Home, R. (1997), *Of Planting and Planning: The Making of British Colonial Cities* (London: E & FN Spon).

Hopgood, D. (1986), 'Metropolitan Adelaide and its Future', in A. Hutchings and R. Bunker (eds.), 'With conscious purpose. A history of town planning in South Australia', (Adelaide: Wakefield Press and RAPI (SA Division)), pp. 109–18.

Hutchings, A. (1988), 'Visions for Adelaide: the Persistence of Planning Ideas', *Urban Policy and Research*, 6(3), 136–9.

—— (2006), 'The Adelaide Plan and the Spanish Laws of the Indies', in C. Garnaut and K. Round (eds.), 'The Adelaide Parklands Symposium. A Balancing Act: Past-Present-Future', Centre for Settlement Studies and the Bob Hawke Prime Ministerial Centre (Adelaide: University of South Australia), pp. 106–14.

Johnson, D. (2004), 'The Kingston/Light Plan of Adelaide and Founding the City', *Journal of the Historical Society of South Australia*, 32, 5–18.

—— (2006), 'Foundations for Adelaide's Park Lands', in C. Garnaut and K. Round (eds.), 'The Adelaide Parklands Symposium. A Balancing Act: Past-Present-Future', Centre for Settlement Studies and the Bob Hawke Prime Ministerial Centre (Adelaide: University of South Australia), pp. 115–27.

Johnson, D. and Langmead, D. (1986), *The Adelaide City Plan: Fiction and Fact* (Adelaide: Wakefield Press).

Jones, D. (2000), 'A Gardenesque Vision for Adelaide: Planning and Planting the Adelaide Park Lands in the 1880s', in C. Garnaut and S. Hamnett (eds.), 'Fifth Australian Urban History/Planning History Conference Proceedings', (Adelaide: University of South Australia), pp. 233–44.

Laidlaw, D. (2001), 'Foreword', in Planning SA (ed.), 'The Future of Open Space in Adelaide: Parklands 21 Strategy', (Adelaide: Planning SA).

Lock-Weir, T. (2005), *Visions of Adelaide 1836–1886* (Adelaide: Art Gallery of South Australia).

Maslen, T. (1830), *The Friend of Australia* (London: Hurst, Chance, and Co.).

Meinig, D. (1962), *On the Margins of the Good Earth* (Adelaide: Rigby).

Miles, J. (n.d.), 'Council Divided on Hall Plan', Festival Hall Newspaper Clippings Book. S270/4/78, LLSAM.

Montgomery, R. (2006), 'The Adelaide Parklands: Framing a Settlement', in C. Garnaut and K. Round (eds.), 'The Adelaide Parklands Symposium. A Balancing Act: Past-Present-Future', Centre for Settlement Studies and the Bob Hawke Prime Ministerial Centre (Adelaide: University of South Australia), pp. 141–58.

Morris, A. (1994), *History of Urban Form Before the Industrial Revolution* (Essex: Longman Scientific and Technical), 3rd edn.

Morton, P. (1996), *After Light: A History of the City of Adelaide and its Council, 1878–1928* (Adelaide: Wakefield Press).

Moscaritolo, M. (2006), 'Balancing Act', *Advertiser* 19 December, 19.

Mugavin, D. (2004), 'Adelaide's Greenway: Torrens Linear Park', *Landscape and Urban Planning*, 68(2–3), 223–40.

Pike, D. (1957), *Paradise of Dissent: South Australia, 1828–1857* (Melbourne: Melbourne University Press).

Planning SA (2001), *The Future of Open Space in Adelaide: Parklands 21 Strategy* (Adelaide: Government of South Australia).

Price, A.G. (1924), 'The Foundation and Settlement of South Australia 1829–1845 (1924)', Facsimile 1973.

Proudfoot, H. (2000), 'Founding Cities in Nineteenth-century Australia', in S. Hamnett and R. Freestone (eds.), 'The Australian Metropolis: A Planning History', (Sydney: Allen and Unwin), pp. 11–26.

Reade, C. (1912), 'Town Planning in Australasia', *Town Planning Review*, 3, 2–10.

—— (1919), *Planning and Development of Towns and Cities in South Australia* (Adelaide: Government Printer).

—— (1927), 'Park-Belts in Australia and New Zealand', in 'Modern Town Planning and Housing. Explanation and Catalogue of Second Exhibition in British Malaya', (Kuala Lumpur: Department of Town Planning).

Reed, T. and Bildstien, C. (2006), 'Grandstand Key to $32m Masterplan', *Advertiser*, 19 December, 4.

Rees, J.S. (1948), *A Brief History of the Adelaide Parklands (and a few suggestions)* (Adelaide: Rees, J. S.).

Reps, J. (1992), *The Making of Urban America* (Princeton: Princeton University Press), reprinted edn.

Ryan to Young (1913), '30 May 1913, GRG 35/1', State Records of South Australia.

Stretton, H. (1970), *Ideas for Australian Cities* (Adelaide: Hugh Stretton).

Sumerling, P. (2006), 'Activities in the Park Lands over Time', in C. Garnaut and K. Round (eds.), 'The Adelaide Parklands Symposium. A Balancing Act: Past-Present-Future', Centre for Settlement Studies and the Bob Hawke Prime Ministerial Centre (Adelaide: University of South Australia), pp. 210–23.

Thorsheim, P. (2006), 'Green Space and Class in Imperial London', in A. Isenberg (ed.), 'The Nature of Cities: Culture, Landscape and Urban Space', (NY: University of Rochester Press), pp. 24–37.

Town Planning Committee South Australia (1962), *Report on the Metropolitan Area of Adelaide* (Adelaide: Government of South Australia).

Veale, W. (1958), *Report on Overseas Visit to the U.S.A. British Isles and Continent*, Parks and Gardens 4, City of Adelaide, Adelaide.

Walkley, G. (1952), *Town and country planning in South Australia: an historical survey* (Adelaide: Royal Geographical Society of South Australia).

—— (1953), 'Why Can't we have a City Plan?', Newspaper Clippings book. S293/16, p. 80, LLSAM.

Williams, M. (1974), *The Making of the South Australian Landscape: A Study in the Historical Geography of Australia* (London: Academic Press).

Winston, D. (1961), 'Adelaide's Development. Problems, Needs of Planning', Newspaper Clippings book. S293/16, p. 209, LLSAM.

CHAPTER 7

Ottawa's Greenbelt Evolves from Urban Separator to Key Ecological Planning Component

David Gordon and Richard Scott

Introduction

Ottawa has a green belt because Canada's seat of government was the focus of several attempts to prepare comprehensive regional plans during the first half of the twentieth century. The Canadian government was determined to improve the appearance and functionality of the capital city, which was established in a compromise location in a remote lumber town on the Québec/Ontario border in the mid-nineteenth century (Taylor, 1986). By coincidence, the plan that was most thoroughly implemented was prepared in 1945–50, when the 1944 Greater London Plan and its green belt were dominant planning ideas.

This chapter briefly introduces the role of open space in national capital plans and how planning for green spaces in Canada's capital evolved over the first half of the twentieth century. It describes the original intention for the green belt in Canada's 1950 Plan for the National Capital, and how the Ottawa green belt evolved from an urban containment measure to an open space and ecological feature of the regional plan. Finally, the chapter presents some lessons from Canada's half century of experience with green belt proposals for its national capital.

National Capitals and Open Space

Most cities have parks, but national capitals often have a larger supply of open space to provide impressive settings for public institutions, monuments and other symbolic content. The plans for 'political capitals' like Ottawa, Canberra, Brasilia and Washington all contained extensive parks systems, which were built over the long term (Gordon, 2006). Although many North American cities prepared open space system plans during the heyday of the Parks Movement (1880s–1914), few cities could find the funds or powers to completely implement them (Schuyler, 1988). The national governments acquired the land for the parks in capital cities early because they had access to the relatively small sums of cash required to pay agricultural prices for land and the legal power to expropriate holdouts. These were crucial advantages when compared to non-capital cities.

The early 20th century model for park system planning in capital cities was Frederick Law Olmsted Jr.'s 1902 plan for Washington, which provided an inter-connected system of open spaces throughout the District of Columbia (Moore, 1902; Peterson, 1985). The 1903, 1915 and 1920s plans for Ottawa were influenced by this model. After World War II, the Ottawa parks system proposals were expanded to include a green belt, following the example of the 1944 Greater London Plan.

Planning for Open Space in Canada's National Capital Region

In 1903, the Ottawa Improvement Commission (OIC) retained Frederick G. Todd (1876–1948) to prepare a preliminary parks plan for the Canadian capital. Todd trained in Frederick Law Olmsted's office, was a founder of the Town Planning Institute of Canada and Canada's first professional landscape architect. His plan for the open space system of the national capital included the first proposal to acquire Gatineau Park in Québec (Todd, 1903). Todd respected Ottawa's unique natural setting and its Gothic Revival parliament buildings, and recommended avoiding any literal planning of a 'Washington of the North'. His inter-connected parks system, regional approach and admiration for natural systems reflected the best of the Olmsted tradition and presaged modern ecological planning principles. Unfortu-nately, the OIC chose to ignore the report and to proceed with incremental additions to the Ottawa parks. However, many of Todd's recommended parks and parkways were incorporated in the future plans of Edward H. Bennett (1915), Noulan Cauchon (1922) and Jacques Gréber (1950).

Only twelve years separate Todd's Preliminary Report and the 1915 Report of the Federal Plan Commission (FPC), prepared by Edward H. Bennett (Federal Plan Commission, 1915). Both documents take a region-wide approach but Bennett's report is perhaps Canada's first comprehensive plan and a national landmark of City Beautiful planning (Gordon, 1998). Although City Beautiful designs are often associated with grand complexes of institutional buildings in the classical style, many of the best plans also incorporated extensive parks systems executed in a natural style (Wilson, 1989). Parks planning for the 1915 FPC report began with population projections showing an increase from 100,000 to 250,000 by 1950 and 'since it is necessary now to plan park areas within the city for all time, [the FPC] have provided parks for a city of 350,000.' (Federal Plan Commission, 1915, 27). Bennett's team established a performance standard that all residents should be within a half-mile of a major park (8–10 acres). The planners compared existing and future residential areas using population density maps. Thirteen new parks and 41 playgrounds were planned using this projection (Figure 7.1). The major parks were connected by a system of eleven new parkways along the rivers and Rideau Canal, in the manner advocated by the 1903 Report (Federal Plan Commission, 1915, 125–30).

The 1915 Federal Plan Commission appropriated Todd's advocacy of large forest

Development of Proposed Park Systems for Ottawa-Hull: 1903-1990

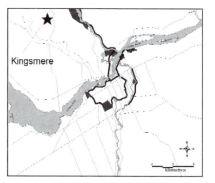

1903 Proposed

1915 Proposed

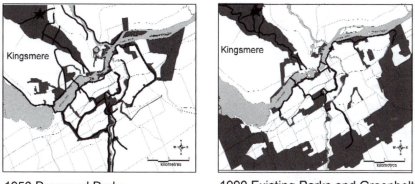

1950 Proposed Parks

1990 Existing Parks and Greenbelt

Figure 7.1: Ottawa parks' evolution

reserves and expanded his proposals by an order of magnitude. Bennett recommended a great green wedge in the Gatineau Hills, extending from the Laurentian mountains almost to Parliament Hill. It was featured in the frontispiece to the 1915 plan as a bird's-eye view of the future capital. Despite its elaborate presentation, the 1915 Federal Plan Commission report sat on the shelf. The Commission was established in late 1913, less than a year before Canada entered World War I, and the nation soon had other priorities. Unfortunately, the report was finally tabled in Parliament only a few weeks after the Centre Block of Parliament Buildings burned in February 1916. Rebuilding the Parliament Buildings diverted any interest in improving the capital in the immediate post-war period.

Some Canadian planning advocates, led by Thomas Adams and Noulan Cauchon, attacked the 1915 report as an impractical City Beautiful plan and advocated a different approach, influenced by City Scientific (Adams, 1916). City Scientific planners advocated extensive technical studies of housing conditions and infrastructure as a scientific basis for planning (Ford, 1913; Adams, 1921). Cauchon was the Chairman of the Ottawa Town Planning Commission (OTPC), where most of his work involved small-scale local improvements. However, he also recommended a regional plan for a larger federal district, including the major parks in the Gatineau Hills (Cauchon, 1922). The federal authorities generally ignored Cauchon's suggestions. The OIC struggled during the 1920s under a new political master, Prime Minister William Lyon Mackenzie King, who dominated planning in Canada's capital from 1921 until his retirement in 1948. In 1927, King replaced the OIC with the Federal District Commission (FDC), although he did not implement a federal district similar to Washington or Canberra. But King did support large-scale open space planning as part of the transformation of the Ottawa region from a lumber town to a national capital. While in opposition in 1931–35, he supported the proposals to acquire the green wedge of Gatineau Park, and implemented them soon after upon returning to power. In 1936, King commissioned French urbanist Jacques Gréber to prepare plans for a central square, and a preliminary design for downtown Ottawa. After World War II ended, Gréber was retained to prepare a comprehensive regional plan for the national capital (Gordon, 2002; Gordon and Osborne, 2004).

Background to the 1950 Plan

Although the early 20th century model for capital city park system planning was Olmsted's 1902 Washington plan, another influential model plan was emerging by 1945. Sir Patrick Abercrombie's 1944 Greater London Plan followed Ebenezer Howard's 1898 prescription for a green belt to encircle the built-up area, and new towns in the periphery to accommodate growth (Abercrombie, 1945; Howard, 1898, Diagram 7).

This sort of plan had been tried in Moscow in the 1930s, and the English government had taken the first steps to assemble the London green belt in the 1930s. But it was Abercrombie's 1944 plan that became a model for many other capital cities including Stockholm, Helsinki, Seoul and Ottawa. Jacques Gréber was certainly aware of the Greater London Plan since he visited England during several of his Atlantic crossings for the commission to plan Canada's capital.

The Green Belt Proposed in the 1950 Plan

The 1950 Plan for the National Capital is a landmark in Canadian planning history (See Figure 7.2). It includes extensive background research, regional land use and transportation plans, urban design schemes for the core, and extensive infrastructure plans (Gréber, 1950; Gordon, 2001). The first half of the Report contained the background studies that surveyed the region. The proposals that followed built upon previous plans by Todd, Bennett, Cauchon and Gréber's 1938 scheme, and included the following elements:

- Relocation of the railway system and industries from the inner city to the suburbs
- Construction of new cross-town boulevards and bridges
- Government offices decentralized to the suburbs
- Slum clearance and urban renewal of the LeBreton Flats district
- Expansion of the urban population from 250,000 to 500,000 in neighbourhood units

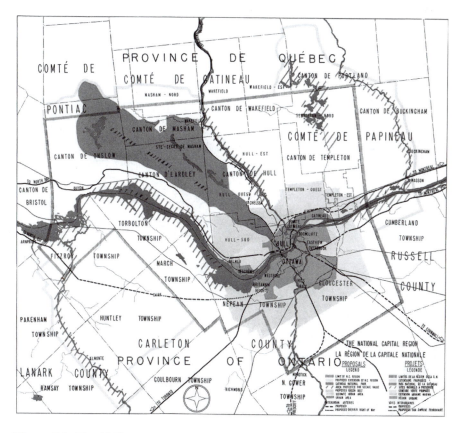

Figure 7.2: The 1950 plan for the National Capital prepared by Jacques Gréber

- A wilderness park in the Gatineau Hill, a parks system along the canal and rivers and an extensive parkways network
- A green belt surrounding the future built-up area

The parks and open space provisions of the 1950 plan drew heavily from both Todd's 1903 Preliminary Report and Bennett's 1915 Federal Plan Commission Report. Gréber's team carried the quasi-scientific approach further, starting with population projections, detailed density analyses, parks inventories and calculations of park space per 1000 people (Gréber, 1950, Chapters, 11, 12).

Gréber's parks system was oriented to active recreation, and began with proposals for a national stadium, playgrounds and local parks. Todd's proposals for riverside parkways were largely adopted. The plan's major open space proposal was a green belt, similar to the one proposed in the Greater London Plan. Finally, Gréber's team noted that it was too late to implement Todd's proposal for a forest reserve in the Gatineau River Valley, and pushed for major additions to the park in the Gatineau Hills, which were assembled in the 1950s and 1960s. These vast land purchases were supported as a tourist resource but also to preserve the national landscape in line with Todd's prescription a half century previously (Gréber, 1950, Chapter 8).

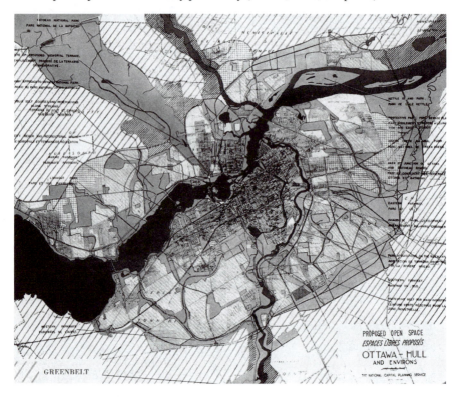

Figure 7.3: Green belt/open spaces from the 1950 plan

A green belt approximately four kilometres wide was planned to surround the suburban areas, to control the outer limits of urbanization (see Figure 7.3). Gréber considered this green belt a 'no-servicing' zone, which would halt tentacular extension of services along main routes into the national capital (Gréber, 1950, 158–60). Land uses on private services would be permitted, as well as farming, industrial estates, and research establishments. Some pockets of land were already federally owned, including two defence facilities (one a bog acquired in the Second World War for bombing practice).

Growth beyond the 500,000 to 600,000 people anticipated within the green belt was to take place in satellite towns in the rural area, although the locations of these towns were not designated. This proposal was clearly rooted upon Ebenezer Howard's 1898 Social Cities scheme, with its green belt and satellite cities. It also drew upon Abercrombie's Greater London Plan, especially in the proposals for the green belt to be implemented by development regulations (Abercrombie, 1945, 8; 24–6). But political relations at the local level were not always smooth and implementation of the green belt proposals suffered.

Problems Implementing the Green Belt Proposals, 1950–1958

Ottawa and Hull were given strong links to the 1950 plan's implementation by appointing both mayors to the Federal District Commission (FDC), while senior staff were appointed to a National Capital Planning Committee. The City of Ottawa supported the FDC by establishing the Ottawa Area Planning Board (OAPB) in 1947 to control unregulated suburban expansion. However, the suburban townships continued to approve low density subdivisions without municipal services. The City reacted in 1948 by attempting to annex all the land to the proposed inside boundary of the green belt (Ottawa City, 1956). The rural townships fought the annexation, and lost.

The FDC sought municipal zoning controls to implement the green belt because the Canadian federal government has no constitutional power for land use control over land it does not own. While the City of Ottawa supported the green belt, the outlying townships of Nepean and Gloucester, where the green belt would be situated, saw their development future dissolving. They did not co-operate, refusing to incorporate the green belt into their zoning bylaws and approving subdivisions. The FDC tried to force the issue through the Ottawa Planning Area Board, but this advisory body could not compel the rural townships to stop subdivision of land for low-density suburbs. The Nepean Township's reeve referred to the green belt as the 'weed belt' and suggested that it be developed with half-acre lots using wells and septic tanks for servicing (Moodie, 1956). After five years of conflict, it became clear that Ontario and Québec planning legislation was not strong enough to establish a green belt by regulation, as in the London and Paris models. Finally, the federal government's housing agency, the Central Mortgage and Housing Corporation, stopped insuring mortgages in the proposed green belt area in 1955, effectively putting a halt to further development until the green belt question could be resolved.

The resulting public outcry led to a parliamentary enquiry. In 1956, a joint committee of the House of Commons and Senate was established to investigate the FDC. The committee endorsed the idea of a green belt as a key recommendation of its inquiry, but advocated further discussions between the FDC and Nepean and Gloucester to negotiate a zoning solution (Joint Committee of the Senate and the House of Commons, 1956). The rural townships refused to co-operate, and the federal government adopted more drastic action to implement the 1950 plan. The federal government abandoned attempts to enforce regional planning objectives through planning regulations. It used land ownership, expropriation power and its infrastructure budget to shape urban form according to its plan. The federal planners also continued to assist some local governments in Québec, while most Ontario municipalities established their own planning departments.

Expropriation and Assembly of the Ottawa Greenbelt 1958–1964

Although the 1950 National Capital Plan was largely a personal initiative of the Liberal prime minister Mackenzie King, he had given it such a mighty push to start implementation that the plan outlasted his 1948 retirement and his party's loss of power in 1956. In 1958, a newly-elected Conservative government decided to create the National Capital Commission (NCC), with the expanded powers required to implement the sweeping proposals of the Gréber plan. The NCC was given the power and the budget to acquire remaining green belt lands through expropriation (Diefenbaker, 1957). The purposes of the green belt upon announcement of federal acquisition were:

- To prevent further haphazard urban sprawl as around the Capital, including ribbon development along approach highways, and so to protect adjacent farming areas from being swallowed up by uncontrolled development;
- To meet long-term national capital planning needs by ensuring that when the central area was built up, an adequate reserve of sites for future buildings, for government and public institutional purposes, was retained;
- To place a practical and economic limit on the growth of the capital by confining intensive building development to an area which could be provided with municipal services at a reasonable cost (McDonald and Cole, 1973).

The permitted land uses in the original green belt included: existing farms and woodlots, existing and new federal uses; 'public developments' covering more than 2 hectares (5 acres) on large lots, private industries occupying more than 10 acres and existing and new residential uses. These initial uses were much more permissive than considered now – the NCC would not allow new residential buildings.

At the time of acquisition, the federal government already owned 2,500 hectares (6,170 acres) of the green belt. Approximately 14,000 hectares (34,600 acres) of land were acquired by negotiation or expropriation between 1958 and 1964; so about 93%

of the area was purchased. The total cost was approximately $40 million in 1966 dollars (2005 $250 million). Many residences built in the 1950–55 period were acquired and leased. One expropriation was appealed to the Supreme Court of Canada, challenging the taking of land for a general purpose, but the federal case prevailed (Supreme Court of Canada, 1966).

Some 600 farms were acquired, many on marginal land. Between 1961 and 1969 leased farm acreage declined from 10,450 to 6,030 hectares (McDonald and Cole, 1973, 21). Within this area, 3,200 hectares came under a long-term forestry agreement with the provincial (Ontario) government, which saw more than 3 million trees planted. The NCC made many investments in farming in 1970s and early 1980s, particularly tile drainage to improve soil productivity (National Capital Commission, 1974a).

In keeping with Gréber's plan, some large areas were transferred to other federal agencies in the 1960s for research purposes to create a large experimental farm, a Communications Research Centre (CRC) and a mining explosives testing site. All these activities benefited from proximity to the urban capital, but required seclusion and security. The CRC helped attract the Northern Electric research center, later to become a foundation of the region's high tech cluster as Nortel Networks (Smart, 2004). Research areas increased from 1,050 ha in 1961 to 3,150 ha in 1969. The 'satellite towns' suggested for development well outside the green belt turned into ordinary suburbs clinging to its edge. Interestingly, and perhaps alarmingly, private developers released early proposals for leap-frogging the green belt in 1964, two years before land acquisition for the green belt was finally completed. Residential developments were proposed for the outer edges of the green belt on portions of its west, south, and east sides. The urban containment role, so much a part of the Gréber vision in 1950, was being undermined even as the green belt came into being.

This change in metropolitan planning vision arose primarily from rapid population increases. The major weakness of the 1950 plan was its population projection. The plan projected that the national capital region would double in population from 250,000 to 500,000 between 1950 and 2000, and the green belt was located to contain the half million people. The post-war baby boom and rapid government expansion were unforeseen by the planners and critics alike (Spence-Sales, 1949). The boom caused the regional population to pass 500,000 by 1966, and one million people by the 2001 census. The concept of urban containment no longer existed (see Figure 7.4).

Regional governments were established in 1969 in Ottawa-Carleton (Ontario) and 1970 for the Outaouais (Québec) to help deal with these growth issues from a metropolitan perspective. This change signalled an inexorable transfer of planning and budgetary influence from federal to regional governments in the capital. Kanata, the westerly outer urban community, was begun in the mid-1960s (Smart, 2004; Timusk, 1976). The 1973 draft Ottawa-Carleton regional plan designated the three outer communities to grow to 100,000 people as a fundamental precept in the future urban growth of the region.

Meanwhile, the idea of a federal green belt in the Québec portion of the national

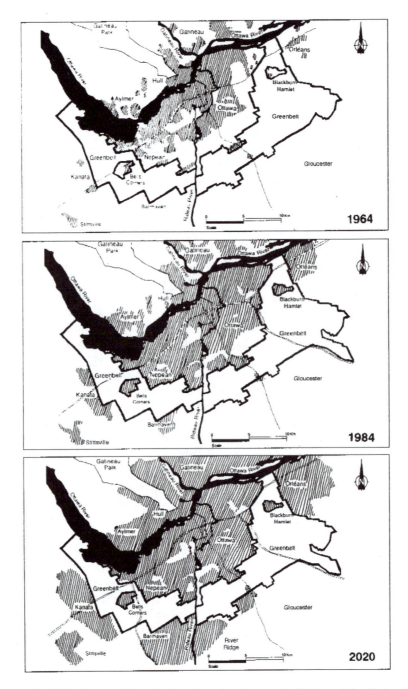

Figure 7.4: The Ottawa Greenbelt and regional growth (National Capital Commission, 1996)

capital region was slowly abandoned. The federal government's 35,600 ha (88,000 acres) Gatineau Park represented a substantial public land intervention in the region. The federal government undertook some preparatory planning work for a Québec green belt, but later studies indicated the need was not sufficient to proceed (McDonald and Cole, 1973, 12). The Québec provincial government was quietly opposed to the federal proposal and slower growth on the north side of the Ottawa River made the need for a green belt less compelling. Ironically, the Québec government's 1978 province-wide agricultural land preservation regulations eventually served the same urban containment objectives in the Gatineau region as the proposed federal green belt.

The federal government's last attempt at unilateral regional planning was *Tomorrow's Capital*, a highly conceptual plan that proposed future urban growth in both the Ontario and Québec portions of the Capital on a SE-NW-trending linear 'spine', with poles of higher density distributed along its length (National Capital Commission, 1974b). The federal and Ontario provincial governments co-operated in initiating the 'Southeast City' part of the concept a satellite community outside the green belt, as Gréber had recommended in the 1950 plan. Land acquisition for this community by the provincial government was complemented by a minor extension of the green belt to the southeast to buffer the proposed city on the east, and the acquisition of a new, non-connected portion of green belt on the city's west side.

The newly-established Regional Municipality of Ottawa-Carleton (RMOC) was outraged that *Tomorrow's Capital* had been developed without consultation and ignored its draft regional plan. RMOC refused to support the federal proposal and approved an official plan that designated the three outer communities proposed by private developers should grow to 100,000 people as the fundamental precept in the future urban growth of the region (Regional Municipality of Ottawa-Carleton, 1974). The proposed federal/provincial 'Southeast City' was not included as a priority urban growth area. Since the RMOC had the statutory authority to plan for the region and the financial resources to build regional utilities and transit routes, its vision prevailed (Fullerton, 2005). The NCC sold most of the proposed buffer in the late 1980s, but retained the part contiguous with the green belt. The province continues to own the land it acquired for the city proper. Two major provincial freeways were also pushed through the green belt in the 1970s to provide high-speed vehicular access to the Capital.

The NCC had no large-scale plan for the Greenbelt lands until a 1972 report undertaken from a largely landscape architectural perspective (Page, 1972). This plan proposed many public amenities such as pathways and recreational areas, but it was never approved. The next effort, the 1982 green belt Management Plan, took much the opposite tact, with a focus on land management of agriculture, forestry, recreation, and natural areas (National Capital Commission, 1982). This plan was inwardly focused, and approved by the NCC as the guidance for its own lands.

Repositioning the Greenbelt, 1990–2003

A change in mandate in 1998 and major budget cuts for the NCC moved the agency away from traditional regional planning and development and towards cultural programming that interprets the capital to the nation. These changes forced the agency to take a more strategic look at the Greenbelt from the standpoint of its role in the capital, not just as a metropolitan asset. At the same time, increasing growth in the outlying communities brought demands to build more roads, sewers, water mains, hydro corridors, and transit lines through the Greenbelt. These new service corridors raised questions about their effect on the role of the Greenbelt, the viability of its natural systems and agriculture, and new demands from a burgeoning urban population for uses such as recreation. A major review was launched in 1990 to come up with a future-oriented plan for the green belt, one that would:

● Reassess and redefine its role(s) as part of the metropolitan area and as part of the capital of Canada.
● Look at the entire green belt system, so that NCC and other federal lands in the green belt would come under one integrated plan.
● Examine the green belt within the context of change beyond its borders, in terms of urban growth and attendant requirements for infrastructure links, land use change, and recreational and other urban pressures (and opportunities), and their effects on cultural and natural systems within the green belt, and their connections beyond, with the intent of assessing prospects for future viability of these systems.
● Provide a framework for land use and land/lease management, landscape character/quality, and public programming and activities in terms of messages.
● Address questions related to natural area management, farm lease management, and residential properties, as some examples.

The review addressed the changing role of the Greenbelt, from urban containment (which was already doomed) to a key element of metropolitan structure and growth strategy for an inner city and three satellite communities. The planning process included an extensive public consultation programme and close liaison with the regional and municipal planners.

An economic analysis examined the effect of the green belt/satellite community model on the character and costs and of the Greenbelt (Nixey, 1991). It revealed suburban density patterns on either side of the Greenbelt to be similar, and that the green belt did not disrupt the suburban land market in terms of residential and commercial land values. The capital costs (operating costs were not measured) of running regional infrastructure (roads, water mains, sewers, etc.) through the Greenbelt were estimated to impose a 2.5% premium in terms of total public and private investment for a 100,000-person satellite community. One must measure these costs against the intangible benefits provided by the Greenbelt. One myth revealed by the study was that the satellite communities were not 'self-contained'.

Except for Kanata, little employment was found, and therefore much cross-green belt commuting to the inner urban area occurred. This phenomenon was partly caused by the immature state of the outer urban communities. Better jobs-housing balance might cause more efficient two-way use of major transport links across the green belt rather than uni-directional peaks in morning and afternoon rush hours.

The ecosystems analysis of the major natural areas in the Greenbelt indicated that the regional growth pattern was starting to impair some ecological links beyond the Greenbelt. Also, the Green-belt edges reflected 1950s thinking, with some ecosystems truncated by the original expropriated boundaries (Hough Stansbury Woodland Limited with Gore and Storrie Limited, 1991). Correcting this problem became a major concept in the new plan.

Five main themes structured and guided the plan, from overall vision/roles, to the overall concept plan, to more detailed implementation actions. They were:

- Continuous Natural Environment,
- Vibrant Rural Community,
- Compatible Built Facilities,
- Distinctive Capital Setting, and
- Accessible Public Activities (National Capital Commission, 1996).

The key regional approach was to 'bundle' major infrastructure into fewer, larger, but sensitively-placed corridors to serve the growing outer urban communities in a way that reduces green belt fragmentation (see Figure 7.5).

The 1996 plan expanded the Greenbelt in two major areas to complete ecosystem ownership. This recommendation has been implemented in two rural areas. The plan also recommended a 'Greenbelt Pathway' to broaden the public experience of the Greenbelt. Although there were clusters of walking and skiing trails through the Greenbelt's natural areas, many areas are not publicly accessible or visible, such as the government complexes and leased farming areas. This recommendation was partly implemented by 2006.

Current Context

The NCC's 1996 plan repositioned the Greenbelt from an urban containment feature to an essential part of the regional ecosystem. This result matched the approach of the 1997 RMOC plan, which also used ecosystem planning techniques (Hostovsky et al., 1995).

After the 2001 amalgamation of the regional and local governments on the Ontario side of the Ottawa River, the new City of Ottawa began to use Smart Growth principles to guide its planning. The 2003 Official Plan intends to increase the 'intensification' of development in the urban area surrounded by the Greenbelt, and to not further expand the urban boundaries of the outer urban communities, which do not have any containment features (Ottawa City, 2003, 1–28). The outer urban

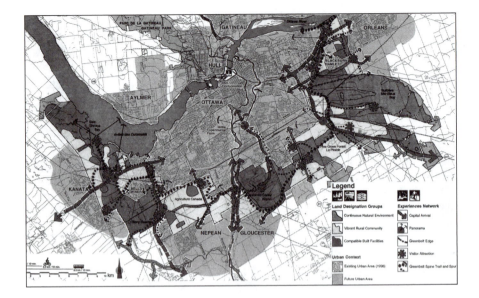

Figure 7.5: The 1996 Greenbelt Concept Plan

Source: National Capital Commission (1996, 13)

communities do not yet have true 'downtowns' and employment is generally lower than ultimately planned. This situation has continued the largely one-way commuting patterns to and from the inner urban area, with the exception of Kanata, which has a healthy (but suburban) high-tech employment node. Current planning challenges within the Greenbelt include infrastructure, land management and sustainability. New infrastructure was pushed through the Greenbelt following the precepts of the 1996 plan, and will test their veracity. Sympathetic landscaping and understated lighting, as well as parallel pathways, have made these corridors less intrusive than they might have been under the older policies.

Land management presents challenges in maintaining leased farms and residential units. Some deteriorating residential units built in the 1950–55 period have been demolished as they are not compatible with the Greenbelt setting and were not profitable. The growth of outer urban communities is changing the nature of farming, with many farmers establishing pick-your-own operations and market gardens to serve the commuting public. This trend, if extended significantly, might contribute to food security and sustainability for the capital's urban areas. Managing farm buildings, 280 leased residences, pathways, and interpretive infrastructure all remain issues in the context of diminishing budgets. Farmers may need some other form of land tenure, such as long-term leases, to allow them to finance farm improvements. Finally, management partnerships are increasing, particularly in recreation. The NCC negotiated agreements with governmental and non-governmental organizations to build and maintain ski trails, pathways, provide interpretation activities, facilities and other public amenities.

Conclusions

The Ottawa Greenbelt was introduced to shape metropolitan form and control suburban expansion, following the Garden City principles advocated by leading planners in the first half of the twentieth century. It also allowed for a green, natural and dignified approach to the downtown area, reinforcing City Beautiful objectives for the symbolic core of the national capital. While the Greenbelt has remained successful in providing a dignified entrance to the capital city, it has clearly failed as a measure to constrain metropolitan expansion. The explosive post-war growth of the region quickly jumped the Greenbelt, and satellite city plans were never completed. The results are rather ordinary agglomerations of conventional suburban development attached to the outside boundaries of three sides of the Greenbelt. However, the Greenbelt did provide a substantial separation between the inner and outer suburbs and its large land parcels later proved useful as components of a new approach to ecological planning and sustainable development. Figure 7.6 shows the

Figure 7.6: Separation of suburban subdivisions by the Greenbelt in eastern Ottawa, looking toward downtown

Source: NCC photography collection

outer suburb, Orleans, in the lower foreground separated by the Greenbelt from the inner suburb named Beacon Hill. This sector of the Greenbelt contains some agricultural land, a popular toboggan hill for winter recreation and buffers the region's largest sewage treatment plant. Green's Creek, running through the centre of the image, is an important ecological corridor connecting to the Ottawa River on the right side of the image.

The Greenbelt offers both benefits and disadvantages from a sustainability context, which is increasingly driving the planning agenda in Canada's capital region and in cities worldwide. The accessibility to natural and open space and recreational amenities bodes well for a healthy and active population. The Greenbelt also offers potential food security, with a permanent, abundant, and high quality supply of farmland within the metropolitan area. It has fostered a coherent urban growth pattern, (despite 'leapfrogging' by urban development) that has provided both community identity and a strong framework for long-range planning. On the negative side are the added financial, energy (and related greenhouse gas emissions), and time penalties associated with the additional travel distance and infrastructure investment the Greenbelt imposes on intra-city travel. Its shape is one that traverses landscapes not flows with them and as a result this form has not adequately protected the regional natural systems that flow across it.

Despite its ecological shortcomings, the 1950 plan's open space network is a visible success story. The parkways are magnificent, with wonderful views along the Ottawa River and Rideau Canal. The Greenbelt and the many parks built by the NCC and its predecessors contribute to an attractive capital for visitors and a high quality of life for its residents. Gatineau Park is an extraordinary natural resource reaching almost to the core of the urban area. The Greenbelt creates a strong edge to the inner urban area and a gracious entrance to the capital by road and air. The good environment and quality of life fostered by these improvements are essential conditions for high technology development and tourism, the two industries the region pursued to expand the economic base beyond the federal government (Gordon et al., 2007).

The considerable public investment in the Greenbelt has shaped municipal and private investment beyond its borders and created an irreplaceable and strongly supported feature of Ottawa's metropolitan landscape. It will likely remain so, but it must continually adapt to retain its relevance. The Greenbelt has changed from a farming and institutional frame of urban development, to the ecological and recreational landscape and urban structuring tool of today. Its future role is not entirely clear, but it is likely to remain as some form of green space. However, some valuable lessons can be learned from the experience in Canada's capital. A government proposing a green belt should ensure that it has the land use powers to implement it. The provincial and municipal governments in Canada held the necessary powers, and the federal government was forced to purchase land to implement its plan. Once acquired, Ottawa's Greenbelt proved completely unsuccessful in containing the urban growth of a rapidly expanding metropolitan area, due to economic and demographic forecasts that were well off the mark. But there

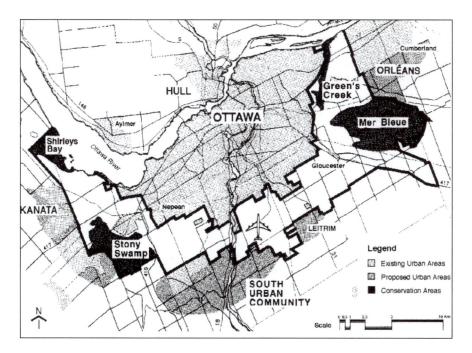

Figure 7.7: The Greenbelt at the end of the 20th century

Source: National Capital Commission (1996, 10)

proved to be many advantages to purchasing large tracts of land at agricultural prices some decades ahead of need. Much riverfront property was acquired for parks and parkways at a small fraction of today's values; some important ecological features were preserved at modest cost, large research facilities were built in convenient locations and vital transportation and utility corridors were available when needed.

The experience in the Québec side of the Ottawa River also offers two lessons for others. The 'green wedge' of Gatineau Park has proven almost as successful as Ottawa's Greenbelt in shaping regional form (Figure 7.7). Its major flaw is that the thin end of the wedge stops just short of the river, losing the opportunity for a natural connection of these two green spaces, and more distinct separation of the two urban communities on the north shore. Secondly, the Québec provincial government's agricultural land protection legislation has proved effective in containing urban development on the north shore for the past thirty years, hinting that a green belt based on natural resource regulations may prove effective in the medium term. The province of Ontario has recently adopted a similar approach to shape the growth of the Greater Toronto Area (Ontario Ministry of Municipal Affairs and Housing, 2005; Ontario Ministry of Public Infrastructure Renewal, 2006). The positioning of Ottawa's Greenbelt from urban growth boundary to open space and ecological resource during the 1990s is another indication of the future potential of the ecosystems approach for green belt proposals, continuing the regional approach first advocated by Olmsted and Todd a century earlier.

References

Abercrombie, P. (1945), *Greater London Plan* (London: HMSO).

Adams, T. (1916), 'Ottawa-Federal Plan', Town Planning and the Conservation of Life, 1(1), 88–9.

—— (1921), 'Editorial: Town Planning is a Science', *Journal of the Town Planning Institute of Canada*, 1(3), 1–3.

Cauchon, N. (1922), 'A Federal District Plan for Ottawa', *Journal of the Town Planning Institute of Canada*, 1(9), 3–6.

Diefenbaker, J. (1957), 'Acquisition of land to establish a green belt around the nations capital', *Community Planning Review*, 8(3), 78–9.

Federal Plan Commission (1915), *Report of the Federal Plan Commission on a General Plan for the Cities of Ottawa and Hull* (Ottawa: Federal Plan Commission).

Ford, G. (1913), 'Principles of Scientific City Planning', *Engineering Contract Record*, 27(21), 42–5.

Fullerton, C. (2005), 'A Changing of the Guard: Regional Planning in Ottawa, 1945–1974', *Urban History Review*, 34(1), 100–13.

Gordon, D. (1998), 'A City Beautiful Plan for Canada's Capital: Edward Bennett and the 1915 Plan for Ottawa and Hull', *Planning Perspectives*, 13, 275–300.

—— (2001), 'Weaving a modern plan for Canada's capital: Jacques Gréber and the 1950 plan for the National Capital Region', *Urban History Review*, 29(2), 43–61.

—— (2002), 'William Lyon Mackenzie King, Town Planning Advocate', *Planning Perspectives*, 17(2), 97–122.

—— (2006), *Planning Twentieth-Century Capital Cities* (London: Routledge).

Gordon, D., Donald, B., and Kozukanich, J. (2007), 'Unanticipated Benefits: The role of planning in the development of Ottawa region technology industries', in R. Tremblay and N. Novakowski (eds.), 'Ottawa in the new economy', (Brussels: Peter Lang). Forthcoming.

Gordon, D. and Osborne, B. (2004), 'Constructing National Identity: Confederation Square and the National War Memorial in Canada's Capital, 1900–2000', *Journal of Historical Geography*, 30(4), 618–42.

Gréber, J. (1950), *Plan for the National Capital: General Report* (Ottawa: Kings Printer).

Hostovsky, C., Miller, D., and Keddy, C. (1995), 'The Natural Environment Systems Strategy: Protecting Ottawa-Carleton's Ecological Areas', *Plan Canada*, 35(6), 26–9.

Hough Stansbury Woodland Limited with Gore and Storrie Limited (1991), *Ecological Analysis of the Greenbelt* (Ottawa: NCC).

Howard, E. (1898), *Tomorrow: A Peaceful Path to Real Reform* (London: Routledge).

Joint Committee of the Senate and the House of Commons (1956), *Report of the Joint Committee of the Senate and the House of Commons set up to Consider the Financial and Other Relationships of the Government and the FDC with the City of Ottawa and the Neighbouring Municipalities* (Ottawa: Joint Committee of the Senate and the House of Commons).

McDonald, D. and Cole, J. (1973), *The Conservation of Urban Greenbelts, with particular reference to the National Capital of Canada* (Ottawa: National Capital Commission).

Moodie, D.A. (1956), *Brief to the Joint Committee in Joint Committee of the Senate and the House of Commons* (Ottawa: King's Printer).

Moore, C. (ed.) (1902), *The improvement of the park system of the District of Columbia, 57th Congress* (Washington DC: U.S. Government Printing Office).

National Capital Commission (1974a), *Agriculture in the Greenbelt: Implementation Program* (Ottawa: NCC).

—— (1974b), *Tomorrow's Capital: An invitation to dialogue* (Ottawa: NCC).

—— (1982), *The Management Plan for the Greenbelt* (Ottawa: NCC).

—— (1996), *Greenbelt Master Plan* (Ottawa: NCC).

Nixey, D. (1991), *The Future Greenbelt – Economic Analysis* (Ottawa: NCC).

Ontario Ministry of Municipal Affairs and Housing (2005), *The Greenbelt Plan* (Toronto: Ontario Ministry of Municipal Affairs and Housing).

Ontario Ministry of Public Infrastructure Renewal (2006), *Growth Plan for the Greater Golden Horseshoe* (Toronto: Ontario Ministry of Public Infrastructure Renewal).

Ottawa City (1956), 'Brief to the Joint Committee', in 'Joint Committee of the Senate and the House of Commons', (Ottawa: Ottawa City).

—— (2003), *2020: Official Plan* (Ottawa: City of Ottawa).

Page, D. (1972), *The Greenbelt* (Ottawa: NCC).

Peterson, J. (1985), 'The Nations First Comprehensive City Plan: A Political Analysis of the McMillan Plan for Washington', *American Planning Association Journal*, 55(2), 134–50.

Regional Municipality of Ottawa-Carleton (1974), *Official Plan of the Ottawa-Carleton Planning Area* (Ottawa: Regional Municipality of Ottawa-Carleton).

Schuyler, D. (1988), *The New Urban Landscape: the redefinition of city form in nineteenth-century America* (Baltimore: Johns Hopkins University Press).

Smart, J. (2004), *A City and a Technology: The Role of Government in The Growth of the Technology Industry in Ottawa, Canada to 1984*, unpublished Ph.D. thesis, Queens University at Kingston.

Spence-Sales, H. (1949), *Layout For Living* (Ottawa: Community Planning Association of Canada), chap. The preliminary report on the plan for the national capital of Canada: a review.

Supreme Court of Canada (1966), 'Munro vs. National Capital Commission [1966]', Supreme Court of Canada.

Taylor, J. (1986), *Ottawa: An Illustrated History* (Toronto, ON: J. Lorimer).

Timusk, C. (1976), 'Kanata: A New Community Approaches its Tenth Year', *Journal of Urban and Environmental Affairs*, 8, 222–32.

Todd, F. (1903), 'Report of Frederick G. Todd, Esq., Landscape Architect, Montréal, to the Ottawa Improvement Commission', in 'Ottawa Improvement Commission', (Ottawa Improvement Commission).

Wilson, W. (1989), *The City Beautiful Movement* (Baltimore MD: Johns Hopkins University Press).

CHAPTER 8

Instruments to Preserve Open Space and Resource Lands in the Seattle, Washington Metropolitan Region – A US Alternative to Green Belts

Alon Bassok

Introduction

While the central Puget Sound region does not have any green belts or green belt policies on the scale of those seen elsewhere around the world (e.g., Korea and the UK), the region has numerous policies in place, including some of the strictest growth management legislation in the US, which aim to achieve similar goals of preserving natural resource lands and open space and containing urban sprawl.

This chapter describes the purposes and techniques employed in local efforts to preserve land and offers an assessment of the effectiveness of these efforts in light of their stated purposes. A brief discussion of the legislative authority through the state's Growth Management Act leads to a discussion of the most crucial of these policies, the establishment of urban growth boundaries (UGBs). The UGBs work well as part of a package of tools, including the transfer and purchase of development rights and land trusts that create options and opportunities for both preservation and landowners wishing to generate wealth from properties subject to environmental regulations. Indeed, the UGBs in concert with other tools are the functional equivalent of a green belt, despite a lack of public ownership in a large amount of the protected lands and efforts by property rights groups to limit state power.

The natural splendor of the Puget Sound region creates a situation by which it is both desirable to preserve land and politically feasible as citizens can rally behind an evident cause. The region is comprised of four counties, King, Kitsap, Pierce and Snohomish and boasts views of the Olympic Mountains to the east, the Cascade Mountains to the west and Mount Rainier to the south. In addition, the region is home to a wide array of wildlife and a temperate climate.

The rich natural features make Puget Sound an attractive place for people and firms to locate in. In 1950 roughly 1.2 million persons, half of Washington State's population resided in the area. In the decades that followed, the region saw steady population increases, leading to a population of nearly 2.8 million by 1990. The high-tech employment boom of the 1990's further fueled migration into the area raising the population to 3.3 million by 2000. Slightly over half of the population and employment activities are located within King County, which is central in the Puget Sound area, with Seattle as its central city and is the location of several corporate headquarters including Microsoft (Redmond), Boeing (Renton) and Amazon (Seattle) among others.

The Washington State Growth Management Act

In 1990, the State of Washington adopted stringent land-use legislation with the passing of the Growth Management Act (GMA), which comprises fourteen goals aimed at containing and curbing sprawl and protecting environmentally critical areas and natural resources while also allowing for growth that would not diminish quality of life (Washington State Legislature, 2007; Washington State Legislature, Revised Code of Washington, 2007b,c,a). The GMA was largely modeled on previous efforts in King County.

King County's early planning efforts prior to the GMA have led to greater success in achieving land preservation than that observed in neighbouring jurisdictions. Beginning in 1964, King County adopted a landmark comprehensive policy plan that laid the groundwork for growth controls by outlining an 'urban centre development concept'. In 1979, frustrated by the loss of agricultural lands, King County voters approved a $50 million purchase of development rights (PDR) bond measure that resulted in the acquisition of nearly 13,000 acres of land (Wolfram, 1981). The 1985 King County Comprehensive Plan revision further developed the notion of land conservation by including a provision for UGBs, similar to those of Boulder, Colorado and Portland, Oregon directing population growth into urban areas and discouraging it from occurring elsewhere.

Under the GMA, land areas are classified into three main categories: urban, rural, and natural resource (agriculture and forestry). In this manner, the GMA is used as a tool to funnel growth into existing urban areas and ensure protection of farmland, forests, rural areas, and habitats for future use.

Furthering the objectives of pushing growth to urbanised areas is the development of urban centers. These centers within urban areas improve access to services, increase housing options, and relieve congestion by creating conditions that support non-motorised travel and make mass transit feasible. While the centers only account for roughly 3% of lands within the UGB, they are forecasted to accommodate slightly over a quarter of the population growth and 40% of jobs by 2040 (Puget Sound Regional Council, 2007).

The primary mechanism for achieving this arrangement is the comprehensive plan, and each jurisdiction in the state (city or county) with a population over 50,000 or a population increase of more than 20% over the past decade must develop plans consistent with the GMA, with robust citizen participation required. Indeed, Washington State has been called the citizen-participation capital of the world. The

GMA directly addresses participation by mandating that planners 'encourage the involvement of citizens in the planning process and ensure coordination between communities and jurisdictions to reconcile conflicts ... providing for early and continuous public participation' and placing minimum notice requirements for public meetings, workshops, or hearings and the opportunity for written comment and citizen advisory committees. (Washington State Legislature, 2007; Washington State Legislature, Revised Code of Washington, 2007b,a). Currently, 29 of Washington's 39 counties, representing 95% of the population, are engaged in planning under GMA requirements.

The plans may be amended annually and are required to be revised every ten years. Further, each comprehensive plan must be consistent with the GMA's goals of critical area protection; resource land conservation; cross-jurisdictional coordination; consistency between land use, infrastructure, and transportation plans; and early and continuous citizen participation. Jurisdictions involved in planning are assisted by the state's Department of Community, Trade, and Economic Development (CTED), a cabinet-level agency that provides technical and financial support for the achievement of GMA requirements.

Each plan must contain eight elements: land use, housing, transportation, capital facilities, utilities, shorelines, economic development, and parks and recreation. While the combined elements of each plan must meet the land conservation and preservation goals of the GMA, the UGB is the strongest required tool to assure that this will occur.

Urban Growth Boundaries

While there has been substantial debate over the effectiveness of UGBs in containing sprawl, (Ding et al., 1999), convincing arguments in favour of such boundaries have been presented (e.g. Nelson, 1992; Nelson and Peterman, 2000). Filtering growth to those areas that are already urbanised allows for the provision of satisfactory public services and facilities in places where they are currently present or can be provided in an economical and timely manner. Beyond the boundary, urban services (e.g., sewers) cannot be extended, and development, in the least stringent of cases, is constrained.

Washington's GMA requires that all jurisdictions engaged in planning efforts implement UGBs. Lands outside of theses boundaries are required to be zoned as rural or resource lands, (agriculture or forestry), cannot be annexed by nearby cities, and have large minimum parcels that discourage development while allowing for the continued functioning of small farming operations.

Designation of Urban Growth Boundaries

Urban Growth Boundaries are established by a public planning process and are not defined arbitrarily; they require an analysis of service capabilities and land capacity and are obligated to meet 20-year population projections as carried out by the State's Office of Financial Management. It is necessary for the boundaries to be large enough not only to allow for future growth but also to ensure that the constraints placed on land supply are not so stringent that they raise land – and as a consequence – home values (Brueckner, 2000; Dawkins and Nelson, 2002). Conversely, if the boundaries are too loose, or are changed frequently to increase the amount of vacant land, the desired higher densities in existing urban areas may not be achieved (Knaap, 2000).

Generally, incorporated cities are included in the boundary, making their designation relatively simple. On the other hand, unincorporated areas require greater consideration because there are no clear boundaries to use. As can be seen in Figure 8.1, the designation of the boundaries around incorporated cities creates a continuous

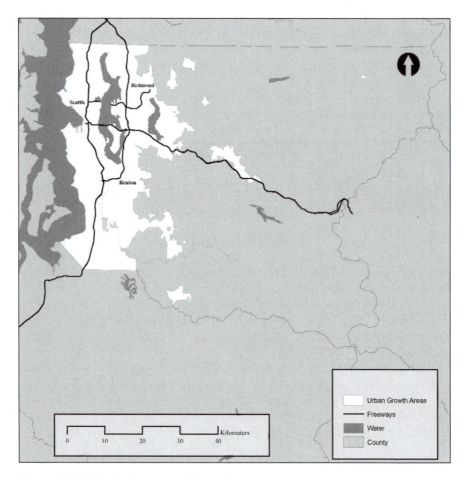

Figure 8.1: UGBs in the central Puget Sound area

Source: PSRC

area, leaving few cities on the outskirts. Unincorporated urban areas that are nearby but not within the contiguous boundary are assumed to eventually become part of the greater urban area.

Buildable Lands Analysis

Implementation of growth management regulations necessitates the ability of jurisdictions to predict private land use activity, especially as increases in population and standards of living place greater demands on urban land supply, infrastructure, and environmental systems (Moudon and Hubner, 2000). Working in conjunction with the mandatory UGB designations, the GMA, under a 1997 amendment, requires that the 6 most populous counties and 97 cities within them carry out a buildable lands analysis in order to determine whether jurisdictions are able to meet the 20-year growth forecasts and whether urban densities are being achieved. The amendment states that a buildable lands analysis will 'determine the quantity and type of land suitable for residential and employment-based activities' (Washington State Legislature, Revised Code of Washington, 2007c). The King County Buildable Lands Program attempts to coordinate 40 jurisdictions through a common methodological framework. All of these jurisdictions collect and analyse data independently within an agreed-upon framework.

The program specifies five elements that are to be achieved with this analysis: (1) data collection on annual development activity, (2) land supply inventory, (3) development capacity analysis, (4) updating of growth targets, and (5) evaluation of capacity to accommodate growth targets. It is recommended that the first three tasks be included in any analysis of land supply (Moudon and Hubner, 2000), and the King County program expands further on this approach by including the elements of updating growth targets and evaluating the capacity to accommodate growth.

The land supply inventory in King County's program is based on a number of factors, such as vacant land, redevelopable land, critical areas land, public use-designated land, and future rights-of-way. The maximum build-out as established by zoning is relatively easy to calculate, especially given tools such as geographic information systems (GISs). However, because GIS cannot predict the future, it is far more difficult to calculate likely or adjusted development capacity, which, according to Berke et al. (2006), 'entails professional judgement about which lands are likely to be developed, how they will be developed, and whether they will be under-built, as well as the effects of political issues about density, timing, and citizen opposition on future development decisions.' As such, the program also pays close attention to market factors, deducting a percentage ranging from 5% to 20% of available land (King County Budget Office, 2002). It is also worth noting that all 40 jurisdictions take the market factors into account separately, which results in a more accurate reflection of each area.

Data are gathered annually, and the analyses are completed in five-year intervals, with the first published reports having been produced in 2002. As shown in Table 8.1, these reports demonstrate the ability of most jurisdictions to meet their growth targets, with the exception of a few small cities.

Table 8.1: Residential capacity in King County

Sub-area	Residential Capacity in Relation to Target				
	Net new units: 1993–2000	20 year housing target	Percent achieved (%)	Remaining target	Current Residential capacity
East County	25,665	48,348	53	22,683	62,771
Sea-Shore	16,375	57,905	28	41,530	122,340
South County	22,957	73,387	31	50,430	68,991
Rural Cities	3,265	8,828	37	5,563	9,178
Urban Area Total	68,262	188,468	36	120,206	268,280
Rural UKC	6,303	7,000	90	697	N/A
King County Total	74,565	195,468	38	120,903	N/A

Source: King County Budget Office (2002)

For those areas that do not have an adequate land supply for their projected growth, mechanisms such as increasing zoning densities are encouraged in lieu of expanding the UGBs. Indeed, the ability to increase densities to reduce sprawl and increase the ability to provide services is still possible and likely because the highest achieved current density is in King County, at roughly seven dwelling units per acre, (State of Washington Department of Community Trade and Economic Development, 2007). In the event that UGBs need be expanded, several factors are considered, including the sufficiency of land for the next 20 years, infrastructure concurrency, resource protection, and citizen preferences. Further, the County utilises a combination of the inventory and event approaches to adjust its boundary.

Under the inventory approach, which is currently used in Portland, Oregon, the amount of developable land that was consumed over a five-year period is calculated. In order to maintain a 20-year supply of buildable land as mandated by Oregon's regulations, an equivalent amount of land is added to the UGA. Knaap and Hopkins (2001) argue in favour of an event-driven approach because rates of development are rarely consistent, which leads to wide fluctuations of the land supply under the inventory approach. When the event-driven approach is used, the UGA is not updated until the quantity of vacant developable land falls beneath a designated threshold, so that development fluctuations are taken into account.

Effectiveness of and Challenges to Urban Growth Boundaries in King County

King County's UGBs have had measured success in filtering growth to urbanised areas. Between 2000 and 2003, roughly 96% of all new housing developments were inside of the boundary (Puget Sound Regional Council, 2005). The fact that this percentage is somewhat higher than those observed in other Puget Sound counties is likely due to the implementation of UGBs a decade earlier in King County, before the passage of the GMA. Nonetheless, even considering the four-county region, 87% of new residential units were within the boundaries, an increase from 78% between 1995 and 1999. In addition, the boundaries have achieved even greater success in funnelling covered employment to urban areas, pushing 96% of all jobs to those areas within the greater four-county region by 2003.

In King County, the UGB has not been modified much and remains virtually unchanged from its original form after several plan updates. Those areas that have seen changes largely fall into the categories of parcels that were split by the boundary's designation and areas that were annexed under previous arrangements. An integral component of King County's success in implementing and maintaining its UGBs is a comprehensive approach to their designation – i.e., a mandate from the state government requiring all jurisdictions to engage in this activity.

In the absence of stringent growth controls of a comprehensive nature, single jurisdictions that may wish to implement a growth boundary may accomplish their own goals while simultaneously spurring leapfrog and sprawling development. For example, the City of Boulder, Colorado has had a boundary in place since 1970, which includes a 27,000-acre green belt and a service boundary provision outside of which utilities cannot be provided. While this has allowed Boulder to control the nature and type of growth in the city, it has led to a rise in home prices and congestion and sprawl outside of the city, while low-density suburban development abuts the city's border, stretching 25 miles to the southeast towards Denver (Pollock, 1998).

While planning efforts in Colorado continue to encourage growth management principles, it is at best difficult to reach consensus and implement a statewide mandate because concerns over property rights complicate such efforts. In recent years, the states of Washington and Oregon have both faced challenges to their respective growth management legislation through property rights initiatives, but with opposite results. In 2004, Oregon voters approved Measure 37, which allows property owners to request compensation or a waiver from regulations the state has imposed for environmental and growth management purposes. At the time of writing, there are nearly 8,000 claims, covering roughly 750,000 acres of land (Portland State University, 2007). Since the cost of compensating all of these landowners is exorbitantly high, all of the settled claims have led to regulatory exemptions. Further, in some of the more extreme cases, the exemptions involve creating a mobile home park on native burial grounds or developing a shopping mall on farmland.

In 2006, Washington voters faced a similar initiative; I-933 'the property fairness initiative' was largely based on Oregon's Measure 37 and would have required retroactive compensation or exemptions to regulations that damaged the use or value of property. Despite the initiative's failure at the polls, nearly a half million people supported the initiative, which, it was projected, would have cost $7.8 billion in the first five years after its passing (Northwest Center for Livable Communities, 2006). Further, the proponents of the initiative are continuing to push for less regulation and controls and are challenging existing growth management tools. While UGBs have weathered this assault thus far, there is a need for environmentalists and property rights proponents to work closely together in reaching cooperative agreements that can be accepted by both groups. To that end, comprehensive analysis of the effects of regulation on property need to be conducted along with the implementation of a wide array of tools that would provide landowners options for financial investments while preserving natural and resource lands.

Other Tools

While UGBs have been shown to be effective at curbing or slowing sprawl, they still have the potential to allow development to 'leak' out of the designated areas and develop in a manner consistent with sprawl, which suggests that UGB policies should be supplemented by other tools, (Carruthers, 2002).

Purchase of Development Rights (PDR)

In King County, the issue of farmland preservation gained importance as the County lost nearly two thirds of its farmland acreage to development between 1959 and 2002, as shown in Table 8.2 (United States Department of Agriculture, 2007a).

Table 8.2: King County farmland area

Year	1950	1959	1969	1982	1992	2002
Area (ha)	62,039	46,425	24,729	24,205	17,114	16,903

Source: USDA

As previously mentioned, the County boasts one of the nation's oldest Purchase of Development Rights (PDR) programs in the United States. In 1979, county voters approved a $50 million bond measure that was largely spent through the Farmland Preservation Program (FPP) in the early 1980s to acquire roughly 13,000 acres of land. To date, $58 million has been spent through the PDR program, with only a minute share of land coming from private donation. Federal aid from the U.S. Department of Agriculture through the Farmland and Ranchland Protection Program has been easier to obtain in recent years, following the passing of the 2002 farm bill. Since 2003, federal aid through this program has given Washington State over a $1 million annually, of which over half has been distributed to King County (United States Department of Agriculture, 2007b).

PDR programs are generally designed to keep lands in agricultural use from converting to housing or commercial development, and they do so by restricting development potential and providing capital to farmers (Freedgood, 1991). Further, this mechanism helps to funnel and intensify development in urban areas and prevent sprawl (Daniels and Lapping, 2005). Under these programs, a jurisdiction pays the landowner (farmer) the difference in value between developing the land and keeping it as a working farm. In return, the jurisdiction places a conservation easement on the land, which allows farming activity to continue but prevents development.

King County's PDR program works in conjunction with growth management tools through the comprehensive plan's zoning requirements and UGBs. There are currently roughly 460 square miles (1,192 square kilometers) within the UGB, slightly less than one fourth of the County's total lands. A 'no net loss' provision within the comprehensive plan requires that when cities annex lands they must provide agricultural lands of equal or greater value than those that will be consumed by the urban area. In some cases, this provision has blocked growth efforts of cities as they encroach on lands already protected under the PDR program. In this way, the

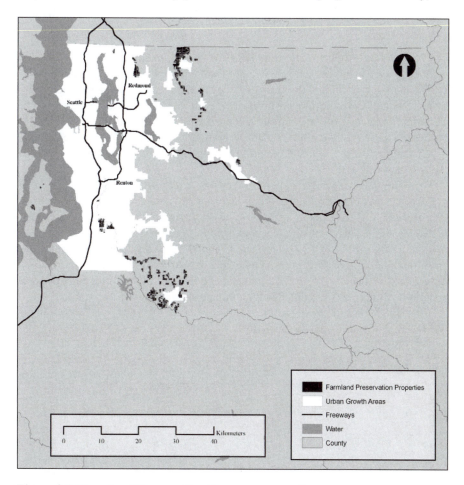

Figure 8.2: Farmland Preservation Program properties

Source: King County

PDRs serve as the second line of defence against development. While the UGB designates areas for urban use, the UGB may be extended as needs arise through an increase in population size. When PDRs are in place in lands adjacent to the UGB, development cannot occur on those lands, which directs the UGB expansion elsewhere.

The designation of areas to be included into the PDR program was based on planning efforts and established three priority areas. As shown in Figure 8.2, almost all of the FPP properties are clustered in Agriculture Production Districts (APDs). The two initial priority areas were in districts deemed to be of high agricultural value. The third priority area included those pieces of land that were contiguous and as such merited special preservation attention.

Transfers of Development Rights (TDRs)

Transfers of development rights (TDRs) work in a manner similar to PDRs in enabling the exchange of zoning privileges from farmland to areas of higher density. Landowners of agricultural or other resource lands in 'sending sites' sell their rights to develop that land to developers in 'receiving sites,' thereby increasing their capital and retaining the use of the land, and a conservation easement is then placed on the property. King County has had a TDR program in place since 1993, predominantly used to retain forest areas, and the program has protected 91,500 acres as of 2005 (King County, 2007).

The sending parcels are in agricultural or rural areas, while the receiving parcels are in urban areas that are part of the unincorporated county or are within specified city areas that operate under agreements with the county. Receiving site criteria include (1) it must have existing linkage to public water service, (2) the project must not require the provision of services, and (3) it must not cause harm to resource and environmentally sensitive areas. Once the development rights are purchased, developers of receiving sites may increase the number of dwelling units per acre above what is normally permitted in the zoning code, as shown in Table 8.3.

Table 8.3: Allowable density increase

Zone	Minimum Density[1]	Maximum Density
R-4	4	6
R-6	6	9
R-8	8	12
R-12	12	18
R-18	18	27
R-24	24	36
R-48	48	72

[1] Dwelling units per acre

Although developers of receiving sites may acquire development rights directly from landowners, the county has had a TDR bank in place since 1999 that uses limited county resources to purchase the development rights to those areas deemed to hold the greatest public benefit. Landowners in the receiving sites may then purchase the rights directly from the county.

Land Trusts

Land trusts directly purchase land and set it aside for particular uses. Currently, there are roughly 1,600 non-profit land trust organisations in the United States working separately from government. While land trusts can only play a minor role in protecting land because they have to purchase lands at market value, those agencies that are particularly skilled at fundraising and obtaining land donations manage to preserve particularly significant lands.

There are at present three major land trusts working locally in King County. The Cascade Land Conservancy has protected nearly 100,000 acres in 65 diverse projects since 1989 (Cascade Land Conservancy, 2007). The PCC Farmland Trust, founded in 1999 by the PCC Natural Markets, focuses on retaining large working farms in organic production and has purchased four farms in Washington State, including the 179-acre Ames Creek Farm in King County. Finally, the Vashon-Maury Island Land Trust has protected roughly 870 acres on 23 parcels on Vashon-Maury Island since its inception in 1990, concentrating on the most critical and significant features.

Another Approach: The Mountains to Sound Greenway

While greenways significantly differ from green belts in both form and function, their importance has been well documented (Little, 1990) and Washington's Mountains to Sound Greenway (MTSG) can be viewed as a successful case study in terms of implementation and use. The MTSG is a 100 mile × 40 mile (161 km × 64 km) area stretching along Interstate 90 (see Figure 8.3) from Puget Sound to Central Washington, encompassing 700,000 acres of land that include public lands, forests, rivers, and historic towns. The program's primary goals are sprawl suppression through economic development incentives for farming and forestry, establishment of visible stewardship projects, and the creative use of preservation tools (Mountains to Sound Greenway, 2007).

As recently illustrated by Rottle (2006), the MTSG differs significantly from other greenway or green belt projects in that it is landscape based: 'a spatial continuum of interrelated functions and meanings integral to the landscape as a whole.'

The positioning of the greenway along I-90, one of the two major corridors in the state, allows the protection of lands that would otherwise be ripe for sprawling development due to easy access to a freeway.

Prior to the establishment of the MTSG, work had already begun on preserving four crucial pieces of land that would later inspire the creation of the greenway

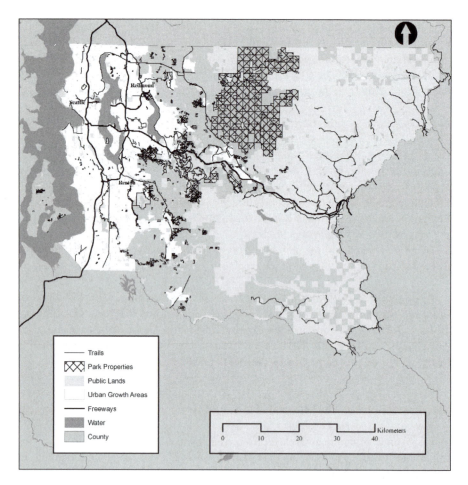

Figure 8.3: Mountains to Sound Greenway

Source: Mountains to Sound Greenway Trust

(Chasan, 1993). In 1984, a 1,000-acre park was established on Cougar Mountain with County bonds to augment nearly 600 nearby acres on top of Squak Mountain that had been previously donated. In 1987, legislation was passed that allowed for the designation of Natural Resource Conservation Areas (NRCAs) which enabled the protection of Tiger Mountain and Mount Si. These four protected areas form the basis of the MTSG and inspire hopes of making connections between them. This notion was highly promoted in the late 1980s by the Issaquah Alps Trails Club, which suggested developing a continuous trail from Puget Sound to the Cascade Mountains and gained support for their ideas through promotion of hiking activities. The success of the hiking club's efforts led to their creation of the MTSG trust in 1991.

Preservation of the greenway is conducted through the non-profit trust, which despite not having ownership or control over the greenway's lands has been successful in coordinating land trades between jurisdictions and forestry companies and preserving historic landscapes to protect small town identities. Indeed, the trust has managed to facilitate the purchase of 125,000 acres of land, rights of way, and development rights with the use of local and federal funds.

Aside from directly protecting lands for public recreation use, the trust has been instrumental in orchestrating the transfer, trade, and purchase of forestry lands for the federal, state, and county departments of natural resources in order to have continuous, working forestry lands as opposed to development. This arrangement, in conjunction with tight UGBs, ensures that the cost of these lands does not rise to a level where the land would be more valuable for development. As a consequence, the remaining lands are priced low enough to support several small working farms.

Applicability to Other Jurisdictions

The success of King County's land preservation policies hinges directly upon the authority of the GMA. As previously discussed, implementing statewide growth management legislation is difficult because of property rights and other concerns. Nonetheless, the attractiveness of UGBs is apparent because jurisdictions do not have to publicly acquire land for preservation, as they do with green belts, and can instead impose regulations that shift the burden to private property owners.

TDR and PDR programs provide means of compensating landowners for voluntarily selling their property development rights and restricting development on publicly valued open space under impending development pressure. These planning techniques have been used in a number of jurisdictions in the United States with varying degrees of success and are most effective when they are actively funded by a jurisdiction and are used in conjunction with other reinforcing policy instruments. The success of King County's TDR and PDR programs to date illustrates their utility and underscores the value of continued exploration of these techniques for preserving open space.

To a large extent, the policies discussed herein are regulatory ones, whereby jurisdictions make little to no expenditures. While land trusts do augment the body of preserved lands, they do so at the expense of private donation and non-profit organisation fundraising. As the costs of land continue to rise in urbanising areas, regulatory tools offer a feasible, albeit difficult-to-implement tool kit for protecting natural and resource lands.

References

Berke, P.R., Godschalk, D.R., and Kaiser, E.J. (2006), *Urban Land Use Planning* (Chicago: University of Illinois Press).

Brueckner, J. (2000), 'Urban Sprawl: Diagnosis and Remedies', *International Regional Science Review*, 23, 160–71.

Carruthers, J. (2002), 'Evaluating the Effectiveness of Regulatory Growth Management Programs: an Analytical Framework', *Journal of Planning Education and Research*, 21, 391–405.

Cascade Land Conservancy (2007), *Conservation Program* (CLC).

Chasan, D. (1993), *Mountains to Sound, the Creation of a Greenway Across the Cascades* (Seattle: Sasquatch Press).

Daniels, T. and Lapping, M. (2005), 'Land Preservation: An Essential Ingredient in Smart Growth', *Journal of Planning Literature*, 19, 316–29.

Dawkins, C. and Nelson, A. (2002), 'Urban Containment Policies and Housing Prices: An International Comparison with Implications for Future Research', *Land Use Policy*, 19, 1–12.

Ding, C., Knaap, G., and Hopkins, L. (1999), 'Managing Urban Growth with Urban Growth Boundaries: A Theoretical Analysis', *Journal of Urban Economics*, 46, 53–68.

Freedgood, J. (1991), 'PDR Programs Take Root in the Northeast', *Journal of Soil and Water Conservation*, 46, 329–31.

King County (2007), *Transfer of Development Rights* (TDR) Program (King County).

King County Budget Office (2002), *King County Buildable Lands Evaluation Report 2002* (KCBO).

Knaap, G. (2000), 'The Urban Growth Boundary in Metropolitan Portland, Oregon: Research, Rhetoric and Reality', in 'Korean Regional Science Association and Korea Research Institute for Human Settlements, Papers and Proceedings of the International Workshop on Urban Growth Management Policies of Korea, Japan and the USA', (Seoul: Seoul National University), pp. 205–32.

Knaap, G. and Hopkins, L. (2001), 'The Inventory Approach to Urban Growth Boundaries', *Journal of the American Planning Association*, 67, 314–26.

Little, C. (1990), *Greenways for America* (Baltimore: Johns Hopkins University Press).

Moudon, A. and Hubner, M. (eds.) (2000), *Monitoring Land Supply With Geographic Information Systems* (New York: Wiley & Sons).

Mountains to Sound Greenway (2007), *100-Mile National Scenic Byway* (MTSG).

Nelson, A. (1992), 'Preserving Prime Farmland in the Face of Urbanization', *Journal of the American Planning Association*, 58, 467–88.

Nelson, A. and Peterman, D. (2000), 'Does Growth Management Matter? The Effect of Growth Management on Economic Performance', *Journal of Planning Education and Research*, 19, 277–85.

Northwest Center for Livable Communities (2006), *The Impacts of Proposed Initiative 933 on Real Property and Land Use in Washington State* (University of Washington: Department of Urban Design and Planning).

Pollock, P. (1998), 'Controlling Sprawl in Boulder: Benefits and Pitfalls', *Land Lines*, 10, [online, http://www.lincolninst.edu/pubs/ accessed 7 March 2007].

Portland State University (2007), *Measure 37: Database Development and Analysis Project* (PSU).

Puget Sound Regional Council (2005), *Urban Growth Trends in Central Puget Sound* (PSRC).

—— (2007), *Destination 2030: Destination 2030 Plan Documents* (PSRC).

Rottle, N. (2006), 'Factors in the Landscape-Based Greenway: A Mountains to Sound Case Study', *Landscape and Urban Planning*, 76, 134–71.

State of Washington Department of Community Trade and Economic Development (2007), *Buildable Lands* (CTED).

United States Department of Agriculture (2007a), *USDA National Agricultural Statistical Service* (USDA).

—— (2007b), *Natural Resources Conservation Service, Washington State* (USDA).

Washington State Legislature (2007), *Growth Management Planning by Selected Counties and Cities* (WSL).

Washington State Legislature, Revised Code of Washington (2007a), *RCW 36.70A.020 Planning Goals* (RCWa).

—— (2007b), *RCW 36.70A.140 Comprehensive Plans – Ensure Public Participation* (RCWb).

—— (2007c), *Review and Evaluation Program, RCW 36.70A.215* (RCWc).

Wolfram, G. (1981), 'The Sale of Development Rights and Zoning in the Preservation of Open Space: Lindahl Equilibrium and a Case Study', *Land Economics*, 57, 398–413.

PART IV
WORKS IN PROGRESS:
PATCHING TOGETHER A
FLEXIBLE GREEN BELT

CHAPTER 9

The Vienna Green Belt: From Localised Protection to a Regional Concept

Meinhard Breiling and Gisa Ruland

Introduction

The Vienna green belt is one of the oldest urban green belts in the world. One hundred and fifty years ago Vienna's citizens realised that an effective protection of urban greenspace was needed. The protection of the *Wienerwald*, the first of the five landscapes of the Vienna green belt, was the first step. By 1905, four additional landscapes – Bisamberg, Marchfeld, Donauraum, Terrassenlandschaft had become part of what was then called the Viennese forest and meadows belt. Later, the aim was to protect single smaller green areas and to unify them with the growing green belt of Vienna. Today, the Vienna green belt comprises about half of Vienna. While the protection of the green belt was realised at an early stage, a connection with the limited urban green in the central parts of Vienna within this green belt has not yet happened. This remains a target for the future, as does the integration of the green belt within a larger regional setting: either the twin city concept Vienna-Bratislava or the even larger concept of the EU level CENTROPE region.

The needs of the Vienna green belt have shifted over time with standards of living. In times of crisis, such as the early post-War periods, the Vienna green belt was a major source of the supply of fuel wood and emergency food and enabled large parts of Vienna's population to survive. In times of abundance, the needs are primarily directed towards recreation and to environmental services like providing clean water and clean air and the provision of high bio diversity in and around Vienna. Together with the inner city parks and remaining green areas of Vienna, the green belt provides environmental safety for the population.

Compared to many other West European cities, Vienna is still growing and development is taking place primarily in the northern, eastern and south-eastern sections of the city. This has to be seen in connection with the opening of Vienna to the north and east. For many decades, any development in this direction was limited and, to some extent, a lifting of this limit is now taking place. The rapid growth of Eastern European cities, and the vicinity of Vienna to some of these cities, pose major challenges for landscape planning. Green corridors should be secured within urban settings. The flora of Vienna, with 2,187 registered wild plants can be considered very rich in species (Erhard, 2005). People have started to discuss the extent to which a much larger green belt could protect the metropolitan area of Vienna-Bratislava or the even larger metropolitan area Vienna-Bratislava-Györ-Brno, currently one of the most dynamic places of economic growth in Europe.

In the following, we mainly limit this discussion to Vienna. The city comprises 415 km^2 of land and approximately half of this is green space. Today, the urban forest covers 75 km^2, agriculturally used land amounts to 65 km^2, meadows extend over 24 km^2, and parks, small house gardens and sports fields together account for 37 km^2. The details of Vienna's green spaces, with regard to the appropriate hectare area and the percentage in the city, can be found in Table 9.1.

Until 1920, Vienna and the surrounding province of Lower Austria were unified. Functionally, the land around today's border between Vienna and Lower Austria belongs together and the green space continues, but is not accounted for Vienna's statistics.

Table 9.1: Current land use in Vienna

Land Use	Area (ha)	%
Total land in Vienna	41,490	100.00
Total green space	20,022	48.25
Forests	7,504	18.09
Agricultural Used Areas	6,506	15.68
Meadows	2,358	5.69
Allotment gardens	1,264	3.05
Parks	1,622	3.91
Sport fields & recreational areas	765	1.85
Water bodies	1,939	4.67

Source: Stadt Wien, Land Use in Vienna 2001, MA 41 Inventory of Use 2001, MA 14 and MA 21A, author's calculation

In the first section, we discuss the historic development of the green belt in Vienna and in the second, we deal with the five particular landscape units, their use and change in use over time, including the expected future uses. The third section covers the upcoming possibilities of urban green belt extension on the international scale.

History, Use and Development of Vienna Green Belt

In the first century AD, the Romans set up a military camp, called Vindobona, which formed part of the large number of similar facilities along the Limes frontier. Around 1150, the Austrian margraves from the Babenberg dynasty moved their residence to Vienna. In this time Vienna developed into a veritable town. By 1500, the city had some 20,000 inhabitants. The medieval town was enclosed by town walls and the glacis and surrounded by fields, villages, vineyards and woods. The glacis was a spacious meadow area, intended for military defence against the Turks, who almost invaded Vienna twice; once in 1529 and again in 1683. After the defeat, several new castles with related green areas were built, including Schönbrunn Castle, the summer residence of Maria Theresia. By 1790, the number of inhabitants had increased to 200,000. Many aristocratic families built residences with baroque gardens outside the glacis such as the Belvedere in the 3rd district. The history of the green belt started when the walls of the inner city were demolished in 1856 and the inner city of Vienna was unified with the surrounding outer suburbs and the even more peripheral districts. At that time, Vienna was already approximately the size of today and had more than 600,000 inhabitants in 1869.

One of the highlights in the history of the Vienna green belt – in former times called the Viennese forest and meadow belt – was the rescue of the *Wienerwald* by Josef Schöffel (1832–1910). In 1870, a crisis in the Austrian state economy following the war against Prussia led to the empire law of 'the sale of state property'. This also concerned the *Wienerwald*, which was to be sold as state property for the

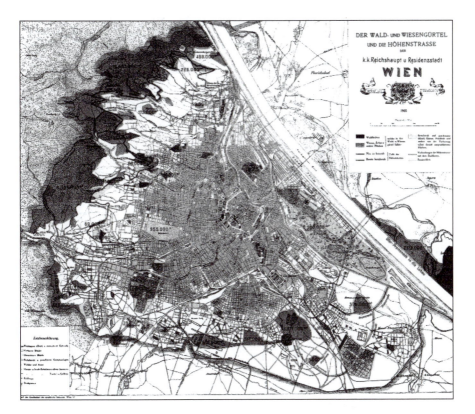

Figure 9.1: The Vienna Woods and Meadows Belt with the 'Höhenstraße' 1905

Source: Stadt Wien (Hg.) (2005a, 76)

replenishment of the empty treasuries. It was expected to raise 20 million guilders. In particular, the Viennese wood dealer Moritz Hirschl profited from this law as he was able to buy the right to cut the forest at favourable conditions. In 1863, the public domain Waidhofen/Ybbs had been sold and the first buyers eagerly cut timber. Hirschl had the option to strike 770,000 *klafters* of wood. One klafter is a cube of 1.8m side length making a total amount of 2.5 million m³, nearly a quarter of the *Wienerwald*.

> The Vienna municipality apathetically neglected to counter the threatening destruction of its forest belt. There was nobody in the imperial state council, who would have arisen against this threatening 'robbery of the state property', because a large part of the representatives profited personally from it' (Museen der Stadt Wien, 1993, 162).

In this situation, the journalist and later mayor of Mödling in Lower Austria, Josef Schöffel started his campaign for that office, in which, as he wrote, 'the boldest swindlers and impostors sat'. In numerous newspaper articles, he mobilised the population and accused individuals of being corrupt. There were murder threats, accusations and bribery attempts, but Schöffel steadfastly continued his campaign. The population responded with a storm of protest and, under Schöffel's leadership, the efforts to save the *Wienerwald* became the first Austrian citizens' initiative. Numerous petitions finally forced the local council to act. In 1872, the law of 1870 was rescinded, the contract with Hirschl was dissolved and the total prohibition to cut timber in the Wienerwald was proclaimed (Seebauer and Weisgram, 1996, 34). 'Schöffel was an uncommonly stubborn person, who fought to overcome all obstacles and thereby made the impossible, possible and brought a law, already sanctioned by the Emperor, to fall' (Schlindner quoted in Lahner, 1999).

Schöffel's commitment also succeeded, for the first time, in demonstrating the tremendous value the *Wienerwald* deserves from ecological and economic viewpoints. The *Wienerwald* was recognised as being the 'green lung' of the city of Vienna. In the year 1905 the *Viennese forest and meadow belt* was formally established as an environmentally protected area by the town council and, since then, has contributed to the Vienna green belt (Figure 9.1). At that time, Vienna reached its highest population level with 2,080,000 people on today's area. A principal purpose for establishing the forest and meadow belt was, at that time, 'to guarantee the supply of pure air' in the city and 'the preservation of the green areas at the western and northern border'. The main winds come from the west and the forest was considered as the source of clean air. For the densely populated southern districts of Vienna 'green areas' were important for a higher supply. Towards the south, new forest and meadow areas came into existence and expanded the Viennese forest and meadow belt. More isolated patches were interconnected through 'broad garden lanes'. The Viennese districts beyond the Danube were predominantly agriculturally used in 1905. Therefore, no concrete preventive measures were undertaken there. An exemption was the Lobau wetland forest in the southeast edge of the city which, at that time, already contributed to the forest and meadow belt. The Viennese forest and meadow belt turned into a recreation place for all levels of the population and contrasted to the urban parks with their ornamental gardens and limited freedom of movement.[1] The report mentions an area of 4,400 hectares while calculations according to the project plan suggest an area of 5,860 hectares (Stadt Wien (Hg.), 2005a, 77).

The development pressure decreased sharply after the two World Wars, as Vienna lost its status as the capital of a large empire in 1918, and because of a major reduction in population ending in 1945. Between the First and Second World Wars Vienna also contained one of the largest Jewish populations, numbering 300,000 out of a total population of 2,000,000. The decrease in development pressure was also the result of the Iron Curtain that had fallen 30km from Vienna and where major ecological zones could flourish safe from human impacts. Vienna's peripheral position benefited the green belt by keeping land prices relatively low for decades. The forest and meadow belt was further closed by purchasing land and forestation (Auböck and Ruland, 1994, 42).

In the 1950s, 1960s and 1970s there was an aim for a clear and modern conception for the green areas of Vienna. Until now protection has been enabled by a dedicated zoning system consisting of 'Forest and Meadow Belt, Protected Zone' (in German: *Schutzzone wald und wiesengürtel* Sww) within the city boundary of Vienna. Further zones within the Vienna Green Belt are: 'Protected Park Zone' (in German: *Parkschutzgebiet* Spk) and 'Agricultural Lands' (in German: *ländiche Gebiete* L). The particularly protected park and landscape areas include: the park of Schönbrunn Castle, the Auer Welsbach Park (1922), the Lainzer Tiergarten (1937), the Laaerberg (1953), parts of the Bisamberg (1965) and the Danube Island (1978).

In recent decades, there was a diversification in the development within different categories of land use and even within the same category. Agricultural use went in two directions. While most of the land is no longer primarily directed towards harvesting but to the provision of a particular traditional type of agricultural, horticultural and viticulture landscape, a minority of land has been developed and devoted to industry-like agriculture using large, concrete greenhouses and producing monocultures with high resource inputs that could also be located in any other highly industrialised city. Less than ten farms produce tomatoes or cucumbers for several million people at world market prices. On the other hand, the health objective of foods and organic agriculture is particularly well developed in Vienna. The largest organic farm of Austria is situated in Vienna and the municipality is also its owner. Without the support of the city, the organic farm could not survive.

A special aspect of the Vienna green belt, sometimes quite isolated in central parts of the city, are the small garden allotments, the so-called *Kleingärten*. They are an important part of the urban green structure and were an important source of personal food supply of vegetables and fruit. It was forbidden to have a house on this land, with only a cottage being allowed. Many owners originated from the working class,

---

1   Citation of the Town Council of Vienna from May 24th, 1905 (Wiener Gemeinderat, 1905).

Table 9.2: Green belt development in Vienna

Year	Size of the green belt (ha)
1905	4,400–5,860
1940	10,700
1995	19,250
2005	21,500

Source: Stadt Wien (Hg.) (2005a, 73)

lived in a city-owned flat and spent much of their time in spring, summer and autumn in the garden. This started to change in the 1980s, when it became possible to build more solid, but still moderately sized, houses for year-round living. Food prices no longer make it necessary to produce one's own supply. If not already in use for permanent living, the gardens are today used for hobbies, gardening, relaxing and recreation. Production and harvest are no longer the most important aspect of forestry. Previously, in particularly in times of crisis, the forest was an important source of energy. Without fuel wood from the *Wienerwald*, many people would have died shortly after World War I when the new state Austria was cut off from major resources. Even at the end of World War II, it was a major relief to have the forest as a resource base and supplier of energy.

Table 9.2, shows the size of the Vienna green belt. As the city has had different extensions over the years, the exact percentage cannot be given. In 1988, the green belt area of the city had grown to 19,250 ha, or 46% of the total area. Some 10,700 ha are dedicated as Sww. In 1994, the 'one thousand hectare program' was decided by city council to secure the landscape in the northeast of Vienna and extend the forest and meadow belt. On 29 November 1995, the Vienna city council approved the plan for the 'Vienna Green Belt 1995'. Accompanying programs and measures were prepared to secure the green belt for future generations (Jedelsky, 2004). A new zone of 'Wood and Meadow Belt, Protected Agricultural Area' was introduced in 1996 and replaced Sww with the inclusion of agricultural land. In 2005, about half of the land in Vienna belonged to the green belt. The population size was 1,638,000, with an increasing tendency to fluctuate during the 20th century.

While the development of the urban green belt has advanced during recent history, there is a lack of urban green in the centre of the city. Unlike the favourable development on the periphery, the patches of small parks and green areas in the inner districts did not merge to a larger entity and still remain isolated.

Types of Landscapes and Particular Uses of Green Belt

The Viennese landscape is unusually varied. There are very few cities in Europe which are comparable in shape and form, because Vienna is geographically and

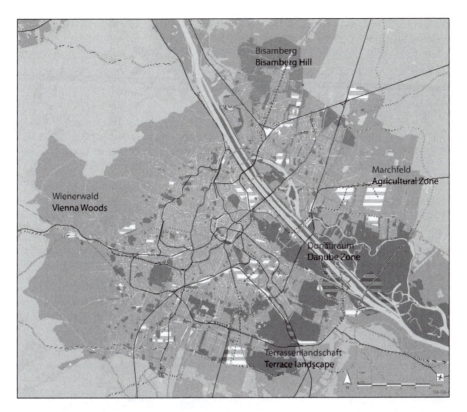

Figure 9.2: Overall concept – green areas of the city region Vienna

Source: Stadt Wien (Hg.) (2005b)

geologically situated at the intersection of different landscape types and climatic areas. Following the sandstone part of the *Wienerwald*, a set of terraces descends in the form of steps to today's city centre and further to the Danube. The set of terraces is caught in the south by the spur of the Wienerberg and the Laaerberg. In the north and northeast, this structure is supplemented by the Bisamberg and the Marchfeld plain with their particular corridor forms and rubble stone ponds (see Auböck and Ruland, 1998, 8–9, 51–2).

The inner city or centre, the suburbs and the urban villages up to the outlying districts stretch out on the individual terraces. In the west, the *Wienerwald* surrounds these urban settings and the Prater terrace, city terrace, Simmering terrace and the Laaerberg terrace form the hilly continuation of the green belt in continuation of the *Wienerwald*. Numerous brooks flow from the *Wienerwald* and have cut the terraces mentioned and formed broad valleys over the course of time. In between, remaining pieces of the original uniform terrace are preserved. This is most clearly recognisable with the Wiental terrace (cf. Auböck and Ruland, 1998, 9).

Vienna is situated at the border of the Central European, the Alpine and the Pannonian climatic zones; continental and oceanic influences are equally valid here. Therefore, the weather in Vienna is described as unbalanced and hardly predictable. The main wind directions are, dependent on the situation, northwest/west/southeast. The vegetation phases are quite different in the individual districts of Vienna. In the west of the city, spring often comes later than in the remaining districts.

The Viennese flora corresponds with the geological and climatic variability and diversity. In Vienna, the region of the European mixed woodland (beech, maple, oak and hornbeam) meets the Pannonian vegetation with its oak forests and drying lawns. In Favoriten, the 10th Viennese municipality district, we find a relict forest of Downy Oaks (*Quercus pubescens*). The far reaching beech forests in the northwest of Vienna, the dense combination of forest edges and meadows in the west, and the unusually various river landscape of the Lobau are considered to be the most beautiful landscapes in Austria.

The Vienna green belt consists of five large landscapes: the *Wienerwald* or Vienna Woods, Bisamberg or Bisamberg Hill, the Marchfeld or Marchfeld Agricultural Zone, the Donauraum or Danube Zone and the Terassenlandschaft or terrace

Photo: Ingrid Gregor

Figure 9.3: *Wienerwald*, **Vienna**

landscapes to the south of Vienna (Figure 9.2). Special protection categories and programs exist for the individual landscapes of the green belt as described below.

The Vienna Woods or Wienerwald

The *Wienerwald* encloses the west of the city in an elbow of more than 20km length, starting from the Danube break-through in the north, called the 'Viennese Gate' to the southern edge of the city. The shady forests, predominantly red beeches, are a popular recreational spot for Viennese people. Most visitors come simply in order to enjoy nature and the view over the city. Hiking in the summer and sledging on the Wienerwald meadows in the winter are very popular. Mountain biking is an attractive activity due to the many ups and downs in the landscape. In 2002, the so-called '*Wienerwald* declaration' was approved by the Vienna Town Council and the local parliament of neighbouring Lower Austria. It is a catalogue of protection and development targets to preserve the *Wienerwald* as a nature protection zone and recreation area for future generations.

In 2005, the *Wienerwald* in Vienna and in large parts of Lower Austria was recognised as a biosphere park (Biosphere Park *Wienerwald*) by UNESCO. It covers a total of more than 105,000 hectares in 51 municipalities of Lower Austria and seven districts in Vienna. The city of Vienna regards the recognition as a biosphere park as an additional possibility to ensure the protection of the *Wienerwald* as an important part of the Viennese green belt. It is planned to be further developed as a landscape and cultural area. The various functional relationships between the individual regions of the biosphere park and adjacent Lower Austria, the combination of uses such as agriculture, forestry, leisure and tourism, and nature protection, are important. The biosphere park forms a new cooperation model between Vienna and Lower Austria, dealing exclusively with the *Wienerwald*. Besides the public actors in the municipalities and districts, we find many private interest groups representing nature protection, agriculture and forestry, tourism, restaurant and catering services and others as important contributors of an, even economically, successful model region.

Bisamberg (Bisamberg Hill)

The Bisamberg in the north of the city is part of the alpine elbow and the continuation of the *Wienerwald* on the other side of the Danube. It takes an outstanding position as a northern entry point into Vienna. The slopes on the west side drop steeply to the Danube. Towards the east, the slopes have more room and fall gently. A thick loess layer and fertile soils are characteristic in the east. Numerous rare plant and animal species make the Bisamberg a valuable nature experience. The vineyards can be explored using the many trails which usually cut underground as so-called 'cellar lanes'. The locals enjoy the wines and the culinary specialities of the *Heurigen* (traditional wine farms with the right to sell their domestic wine to visitors) during their weekend and evening trips. In a 'landscape and open space concept' for the

Photo: Meinhard Breiling

Figure 9.4: Bisamberg Hill, Vienna

northeast of Vienna from 1994, large parts of the Bisamberg were regarded as being a highly valuable cultural landscape. The wine quarters were included in the green belt concept and resulted in an intensified cooperation between wine farmers and planners. An association for the development of a common recreation region between Lower Austria and Vienna was created.

A concept to unify individual biotope patches on the Bisamberg emerged in the year 2000. It considered the special meaning of individual elements within this landscape, for example, three defence constructions against Turkish invaders from the 17th century (*Alte Schanzen*). Now, a hiking path links them. The 'Agricultural Structural Development Plan' of 2004 designates the vineyards on the Bisamberg as an agricultural preference area. Many farmers also take part in a contract-based nature protection program: the 'habitat field' emphasising the important role of farming in the bio diversity of Vienna. Here, suitable care measures are used to convert agricultural areas into nature protection zones. Further programs with the same intention are the 'habitat vineyard' and 'habitat hedge' programs.

At present, a trans-boundary green belt concept between Vienna and Lower

Austria is under consideration: the Vienna green belt should be integrated into the landscape of Lower Austria. A possible instrument for this would be a transboundary regional park.

Marchfeld (Agricultural Zone)

North of the Danube, the landscape is characterised by predominantly gentle transitions and the hardly recognisable borders between the individual landscape units. The Marchfeld is a landscape area and part of the Viennese basin and slopes gently towards the southeast. Here, in the northeast, the majority of the agriculturally used land of Vienna is situated, altogether 17% of the city. It is 'the granary' and 'vegetable garden' of the city. The landscape of the Marchfeld stretches to the March River and the border to Slovakia. The strongly increasing settlement activity in this part of the city is changing the landscape and the new inhabitants are seeking opportunities for leisure activities: jogging, bicycling, walking among other activities.

The Agricultural Structural Development Plan of 2004, points to an expansion of urban agriculture as well as the promotion of urban agriculture. It investigates the options of improved marketing, new branches of production and cooperation possibilities between the city administration and farmers (see PlannSinn in Stadt Wien (Hg.), 2005a).

The Austrian agro-environmental program, ÖPUL 2000, supports the farmers with the advancement of environmentally friendly production methods. Among other things, we find a 'groundwater care program' and the previously mentioned programs with a contract nature such as the 'habitat field' and others. One goal is agriculture in the service of nature protection where all the partners involved profit: the farmers, the citizens, the endangered plants and animals.

Besides the programs for agriculture in this part of the green belt, there is another idea of a 'Cultural Landscape Park Marchfeld'. The value for tourists should increase and the newly restored *Schloß Hof* or 'Hof Castle' in Lower Austria, near the Slovakian border, should become a main attraction in this context.

A development concept for the northeast surroundings of Vienna, a by-product of the strategic environmental impact assessment of the planned northeast motorway by-pass, is currently being elaborated. Here, the emphasis lies on agricultural development. There are considerations of new landscape types such as a 'pond landscape' for recreational purposes in which agricultural use is excluded.

Donauraum (Danube Zone)

The settlement history of Vienna is closely related to the development of the Danube and the alteration in the river landscape. At the 'Viennese Gate' between Leopoldsberg and Bisamberg, as the natural gate and border to the Viennese basin, the Danube reaches the urban space and leaves it again after 21km in the southeast in the wetlands of the National Park Lobau. The many floods, inundations and channel regulations over the centuries have determined the development of today's differentiation into the Danube Channel, the actual Danube stream, the new Danube and the Old Danube. This entire river area forms one of the most important close-to-the-city recreational landscapes in Vienna. The Danube Island was developed in the course of the last Danube regulation in the 1970s. Up to 200,000 visitors visit the Danube Island on beautiful summer days: swimming, sunbathing, walking, jogging, playing, skating, rowing, or doing something else. The Danube Island Festival at the end of June is a three-day festival which attracts more than 2 million visitors. Vienna and Lower Austria declared the water dominated landscape (*Aulandschaft*) in the south of Vienna along the Danube towards the Slovakian border as a national park in October 1996. In 1997, the IUCN recognized the 'Donauauen' National Park according to the criteria of the category II as a protected area for conservation and recreation purpose.

Important objectives for the development are the promotion and preservation of the area as a close-to-nature and highly valuable landscape of national and international importance including the opening of the area for the purposes of education, recreation, science and research (cf. Stadtentwicklung Wien (Hg.), 2001).

In addition to flood protection, the 2000 'Vienna Danube Zone Structure Plan' particularly concentrates on aspects of recreation along the Danube area and its improved accessibility and unrestricted passage. The Danube area takes on two important tasks within the green belt. It belongs to the most important local recreation areas inside Vienna with a large offer of activities in, at, and on the water and, as a national park, simultaneously represents one of the most interesting habitats for animal and plant species in the southeast of the city.

At present, a motorway circuit around Vienna is being planned and construction is already completed in the south. In the Danube area, a tunnel is under discussion as the only alternative to preserve the devoted use as a national park. This solution was the result of a strategic environmental impact assessment. The effects on the National Park 'Donauauen' and the possible development of the green belt in the northeast of Vienna are being discussed. The completion of the motor circuit can result in a further carving into and/or reduction of the remaining areas which are applicable for the advancement of the green belt in the northeast of the city.

Terrassenlandschaft (Terrace Landscape in the South of Vienna)

The terrace landscapes in the south of Vienna include the Goldberg, the Laaerberg and the Wienerberg, all deposited by the *Urdonau* (the original course of the Danube in the south), which, over the centuries, were covered with a fertile loess soil layer. Clay excavation and viticulture were the principal forms of development in these areas. Today, there is a recreational landscape with ponds and hiking paths framed by the settlements of the urban extension in the south of Vienna. For the densely populated southern quarters of Vienna, the Wienerberg and Laaerberg belong to the most important local recreation areas.

For the improvement of the functionality of the terrace landscape in the south, some single projects were developed in the course of the years: the afforestation measures on the Laaerberg in the 1950s, the Viennese International Horticultural Exhibition in 1974 for the development of the Oberlaa Spa Park – WIG 74, the landscape concept for the Wienerberg in 1983, and the reorganisation of the waste dumps at Wienerberg West in 1995.

As urban development is particularly intensive here, the green islands and the combination of green patches are particularly important. The green course of the Liesingtal is an important liaison in the green belt of Vienna. The river Liesing, until then canalised in concrete, started to be reopened in 1992 as a pilot project in the context of the EU-LIFE program (Goldschmied and Schmid, 2006; Birli, 2006). A goal is to achieve the 'maximum ecological potential' for a 'heavily modified water body' as demanded by the EU water framework directive of 2000 (Breiling, 2006).

Among other things, that means an improvement of the water quality to grade II of the sapro-biological system and creation of new habitats for priority species (see European Union, 1992) for the Liesingtal. Current projects, besides the ecological restoration of the Liesing River and its surrounding landscape, include improved access for pedestrians and cyclists to use the area for recreational purposes. An accompanying measure is the information of citizens in these relatively densely settled, primarily industrial, areas in the south of Vienna. Information is displayed in small parks, green spots or other information points.

Current Activities and Future Plans to Develop the Vienna Green Belt and a Larger Scale Metropolitan Green Belt

Today's objectives for the Vienna green belt go beyond the city borders of Vienna and are oriented on landscape, and no longer political, borders. The green belt is divided into different protection categories with particular development concepts to achieve the aims for protection, preservation and development. Very often, this is performed in cooperation with the adjacent province of Lower Austria. The nature protection law of Vienna includes the following protection categories: national park, protected area, landscape protection area, protected landscape.

Large parts of the Danube area in the southeast of Vienna are protected as the 'Nationalpark Donau Auen' and Vienna is probably the only city of a comparable size to have a share of its area in a national park. The Lainzer Tiergarten (part of the *Wienerwald*) and the Lobau (part of the Danube zone in the southeast of the city) are protected areas. The River Liesing – the combining element of the green belt in the south of Vienna – the upper part of the Lobau and parts of the Bisamberg are landscape protection areas, the Wienerberg (part of the terrace landscape in the south of the city) is a protected landscape section.

Many of the larger areas, such as the *Wienerwald* in the west, the Lobau in the southeast, Wienerberg, Laaerberg and Goldberg areas in the south and the Bisamberg in the north, are secured under particular protection categories in the Viennese building ordinance as a part of the master plan of Vienna. The most important protection categories are: protected area forest and meadow belt, Sww, and the supplementary category SwwL (Wood and Meadow Belt, Protected Agricultural Area), category L (Agricultural land) and as park protected areas, SPK (Protected park zone).

Some of the areas of the green belt are additionally protected by the so-called NATURA 2000 directive of the European Union for the protection of natural habitats and endogenous species: the National Park Donau-Auen (Viennese part), the protected area Lainzer Tiergarten, the landscape protection area Liesing and all parts of the Bisamberg that are under landscape protection.

In the Viennese species and habitat program – 'nature network' nature protection guidelines have been developed for individual districts of Vienna. Here, one protects and/or promotes rare habitats in particular areas of the green belt with concrete projects of primarily important animal and plant types. A goal is to increase biodiversity and link biotopes and promote the nature experience of the city dweller inside Stadt Wien, Geschäftgruppe Umwelt, MA 22 (Hg.) (2002).

At present, everywhere in the European Union, the water framework directive has to be implemented. The ecological restoration of the River Liesing was undertaken to fulfil the objectives the water framework directive.

Future Perspectives for the Vienna Green Belt

The 'green belt' project to be regarded as an attempt of a large-scale open space planning exercise to secure the existing qualities in Vienna. Open spaces are regarded as an important feature of urban development where they take on a role of mediation between the city and nature. Three strategies contributed to the situation today. First, the unification of single green areas to larger ones with a higher protection status was aimed at in recent decades. Second, the purchase of new land by the city was very important. The '1,000 hectare program' of the Vienna town council between 1994 and 1995, which was, in particular, established to increase and develop the Vienna green belt, was an important step towards safeguarding and altering the green belt. Third, the improvement of second-class open spaces to first-class green recreation areas as is currently the case with the River Liesing.

The development of the individual landscape areas takes place in the context of many individual measures and under various names and programs. Depending upon the landscape area – as we described above – different cooperation agreements and financing models are needed and also partly established. The green belt is a common frame for the remaining fragments that are not, or not sufficiently, well integrated into urban planning and where single areas do not relate to each other. In meetings, publications and discussions to celebrate the 100 year anniversary of the establishment of the Vienna green belt in 2005, the people involved repeatedly stressed the privilege of Vienna with its five landscapes described above. There is a hiking pass around the green belt of Vienna called *Rundumadum*. Throughout the year, walking tours were organised along particular sectors to increase awareness and promote the green belt, with the participation of prominent persons along with the resident population (cf. Stadt Wien, Geschäftgruppe Umwelt, MA 22 (Hg.), 2005). However, at the latest, this showed that the green belt is not complete. In some places, in particular in the south in the 23rd district Liesing and in the northeast in parts of the 21st and 22nd districts called Floridsdorf and Donaustadt, improvements are necessary as the green belt is partly missing or, to some degree, too narrow. Besides closing and extending the green belt on the outskirts of Vienna, it has to be complemented within the boundaries of the city. The existing green areas within the city are understood as green patches and relate to the green belt. However, unlike Hamburg, the German partner town of Vienna, where we no longer find a single green belt, but a green net, Vienna has not yet developed instruments to consider such a development with connected green spaces in urban planning (Fachamt für Landschaftsplanung Hamburg (Hg), 1997). This may become a challenge for the coming years.

In the south and northeast of the city, the current urban development of Vienna has set different priorities from the green belt. Here, residential, manufacturing and industrial development receives the highest priority. The traffic planning with a motorway circuit around the south and northeast part of the city creates new opportunities for additional large-scale project development. South of Vienna, there is the largest shopping center in Europe, the 'Shopping City Süd' and competing centres are planned in the vicinity of, or even inside, the borders of Vienna. This is in strong conflict with the aim of strengthening the Vienna green belt. On the other hand, the most expensive variant of the motor circuit under the Lobau and Danube was recently approved by the town council and tempered the conflict over the motor circuit with the Lobau area.

The expansion of the green belt into the adjacent regions of Lower Austria is an expressed aim of the town development plan of 2005 (STEP 2005) (Stadt Wien (Hg.), 2005b). There are more opportunities to protect and alter the value of the landscapes of the Vienna green belt in an ensemble with the neighbouring municipalities. The political borders between the provinces should become insignificant for planning considerations. A goal is to regard the green belt regionally and use it together with the adjacent municipalities of Lower Austria in order to gain a maximum of synergetic potential for protecting the landscapes. In the west, there is already a common development of the green belt between Vienna and Lower Austria and an established biosphere park *Wienerwald*. The topographic conditions – the *Wienerwald* is the eastern starting point of the Alps – favoured this cooperation from the very beginning. In particular, towards the northeast and southeast, agriculture is the prime use of the greenbelt and was also highlighted in the Agricultural Development Plan (Stadt Wien (Hg.), 2004). A main reason for the recent increased attention to urban agriculture is the trend to supply fresh and healthy food locally, combined with its value as an inexpensive recreational activity. The concern in Vienna is probably higher than in most other European cities as Vienna has a distinct strategy for agriculture in the current town development plan STEP 2005, while many urban planning divisions in other European cities do not yet consider agriculture as their task of interest (Lohrberg, 2001).

In the north and the east, the concepts of the twin city region Vienna–Bratislava and CENTROPE region, have been under discussion, starting with the fall of the Iron Curtain in 1991 and, in particular, since the accession of Slovakia to the European Union in 2004. The distance Vienna–Bratislava is only 40km and nowhere in the world are two national capitals situated so close together. A goal is for an extended cooperation within a European region. In the twin city region we find 3.4 million inhabitants. The direct connection is the Danube. There are two development axes north and south of the Danube. The National Park *Donauauen* between these two cities is regarded as a source for a high quality of life. The national park connects the two cities and pulls the green belt along the river into Slovakia. Bratislava has qualities similar to Vienna but on a smaller scale. It is like a mirror of Vienna, where east and west are mirrored. The Carpathian Mountains rise to the northeast of Bratislava and the south is an open landscape. Many of the concepts and experiences of Vienna could be used to develop the green belt in a twin city approach.

The CENTROPE region goes beyond the twin city region and is strategically located in 'new Europe'. It is even larger than the capitals Vienna and Bratislava with their surroundings and four countries contribute to the region. The CENTROPE region includes the Czech city Brno and the Hungarian town Györ with their surroundings and represents one of the continent's most dynamic economic regions with more than 5 million inhabitants. Economic cooperation should be multiplied here. In particular, the growth of tourism along the Danube with its tributary March/Morava and the Neusiedler See/Fertöd Lake region is considered a possibility. CENTROPE should also be a platform for small-scale initiatives coming from the region. The urban green of the cities should be linked with green corridors including many of the existing cultural and natural treasures within this region and complement the new developments going on just now.

Conclusions

The development of the Vienna green belt has not finished. Major aims were established in closing the green belt while unification with the green of the inner city remains a target for the future. Larger visions of a Vienna green belt, or even a larger regional belt, are an important stimulus to preserving the surrounding landscapes and developing the green belt in an international context for the larger region. On the other hand, we have experienced an acceleration in urban development since the fall of the Iron Curtain and, in particular, since the accession of the Czech Republic, Slovakia and Hungary to the EU in 2004; all of them less than 100km away. What was not possible for decades is now happening and is likely to continue for some time. Major conflicting projects, like the enlargement of the traffic system, new shopping centres, settlements and new industrial zones, challenge the ideas of a larger green belt on the local Viennese level and on the international level of a larger region. Development initiatives have to be combined in such a way that the growth of urban green can continue, at least proportionally, to what was the case in the past.

References

Auböck M. and Ruland, G. (1994), *Grün in Wien* (Wien: Falter-Verlag).

—— (1998), *Paradies(t)räume, Parks, Gärten und Landschaften in Wien* (Wien: Holzhausenverlag).

Birli, B. (2006), 'The Role of the European Water Directive on Reconstructing Liesing River, Vienna', in M. Breiling (ed.), 'The Implementation of the EU Water Framework Directive from International, National and Local Perspectives', pp. 55–8.

Breiling, M. (ed.) (2006), *The Implementation of the EU Water Framework Directive from International, National and Local Perspectives. Proceedings of extended abstracts*.

Erhard, E. (2005), 'Vienna', in 'COST Action C11: Green structure and urban planning, Final report', EUR 21731, pp. 200–205.

European Union (1992), 'Council directive 92/43/EEC on the conservation of natural habitats and of wild fauna and flora', European Union.

Fachamt für Landschaftsplanung Hamburg (Hg) (1997), *Grünes Netz Hamburg* (Hamburg: Landschaftsprogramm Hamburg).

Goldschmied, U. and Schmid, J. (2006), 'Living River Liesing – A LIFE-project on rehabilitation of a heavily modified waterbody in Vienna's urban environment', in M. Breiling (ed.), 'The 304 Implementation of the EU Water Framework Directive from International, National and Local Perspectives', pp. 65–73.

Jedelsky, B. (2004), 'Grüngürtel Wien 1995. Von Lueger (1905) bis Häupl (2004)', in D. Bruns (ed.), 'Ballungsräme und ihre Freiflächen' (Kassel: University of Kassel), pp. 48–55.

Lahner, S. (1999), 'Der Wienerwald', *Ambiente*, 25(4).

Lohrberg, F. (2001), *Stadtnahe Landwirtschaft in der Stadt und Freiraumplanung*, Dissertation, University of Stuttgart.

Museen der Stadt Wien (1993), *Wiener Landschaften* (Wien: Eigenverlag).

Seebauer, V. and Weisgram, W. (1996), *Der Wienerwald und die Thermenregion* (Wien: Falter-Verlag).

Stadt Wien, Geschäftsgruppe Umwelt, MA 22 (Hg.) (2002), *Wiener Arten und Lebensraumschutzprogramm Netzwerk Natur* (Wien: Stadt Wien).

—— (2005), *Rundumadum, der Wanderplan durch den Grüngürtel* (Wien: Stadt Wien).

Stadt Wien (Hg.) (2004), *Agrarstruktureller Entwicklungsplan Wien* (Wien: Abschlussbericht).

—— (2005a), *100 Jahre Wiener Wald und Wiesengürtel, 1905–2005* (Wien: Stadt Wien).

—— (2005b), *STEP 05 – Stadtentwicklungsplan Wien 2005* (Wien: Stadt Wien).

Stadtentwicklung Wien (Hg.) (2001), *Donauraum wien* (Wien: Stadtentwicklung).

Wiener Gemeinderat (1905), *Der Wald und Wiesengürtel und die Höhnstraße Gemeinderatsbeschluss vom* (Wien: Wiener Gemeinderat).

CHAPTER 10

From Green Belts to Regional Parks: History and Challenges of Suburban Landscape Planning in Berlin

Manfred Kühn and Ludger Gailing

Introduction

Within the context of international discourse on the compact city as a sustainable form of settlement (see Jenks et al., 1996) and green belts as models for urban containment, this chapter examines two central themes as exemplified by Berlin, the capital of Germany. The themes are, first, the evolution of the green belt idea in the city region of Berlin since the nineteenth century (first part) and, second, the current application and innovation of the green belt idea in the concept of the Berlin-Brandenburg Regional Parks (second part). In the third part we will summarise the results of the case study on Berlin and draw some conclusions, addressing the question as to whether the traditional idea of the green belt can still serve as a planning model for the twenty-first century.

The Development of the Green Belt Idea in Berlin Since the Nineteenth Century

Urban Growth and Suburbanisation

After Berlin became the capital of Germany in 1871, it grew rapidly and developed into one of the largest industrial cities in Europe within a few decades. While the city had a population of 420,000 in 1850, the number of inhabitants had already reached the one million mark by 1877. By 1905, the population had grown to over two million. Concentric rings of tenement buildings, which were initially bounded by the circular railway constructed in the 1870s, grew up around the centre of the city. The rising price of land, real-estate speculation and a shortage of housing resulted in high-density urban residential developments with little in the way of greenspaces. Those developments comprised five-storey blocks with lower-quality buildings constructed around up to six courtyards at the rear (*Hinterhöfe*) to house the lower classes. By contrast, leafy residential districts with villas for the wealthy middle classes developed on the south-western outskirts of the city in Grunewald, Wannsee,

Nikolassee, Zehlendorf and Lichterfelde as an early form of suburbanisation. An area of country homes, which was the largest in Europe at that time, developed in the south-western part of Berlin. As the density of the inner city bounded by the circular railway increased, industrial enterprises and inhabitants alike began to move to the periphery of the city at the beginning of the twentieth century. Berlin expanded far into the surrounding countryside as a result of the migration to the outskirts and the development of the local railway network. By around 1920, the population of the suburbs and outskirts had almost reached that of the inner city. Development no longer took the form of concentric rings but followed the radial pattern of the local and main-line railway lines instead. Further developments grew up around the stations in the surburbs, spurring the growth of a radial and polycentric settlement structure (see Senatsverwaltung für Stadtentwicklung, Umweltschutz und Technologie, 1995).

From the 1870s up to the beginning of the twentieth century, the city administration bought a total of 14 agricultural properties to the north-east and south of the city to dispose of the waste water produced by the expanding city and to secure recreational areas for the city's inhabitants as these were being lost in the turbulent process of development. The properties covered an area of more than 25,000 ha and were managed by the public authorities as municipal farms throughout the twentieth century up until their privatisation in recent years. The extensive sewage farms established for the handling of waste water also served to secure the city's food supply (see Betriebsgesellschaft Stadtgüter mbH, 1996). In addition to this, the city administration purchased more than 10,000 ha of forest in the city and the surrounding areas which were protected as permanent woodlands by law and were reserved for recreation and securing the water supply as from 1915. This far-sighted open-space policy succeeded in limiting urban sprawl in some districts at least and protected important recreational areas close to the city, such as Grunewald Forest, for example (see Senatsverwaltung für Stadtentwicklung, Umweltschutz und Technologie, 1995). The acquisition of connected open spaces also contained real-estate speculation which had been boosted by the steep increases in land prices during the growth phase.

The turbulent growth of Berlin into a large city with over a million inhabitants and the increasing development of links between the city and the surrounding area, which comprised numerous municipalities and communities, continued until after the First World War. Planning for the city region as a whole did not exist at that time. In 1920, eight independent towns, 59 rural communities and 27 forest and agricultural areas were merged to form Greater Berlin which, with 3,803,000 inhabitants, temporarily became the third largest city in the world after London and New York. The city area increased thirteen-fold to a figure which is still valid today. As many of the incorporated villages and towns had large forest and agricultural areas the population density of Berlin decreased considerably and villages and countryside became part of the city. The city of Berlin thus became a city region within its own administrative boundaries (see Senatsverwaltung für Bau- und Wohnungswesen, 1995).

During the National Socialist period from 1933 to 1945, the population of Berlin reached 4.3 million, its highest figure to date. After the Second World War, in which the city suffered large-scale destruction, the population fell to 3.1 million. The political division of Berlin into western and eastern parts in 1948/49 put a stop to collective planning for the city region as a whole. By 1978, the population had fallen to around three million as many people left the western part of the city. In stark contrast to the trends in other European city regions, the population of the communities bordering Berlin also fell between 1960 and 1990.

West Berlin was completely cut off from the surrounding area by the construction of the Berlin Wall in 1961. Suburbanisation around the western part of the city was prevented entirely in the following four decades, up to the reunification of Germany in 1990. During that period, the only recreational areas for the inhabitants were within the city boundaries. West Berlin was forced to develop into a compact city. Many large housing estates, some with high-rise blocks, were built along the periphery of the city and even now mark the 'edge' of Berlin. East Berlin, the capital of the German Democratic Republic, expanded, with large housing estates being built on the outskirts of the city. Development was also based on the concept of the compact, socialist city. Plans for open spaces provided for green wedges extending into the city centre (see Senatsverwaltung für Stadtentwicklung und Umweltschutz, 1990).

Suburbanisation resumed after the fall of the Berlin Wall and the reunification of Germany in 1989/1990. Many middle-class households built detached houses in the areas around Berlin, attracted by the much lower land prices there. Between 1990 and 2000, the city of Berlin experienced a net loss of 150,000 inhabitants to the communities in the surrounding areas. However, migration out of the city has been decreasing over the past few years. The ratio of 80:20 between the population of the city and that of the surrounding areas is still far higher for the city region of Berlin than for other large cities in Germany. The ratio for Hamburg or Munich is around 50:50. Thus the suburban areas around Berlin are, even today, relatively thinly populated. However, some suburban areas around the Berlin orbital motorway are developing into preferred locations for extensive infrastructure projects (including the new Berlin-Brandenburg International Airport Schönefeld, several logistic centres and shopping centres).

History of Green Belt Planning in Berlin

In 1840, the Prussian Garden Director Peter Joseph Lenné submitted a plan for 'Schmuck- und Grenzzüge for parkways and gardens in and around Berlin (see Figure 10.1). According to Lenné, the plan was 'designed to meet the needs ... of the distant future' and included a ring of promenades – based on those in Paris – and avenues with several rows of trees which were to be planted 'not solely for pleasure but also for health considerations'. The parkways and gardens were to connect the Tiergarten Park in the west of the city with a new public park planned in the north-eastern part of the city, which was later named Friedrichshain. A romantic planner during the Age of Absolutism, Lenné still attempted to limit the expansion of the city and to design its outskirts according to aesthetic principles (Hennebo, 1979, 429).

Figure 10.1: Peter J. Lenné: 'Schmuck- und Grenzzüge' – Plan of 1840

Lenné's plan was soon upset by the onset of urban growth in Berlin. It was precisely because of this that the green belt idea gained in popularity in Germany at the end of the nineteenth century. In 1874, the green belt idea in Germany was promoted in the book 'Housing Shortages in Cities and Principles for Radical Remedies' by Arminius. Writing under that pseudonym, the author, Countess Adelheid Dohna-Poninski, called for an 'outer green ring' to limit the expansion of the 'compact mass of housing' in the city so that 'the right of each and every inhabitant to be able to reach the open countryside within half an hour's journey from their homes would not be violated' (Arminius, 1874, 94). At the turn of the last century, the green belt idea was propagated by two more influential works. These were Theodor Fritsch's book *The City of the Future* (Fritsch, 1912) and Ebenezer Howard's book *Garden Cities of Tomorrow* (Howard, 1946). Urban planning in many of the cities of Europe and Germany was inspired by Howard in particular.

In 1909, entries were invited for the 'Competition for a Basic Plan for the Urban Development of Greater Berlin'. The aim of the competition was to establish a blueprint for the expansion of the city within a radius of 25 km, with Potsdamer Platz at the centre. It was assumed at the time that the population of the city would more or less double. Two prize-winning entries turned out to be particularly significant for the subsequent development of planning concepts for settlements and open spaces in Berlin. They were Herrmann Jansen's plan for a 'belt of forests and meadows' (see Figure 10.2) and the concept for radial greenways put forward by a group comprising Rudolf Eberstadt, Bruno Möhring and Richard Petersen.

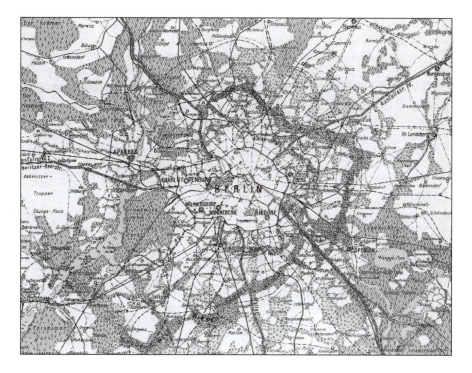

Figure 10.2: Hermann Jansen: Belt of forests and meadows around Greater Berlin including radial links, 1908

Hermann Jansen developed a system of open spaces from a small belt of forests and meadows in the immediate vicinity of the existing settlement areas and a large green belt beyond a ring of new settlements. They were to be linked to each other and to the city by radial parkways to ensure that the greenways were accessible to the city dwellers. The main aim of the plan was to achieve a balance between the middle-class suburbs in the west of the city, which had an abundance of green spaces, and the working-class residential districts with few green areas in the east, north and south of the city. Jansen based his proposals on the plans for a green belt in Vienna where the first attempt to realise a green belt in Europe commenced in 1905. Although Jansen's concept won the first prize in the competition it was never realised in its intended form in Berlin (see Senatsverwaltung für Stadtentwicklung und Umweltschutz, 1990).

By contrast, Eberstadt, Möhring and Petersen rejected concepts for urban expansion based on concentric rings which, in their opinion, had previously determined urban development in the form of medieval fortifications and absolutist customs walls, not to mention circular roads and railways. The authors took the view that a green belt would have a detrimental effect on the development of the city as far as land management and transport were concerned. They therefore proposed a model of radial urban expansion in which the settlements grew along the railway lines and the open spaces formed green wedges extending into the city. Although the green belt idea was referred to as a 'laudable concept' it was regarded as unrealistic. To quote the authors: 'One cannot deny that an entirely closed ring would be highly problematic as it can almost only be appreciated on paper and could hardly be realised in full, even if great sacrifices were made. Its realisation is prevented, for instance, by the railways along which industries are spreading' (Eberstadt et al., 1910, 45).

The history of urban planning in Berlin was characterised throughout the twentieth century by the constant competition between two basic models of urban growth: the concentric ring model and the radial model. While green belts based on the concentric ring model were planned time and again, the advocates of the radial model developed the idea of green wedges. The competition between the concentric ring model and the radial model in the city region of Berlin, which has continued until this day, will be illustrated below using selected examples of planning proposals (Table 10.1).

Table 10.1: Planning approaches of different models in Berlin

Year	Concentric ring model/Greenbelt	Radial model/Green wedges
1840	Peter Josef Lenné	
1908	Hermann Jansen	Rudolf Eberstadt, Bruno Möhring and Richard Petersen
1929		Walter Koeppen and Martin Wagner
1932		Gustav Langen
1946		Hans Scharoun et al.
1990		Planning group Potsdam
1998	Joint State Planning Berlin and Brandenburg	

After the establishment of Greater Berlin it was not until 1929 that a new concept for Berlin and the surrounding area was put forward. The concept, known as the 'Open spaces programme for the municipality of Berlin and the surrounding zone', was submitted by Walter Koeppen and Martin Wagner, the latter being the head of the Municipal Planning and Building Authority of Berlin from 1926 to 1933. The plan linked the existing open spaces, above all forests, water, sewage farms and agricultural areas in Berlin and its surrounding areas. Green wedges extending into the inner city were planned. Their purpose was to provide recreational spaces close to residential areas and improve air quality. Koeppen and Wagner regarded the surrounding countryside primarily as 'Berlin's garden' and any further destruction of the landscape by suburbanisation was to be avoided.

However, the Regional Planning Association pursued a different concept. By way

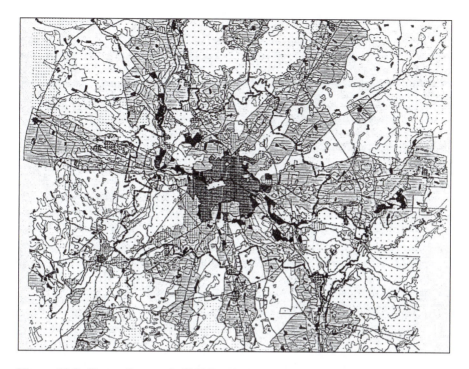

Figure 10.3: Gustav Langen's 1932 Radial Plan for the area around Berlin (1932)

of preliminary work for an extensive general settlement plan, the technical advisor Gustav Langen developed a 'radial plan for the surrounding countryside' which included the generous expansion of settlements along the radial railway lines while retaining the open spaces in the areas between the axes (see Figure 10.3).

After the National Socialists seized power in 1933, the development of open spaces, which had been geared to the recreational and health needs of the inhabitants during the Weimar Republic, was relinquished in favour of the mammoth plans for the growth of the capital of the German Reich. The 1939 draft Master Plan for the development of the city was based on the assumption that the population would increase from 4.4 million to 7.5 million. Compared with the planned built-up areas, it included few green areas. There was no superordinate concept for developing the open spaces. Indeed, the construction of an orbital motorway took priority over a green belt during the National Socialist period.

The Structure Plan for the Berlin region put forward in 1946 by a group including Hans Scharoun, Reinhold Lingner and others was based on the principle of the 'organic urban landscape'. Starting with the fact that Berlin lies in the Spree Valley (a glacial valley) between the plateaus of Teltow and Barnim, Scharoun's plan focused on opening up the structure of the city and linking the city with the countryside. A wide belt of horticulture aimed at providing the city's food supply was planned between the city and the orbital motorway. The plan was based on greatly reduced expectations of growth (see Senatsverwaltung für Stadtentwicklung und Umweltschutz, 1990).

The political division of Berlin into eastern and western halves in 1948/49 and the construction of the Berlin Wall in 1961 meant that planning concepts for the city region as a whole were increasingly put on hold. The prospect of being able to draw up a comprehensive plan for settlements and open spaces in the city region of Berlin was revived after the fall of the Berlin Wall in 1989. The 1990 report of the Potsdam Planning Group entitled 'Principles and Objectives for the Development of the Berlin Region' put forward the first joint concept for the development of the city of Berlin as a whole and the surrounding areas belonging to the newly established federal state of Brandenburg. The development plan, also known as the 'Star Model' (see Figure 10.4), was based on the radial growth of settlements in the city region along the traffic routes and on the assumption that the population would grow considerably. Open

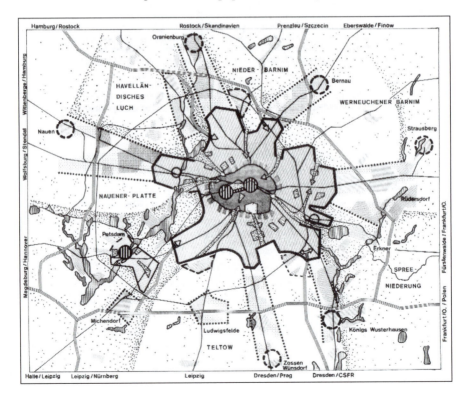

Figure 10.4: 'Star Model'

Source: Provisorischer Regionalausschuss Planungsgruppe Potsdam (1990)

spaces were largely limited to the areas between the radial ribbon developments (Provisorischer Regionalausschuss Planungsgruppe Potsdam, 1990).

Regional Parks in Berlin and Brandenburg – Developing the Green Belt Idea

The suburbanisation processes typical of western city regions did not occur in Berlin owing to the isolation of West Berlin over many decades and the absence of market mechanisms in the eastern part of the city up until the beginning of the 1990s. The stark division between city and countryside, due to a high-density city bordering on a sparsely populated surrounding area, was described as follows: 'When the wall fell it gave rise to a situation unique among all the world's metropolises – a city's edge as sharply defined as if it had been cut with a knife' (Joint Spatial Planning Department for Berlin and Brandenburg, 2000, 4).

The renaissance of the green belt idea around Berlin owes its origin in particular to the desire to preserve this extraordinary situation in view of the increase in the growth of settlements and traffic areas since the fall of the Berlin Wall. For example, the Berlin Regional Association of BUND (Bund für Umwelt und Naturschutz Deutschland), one of the most influential German nature conservation assocations, spoke out in favour of reviving the idea of a green belt around Berlin (see Salinger, 1993). In this case, the term 'green belt' was taken to mean a mosaic of different landscapes, with the extensive forest areas and the agricultural areas of Berlin's municipal farms at its core. The green belt idea was revived by spatial planners in the first half of the 1990s in the shape of a concept for regional parks around Berlin. The establishment of eight regional parks around Berlin was proposed for the first time in a preliminary study addressing the subject of such parks which was commissioned by the Brandenburg Ministry of the Environment in 1993. Regional parks were regarded in the study as

a specific kind of green belt around a large city with associated economic functions. Regional parks in this sense are countryside and recreational spaces in the vicinity of a town or city, whose economic aspects are based on preserving them as open spaces and not converting them into building land. They must be developed into a multifunctional and attractive cultural landscape by means of landscape architecture projects, by introducing interesting features relating to the landscape and establishing areas for recreational activities, whilst allowing for the preservation and reorientation of the agriculture and forestry which characterise the landscape (Wünsche and Louafi, 1993, 2).

The concept of regional parks was first taken into account in formal spatial planning when it was incorporated into the Joint State Development Programme drawn up by the federal states of Berlin and Brandenburg and in the Joint State Development Plan 'LEPeV', which is a formal plan for Berlin and the surrounding area. The two documents, which became legally valid planning documents in 1998, call for the establishment of regional parks to form a green belt around the capital. In addition, to quote from the Joint State Development Programme: 'A green belt is to be secured and developed in the suburban areas by establishing a chain of regional parks, taking the areas within the Berlin city boundaries into consideration' (Ministerium für Umwelt, Naturschutz und Raumordnung and Senatsverwaltung für Stadtentwicklung, Umweltschutz und Technologie, 1998, 56).

Despite their inclusion in the Joint State Development Plan, regional parks must not be regarded as an administrative planning instrument, on the same level as extensive natural conservation areas established by law, for example, but as a proposal put forward by regional planners (Ermer et al., 1997, 874). The ecological protection of the open spaces in the regional parks is deliberately meant to be linked with prospects for socio-economic development. The Joint State Development Plan for the suburban areas in Brandenburg and Berlin expresses those prospects in concrete terms. It states that the aim of the chain of regional parks is to 'secure the social and economic needs of the resident population within the framework of the development of their settlements and to meet the criteria for ecological compensatory spaces and the recreational needs of the inhabitants of the densely populated areas. The structure of individual regional parks should be such that the development of rural settlements, nature conservation areas, different types of recreation and ecologically sound land use by agriculture and forestry are compatible with each other, depending on the characteristics of the landscape' (Ministerium für Umwelt, Naturschutz und Raumordnung and Senatsverwaltung für Stadtentwicklung, Umweltschutz und Technologie, 1998, 89). The regional parks cover not only the open spaces but also villages and urban fringe developments.

The idea of regional parks is an innovation in the traditional German system of planning which tends to be based on restrictions and formal plans. Although the regional planners in Berlin and Brandenburg were able to draw on experience in other German city regions when drafting the objectives and concepts for the regional parks – for example, the Ruhr Area or the area around Frankfurt where the Emscher Landschaftspark and the Regionalpark Rhein-Main respectively were established in the early 1990s (see Gailing, 2005) – they still had to apply that experience to the particular situation of a monocentric city region with a comparatively clear-cut division between town and country. A spatial model comprising a chain of eight regional parks was developed (see Figure 10.5). The parks in the model form a ring around Berlin with a radius of around fifteen kilometres and an area of more than 2,500 km^2 which is interrupted only by the settlement axes.

The division of the green belt into eight separate regional parks, each with its own designation referring to an area of the local countryside (for example, Barnimer Feldmark, Krämer Forst, Döberitzer Heide), reflects the reality of the heterogeneously structured area around Berlin to a far greater extent than the definition of a single monostructural green belt which would have included all areas of the suburban landscape, disregarding the settlement axes. The subdivision of the green belt into separate regional parks thus opens up opportunities for landscape policies based on regional identities, specific features of individual landscapes and decentralised cooperation networks.

In opposition to traditional green belt approaches whose landscape protection status is based on formal planning instruments such as landscape conservation areas,

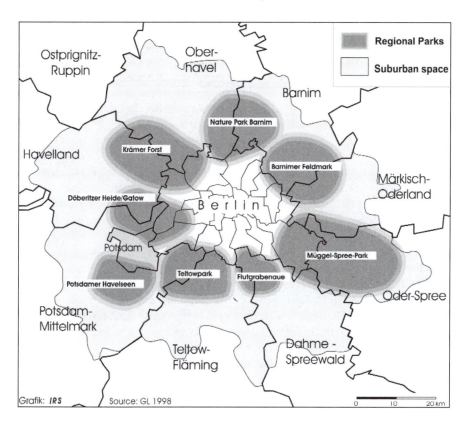

Figure 10.5: Map of regional Parks in Berlin and Brandenburg

Source: Ministerium für Umwelt, Naturschutz und Raumordnung and Senatsverwaltung für Stadtentwicklung, Umweltschutz und Technologie (1998)

the regional parks around Berlin are new forms of flexible landscape governance without any binding protection status. The regional parks are supposed to produce value for the open spaces by means of project-oriented regional management and thus prevent further suburban development of settlement or infrastructure. These new governance structures do not present themselves as a substitute for classical formal planning instruments, but supplement them in their efficiency by models of stakeholder participation or their project orientation.

In the absence of legal instruments, administrative structures or funding, the successful development of the regional parks – in terms of the objectives of regional planning – depends essentially on local decision-makers in Brandenburg and Berlin and on the stakeholders and land users who preserve the open spaces in the individual regional parks. The originators relied primarily on the self-organising ability of voluntary actors and the cogency of their idea. The motivation and the willingness of local actors to become involved and to cooperate as well as their ability not only to consult external experts but also to attract funding are essential if the development of the regional parks is to be a success. Consequently, it has only been possible to develop effective management in a few of the regional parks (see Table 10.2). In several areas in which regional parks should have been developed (for example, the Flutgrabenaue meadows near the new Berlin-Brandenburg International airport), it has not been possible to establish any cooperation structures at all, with the result that such areas are no more than planning elements at present.

The idea of developing a regional park has only been greeted with enthusiasm in areas with relatively little potential for other forms of development or with natural conditions suitable for recreational activities. Attempts to combine the preservation of open spaces with economic development only seem to be successful where 'serious' development issues do not predominate (see Römer, 2001; Gailing, 2005). The supply-oriented instrument of the regional parks is dependent on the economic uses that are linked with the preservation of the open spaces enjoying at least the equivalent potential for development in individual subspaces so that they can be taken into account appropriately in specific decisions on land use. Tourism and recreation seem to be the only viable prospects in the conflict-laden suburban space (see Kühn, 2003, 22–3). Under the present conditions, agriculture is likely to be of similar importance only in disadvantaged areas.

In spite of the serious difficulties encountered in realising the regional parks around the German capital, the Joint Spatial Planning Department for Berlin and Brandenburg regards them as a successful cooperation project. The citizens' and inter-municipal organisational and funding structures must be highlighted in particular. The strategy of delegating responsibility to local actors, which must be criticised from the point of view of efficiency, has also had positive effects. Cooperation has been encouraged in areas in which the willingness to cooperate was previously non-existent and – especially in the case of the Barnimer Feldmark Regional Park to the north-east of Berlin – existing networks of active, involved citizens have been strengthened. Farmers, conservationists and the tourist trade have all become involved in regional development. It has been possible to persuade municipal actors, civil society and even economic actors to become involved in spite of the poor incentive structures. Funding for the development of the regional parks has generally been provided by associations or municipal committees. Even so, around 130 projects in total have been realised in the regional parks. They include, for example, the marketing of regional products, landscape conservation measures, signposting networks of cycle and hiking paths, projects to restructure villages and biotopes or setting up tourist information centres (see Gemeinsame Landesplanungsabteilung der Länder Berlin und Brandenburg, 2005).

In view of the lack of funding and the absence of efficient top-down management structures, the development of the regional parks is a long-term undertaking. Owing to this 'institutional void' (Röhring and Gailing, 2005, 12), the processes of persuasion and awareness-raising are particularly important. The willingness of

Table 10.2: Regional parks in Berlin and Brandenburg: summary of characteristics

Name of regional park	Inhabitants in 1999 (approx. 000s)	Size (km²)	People employed	No. projects	Funded by	Main focus of activities
Krämer Forst Regional Park	25	323	6	4	Association	Recreation, regional
Barnim Nature Park	147	964	12	25	Authority under the Brandenburg Department of the Environment	Nature conservation, recreation, sustainable land use
Barnimer Feldmark Regional Park	71	423	656	70	Association and network of associations	Landscape development, recreation
Müggel-Spree Regional Park	89	449	237	7	Municipal committee	Nature conservation and water pollution control, recreation
Flutgrabenaue Regional Park	No data	No data	0	0	None	No activities
Teltow Park	91	297	77	13	Associaiton	Landscape development, recreation
Potsdamer Havelseen Regional Park	160	266	39	9		Landscape conservation
Döberitzer Heide Regional Park	17	144	0	0	None	No activities

Source: Joint Spatial Planning Department for berlin and Brandenburg (2000); Gemeinsame Landesplanungsabteilung der Länder Berlin und Brandenburg (2005)

regional and municipal politicians to support the development of regional parks, inter-municipal and inter-departmental cooperation, not to mention the approval and awareness of the population, are only growing slowly and need to be furthered by persevering actors and lobbyists. It was for these reasons that an umbrella organisation for the regional parks was set up in 2003. An official advisory committee for the umbrella organisation was established in 2004 in order to seek partners in the political and administrative bodies of the states of Berlin and Brandenburg with the aim of involving them in the development of the regional parks in addition to the actors in the individual regional parks who are often unpaid volunteers. The objective is to seek funding from government and European bodies. The new forms of cooperation in the city region, which have come about with the aim of developing the regional parks, are committed to furthering the common key issues set out by the bodies responsible for the regional parks (cf. Büro complan, 2001). The issues are as follows:

● strengthening regional economic activity
● the economic importance of day trippers
● cultural landscapes as signature features
● regional pools of compensation measures as a means of promoting the development of the regional parks.

Landscape policies in the areas surrounding large cities are always faced with problems to which there are no easy solutions. The same applies to the area around Berlin in which problems caused by the fragmentation of administrative responsibilities and the specific competition between, and intertwining, of urban and rural land uses are rife. The approach to the development of the regional parks around Berlin, which relies on cooperation, changing awareness and the self-organisation of citizens or different municipalities, is an innovative way of seeking solutions even though it is not yet apparent whether the planned enhancement of cultural landscapes close to the city has been successful owing to the simultaneous process of suburbanisation.

Conclusion

The popular idea of the green belt in Berlin can be traced from the plans drawn up by Lenné in the Absolutist period in the first half of the nineteenth century, through Jansen's belt of forests and meadows in the early twentieth century to the Joint State Development Plan for Berlin and Brandenburg established in the 1990s after the reunification of Berlin. In the case of Berlin, the closed green belt model has so far remained a planners' construct. In contrast to other European cities such as London, Vienna, Edinburgh or Cologne, it has not been possible to realise that planning concept in the city region of Berlin. The reasons for this are summarised below.

The growth of settlements in the city region of Berlin followed less and less in the twentieth century the concentric ring model, which characterised the development of the city up until the nineteenth century. The settlement structure of the city region is marked instead by radial developments (Senatsverwaltung für Stadtentwicklung und Umweltschutz, 1990) which have been spreading along the axes of the railway lines since the first half of the twentieth century. The history of urban planning in Berlin is thus characterised by the competition between the concentric-ring model and the radial model.

Relatively restrictive planning aimed at protecting a green belt was pursued in the open space policies of the Berlin city administration at the end of the nineteenth century. Extensive areas of land were purchased to protect them from being destroyed by urban sprawl. However, it was never intended to limit urban development in Berlin by creating a closed green belt on the periphery of the city but, at most, to channel growth spatially instead. In certain phases of the city's history (National Socialist period and the 1990s) urban planners' expectations of growth far exceeded actual developments.

Since the establishment of Greater Berlin in 1920, the city has been a city region within its administrative boundaries so that both urban and suburban districts lie within the city. Since reunification, the city region of Berlin has been faced with the particular problem that the city and the surrounding area are not only divided by a municipal boundary but also by the boundary between two federal states, which makes cooperation more difficult.

The length of the notional green belt around Berlin is around 250 kilometres. This spatial dimension means that a green belt is too big to be perceived as such by individuals visiting the green spaces for recreational purposes. Therefore, the protection of a green belt is rarely based on initiatives of inhabitants. A green belt around a metropolis is a professional construct which can only be appreciated on large-scale planning maps. London's green belt has also been criticised for this. To quote: 'From a plane circling London, the green belt is highly visible and immensely pleasing; and one senses some of the order and symmetry apparent on the planners's map. On the ground, however, the green belt is not so easy to see' (Whyte, 2002, 162).

Restrictive and centralised urban planning is always the prerequisite for pursuing extensive idealistic models such as green belts or green wedges (see Tessin, 1979). This prerequisite no longer exists in many market-driven and pluralistic countries. In countries which used to have a planned economy, such as China, concepts for green belts around the rapidly growing cities of Beijing and Hong Kong are therefore threatened. To avoid this, planning for the city regions of the twenty-first century should secure suburban landscapes and open space structures by bottom-up measures based on small-scale features and requirements instead.

The central planning concept for the green belt, which is based on a concentric ring structure, idealises the reality of suburban spaces in city regions as it is ultimately founded on a romantic image handed down from earlier periods and smaller cities. The concept of a closed form of city, which is linked with that of the 'compact city', now seems obsolete in view of the modern-day level of integration and mobility in city regions (see Fishman, 1990). A backward-looking and restorative view of the city underlies the green belt model if it is understood to be no more than a growth-inhibiting element on the periphery of the city (see Hennebo, 1979). In his model for a garden city, Howard drew a distinction between settlement forms and patterns of interaction and he interpreted the green belts as structural elements in the settlement structure of city regions which were intended to be overcome by fast means of transport (see Howard, 1946).

The new concept for the regional parks has reformed the previous green belt idea by replacing the strict separation of urban built-up areas and rural open spaces with a more realistic view of suburban spaces. The purpose of the regional parks is not primarily to preserve open spaces but to maintain and structure suburban landscapes. This is not a negative, restrictive form of planning but a forward-looking way of planning the development of suburban landscapes. It is an important prerequisite if the shortcomings of previous plans for a green belt are to be overcome, as those were due, at least in part, to a lack of acceptance in the communities in the areas surrounding the city (see Amati and Yokohari, 2006). The New York planner William H. Whyte recognised this fact as far back as the 1960s, when he wrote of London's green belt: 'Growth can, indeed, be contained; but it cannot be contained by a vacuum. The only way open land can be maintained against growth pressure is function, and it is in this respect that the green belt is wanting. Absence of development is not a function. The space must be useable for people, and not just a few people, but the people of the metropolis. They must be able to use the land for recreation, to see it, and to enjoy it. Lack of access is the trouble with the London green belt' (Whyte, 2002, 156–62).

The suburban spaces and the areas surrounding large cities are always characterised by a variety of urban and rural land uses. They reflect different ways of life and different types of policy which cannot be guided solely by one-sided restrictive policy and planning approaches or by one-dimensional key planning concepts. The governance concept for the regional parks in Berlin and Brandenburg demonstrates that there is potential for the renewal of the green belt idea – in spite of all the weaknesses explained above. Thanks to their active and economic support for the landscape, the inhabitants of the city region have become a significant development resource. The success of individual regional parks and thus of the entire green belt depends to a great extent on the inhabitants' ideas for use and development, their self-organising ability and cooperation in local and regional governance structures.

References

Amati, M. and Yokohari, M. (2006), 'Temporal changes and local variations in the functions of London's green belt', *Landscape and Urban Planning*, 75, 125–42.

Arminius (1874), *Die Großstädte in ihrer Wohnungsnoth und die Grundlagen einer durchgreifenden Abhilfe* (Leipzig: Duncker & Humblot).

Betriebsgesellschaft Stadtgüter mbH (ed.) (1996), *Entdecken Sie die Berliner Stadtgüter* (Berlin).

Büro complan (2001), *Untersuchung über die Regionalparkentwicklung als raumordnerisches Modell für eine nachhaltige Stadt-Umlandentwicklung und für ein raumwirksames Regionalmanagement, Endbericht*, vol. 1 (Langerwisch).

Eberstadt, R., Möhring, B., and Petersen, R. (1910), *Groß-Berlin, ein Problem für die Planung der neuzeitlichen Großstadt* (Berlin: Wasmuth).

Ermer, K., Hoff, R., and Mohrmann, R. (1997), 'Regionalparks in Berlin und Brandenburg', *Stadt und Grün*, 12, 873–7.

Fishman, R. (1990), 'Americas New City. Megalopolis Unbound', *Wilson Quarterly*, Winter, 25–45.

Fritsch, T. (1912), *Die Stadt der Zukunft* (Leipzig: Hammer). Originally published in 1896.

Gailing, L. (2005), *Regionalparks – Grundlagen und Instrumente der Freiraumpolitik in Verdichtungsräumen* (Dortmund: Dortmunder Beiträge zur Raumplanung).

Gemeinsame Landesplanungsabteilung der Länder Berlin und Brandenburg (ed.) (2005), *Perspektiven für die Regionalparks in Brandenburg und Berlin* (Potsdam).

Hennebo, D. (1979), 'Vom grünen Ringe der Grosstådte … Zur Geschichte einer städtebaulichen Idee', *Das Gartenamt*, 28, 423–33.

Howard, E. (1946), *Garden Cities of Tomorrow* (London: Faber & Faber). Originally published in 1898.

Jenks, M., Burton, E., and Williams, K. (eds.) (1996), *The Compact City. A Sustainable Form?* (London: E & FN Spon).

Joint Spatial Planning Department for Berlin and Brandenburg (ed.) (2000), *Regionalparks in Brandenburg and Berlin. Strategies for Sustainable Development in the Metropolitan Area*.

Kühn, M. (2003), 'Greenbelt and Green Heart: separating and integrating landscapes in European city regions', *Landscape and Urban Planning*, 64, 19–27.

Ministerium für Umwelt, Naturschutz und Raumordnung and Senatsverwaltung für Stadtentwicklung, Umweltschutz und Technologie (ed.) (1998), *Gemeinsam planen für Berlin und Brandenburg* (Potsdam: Ministerium für Umwelt, Naturschutz und Raumordnung und Senatsverwaltung für Stadtentwicklung, Umweltschutz und Technologie).

Provisorischer Regionalausschuss Planungsgruppe Potsdam (1990), 'Grundlagen und Zielvorstellungen für die Entwicklung der Region Berlin, 1', Bericht 5/90.

Röhring, A. and Gailing, L. (2005), 'Institutional problems and management aspects of shared cultural landscapes', published online: http://www.irs-net.de/download/shared-landscape.pdf, accessed 20 December 2005.

Römer, R. (2001), *Regionalparks um Berlin: Anwendung der neuen Planungskultur für eine nachhaltige Regionalentwicklung* (Berlin: VWF).

Salinger, S. (1993), *Ein Grüngürtel für Berlin. Eine Kampagne des BUND Berlin* (Berlin: BUND).

Senatsverwaltung für Bau- und Wohnungswesen (ed.) (1995), *Topographischer Atlas Berlin* (Berlin).

Senatsverwaltung für Stadtentwicklung, Umweltschutz und Technologie (ed.) (1995), *Freiraumerholung in Berlin, Arbeitsmaterialien der Berliner Forsten 5* (Berlin).

Senatsverwaltung für Stadtentwicklung und Umweltschutz (ed.) (1990), *Räumliche Entwicklung in der Region Berlin – Planungsgrundlagen* (Berlin).

Tessin, W. (1979), 'Restriktives Baurecht im Stadtumland. Zur Praxis der Green-Belt-Politik', *Stadtbauwelt*, 64/1979, 413–16.

Whyte, W. (2002), *The Last Landscape* (Philadelphia: University of Pennsylvania Press). Originally published in 1968.

Wünsche, G. and Louafi, K. (1993), *Vorstudie Regionalpark. Grundsätze und Rahmenkonzepte für die Entwicklung von Regionalparks im Randgebiet von Berlin* (Berlin: Gutachten).

CHAPTER 11

Controlling Urban Expansion in Italy with Green Belts

Giulio Senes, Alessandro Toccalini, Paolo Stefano Ferrario,
Raffaele Lafortezza and Pasquale Dal Sasso

Introduction

In Italy since the 1980s attempts have been made by a number of municipalities to implement green belts or greenways. The underlying rationale for these attempts has been to control urban growth and mitigate the environmental damage caused by Italy's rampant post-war development. The residents of Italy's cities have increasingly used green belts and greenways to connect them to areas of urban agriculture and forestry.

The linking-up of large areas of forests, public reserves and agricultural areas has necessitated the expenditure of funds and the formation of political alliances. It has not been a smooth process however and only since the 1990s have greenspace initiatives been enforced through the main planning document the 'General Municipal Regulatory Plan' (or in Italian: *Piano Regolatore Generale Comunale* PRGC), remaining up until then at the periphery of local politics and reliant on the enthusiasm and commitment of a few individuals.

In the following chapter we trace the development of the greenspace ideas in Italy. We first highlight the politics behind the development of the various initiatives that have been taken, highlighting a key moment in the adoption of greenspace initiatives. We also review the current state of greenspace policy implementation in Italy. We then trace the history of the most influential of these various greenspace initiatives – the 'South Milan Agricultural Park' – and report the findings of a study that sought to show its impact on shaping Milan's growth.

The History of Italy's Greenspace Schemes

The employment of greenspace schemes in Italy goes as far back as the 1970s when Ferrara launched its scheme to preserve the city's medieval backdrop (Table 11.1). Since that time a number of initiatives have been launched that have had a variety of objectives. From Table 11.1 we can see the following characteristics of greenspace planning in Italy. In the large number of the cities that have a population of less than

Table 11.1: Summary of green belt provisions in Italy

City	Year	Enforcing policies	Objectives	References
Ferrara	1970s	Municipality of Ferrara proposal for agri-cultural park	Green belt: acquisition of the cultivated land from the walls of the city to the River Po	Community project
Province of Milan	1990	Establishment of the Metropolitan Belt Regional Park known as the South Milan Agricultural Park	Protection, assessment and support of agriculture in order to prevent development	Regional Law 23 April 1990, no. 24
Florence	1992	General municipal regulatory plan (GMRP)	Green belt: proposal for a 'green wall' and a 'hill park': a greenspace system of wooded and terraced areas accessible by bicycle and on foot along the walls that circle Florence's historical centre. Echoing the walls' historic protection of the city and its delineation from the surrounding hinterland	Interview with Marcello Vittorini (Urban characteristics and urban planning) held during a course in urbanism (by Prof. A.L. Palazzo) 23 April 2003. The meeting was coordinated by Mario Cerasoli
Turin	1993, 2001, 2002 & 2003	Regional level proposal of the 'Green hinter-land' committee. In 2003 the Piemonte region sought approval to use state funds for the 'green hinterland system'	Green belt: project to preserve a circular green area and establish paths in the hills surrounding the town and a 'green crown' (management of the regions parks and reserves) and 'Turin – city of water' (a greenspace system to link rivers, hills and urban greenspace)	Planning proposal adopted from the management bodies of Turin's peri-urban parks
Ravenna	1993	General regulatory plan and local Agenda 21	Green belt: preservation of the greenspace for public recreation, thus alleviating the environmental harm to fragile pine-based coastal ecosystems; an appraisal of the greenspaces within the city and a definition of the physical boundaries of the city	Greenspace plan
Palermo	1996	Variation in the general regulatory plan. The parks project was funded out of the EU's LIFE-DG XI funds and the Mun. of Palermo	Green belt: definition of the urban agricultural park. The parks projects act as a management tool for enhancing agricultural activity, leisure, environmental education and aesthetic preservation so as to retain the characteristic of the area as a 'Mediterranean garden'	'Urban greenspace plan' – Synthesis of the material from a seminar of the 16 February 1998 available from Luigi Latini

Continued on the next page

City	Year	Enforcing policies	Objectives	References
Naples	1999/ 2004	Variation in the general regulatory plan. Institution of the Regional Neapolitan Hills Park of Naples	Green belt: Metropolitan park of the hills of Naples – peri-urban area made up of agricultural areas and public parks	Agency for the management of the Neapolitan Hills Park
Modena	2000	Variation to the plan applying to productive areas	Green belt: linking the productive plains and the urban forests	Municipality of Modena – Plans service
Milan	2002	Framework accord 2002 Ministry of the Environment, Treasury, from the Economic Programme of the Regional of Lombardy & Province of Milan and Mun. of Milan	Green belt: Parks and region have decided on the guidelines of the 'Intervention for environmental restoration' – afforestry and planting in the Parco Agricolo Sud Milano the 'Metro-forest': linking of the woods in the extra-urban parks and those within the green belt and connecting this and the greenery within the city along radial greenways (pedestrian and cycleways)	Framework agreement
Padova	2003	Green network and greenspace plan – Plan of services and transport (Agenda 21) Munici-plity of Padova – integrated system between the province and the region a consortium of volunteers, civil groups, public transport and forestry agencies and the University	Green belt: green network and greenspace plan consisting of a peri-urban green belt and a green network in the city	V Congresso Legambiente di Padova *'Dal rischio ambiente alla città sostenibile – la forza della partecipazione'.* Objective: green network (& land-use control) R. Gonzato & S. Lironi from the Local Agenda 21 plan. Nov. 2003
Cremona	2003	Lombardy region in collaboration with the Italian Federation of Friends of the Bicycle and other groups as part of an Agenda 21 development. Municipality and Province of Cremona: Projection of the ecological network	Greenway: bicycle route – connection between the parks of the Adda, Serio, Oglio Ecological network – area to attract fauna and increase biodiversity	Il Verde Editoriale: RETI ECOLOGICHE N 1 – (2004) Aree di potenziamento Agroecosistemi in primo piano by *Riccardo Groppali*

Continued on next page

City	Year	Enforcing policies	Objectives	References
Rome	2003	GMRP ecological network	Greenways: characterised by metropolitan parks (a system of parks at the regional level), agricultural areas in Rome's hinterland, and other areas of public greenspace	RI-VISTA-Ricerche per la progettazione del paesaggio. Doctorate of research in Landscape research – University of Florence Anno 1 – numero 2 – settembre/ dicembre 2004 University of Rome 'La Sapienza' Dept. of Agriculture and analysis of the city – *Rome Third Millenium*
Novara	2004	Preliminary project as part of the preparation of the GMRP (2000)	Variation to the Municipality of Novara (2004) GMRP for the green belt: compensation for the environmental harm from the impact of 'large infrastructure' already constructed. Forms part of a 'greenspace system' comprising a green belt around the city, the forested zone between S. Agabio and Olengo, ecological corridors (accessible on foot or by bicycle), which link to each other and link the city to its provincial parks (Ticino, Sessia, Casalbeltrame)	Newspaper 'Corriere di Novara' 11 May 2006 – *Ambiente a Novara: domande delle associazioni ai canditi Sindaci*
Bergamo	2004	Environmental associations (Italia Nostra, WWF, Legambiente) Municipal administration – Plan for the governance of the region	Green belt: agricultural and ecological park and green belt in the region south of Bergamo	Documenti di Italia Nostra sezione di Bergamo
Asti	2005–2006	Study of the feasibility of a rural park/ University of Turin, studies for the rural development of the hills). Municipality conducted the project the Region formulated the strategic plan	Green belt: the rural park in Asti. Guidance and development of the rural areas, support for local produce	Proceedings of a seminar Udine 26–27 October 2006 'Rarita utilita e bellezza nell educazione sostenibile del mosaico paesisticoculturale' edited by B. Giau, S. Novelli and E. Xausa
Arezzo	2006	Preliminary structural plan of the city of Arezzo	Green belt: preservation and identification of the existing green areas and a structuring of spaces to link the urban center and the rural areas	Municipality of Arezzo Sistema Informativo Territoriale

100,000 (for example, Ferrara and Cremona), the green belt or greenway is used to enhance the historic feel of the city and preserve its medieval aesthetic. Indeed, Florence has gone so far as to employ a 'green wall' around the city tracing the course of the medieval battlements. In addition to this essentially aesthetic objective, of notable interest is the City of Palermo's 'Mediterranean garden', a green belt that preserves the area's typical agriculture and protects products that are specific to the region. Another main function of greenspaces in Italy has been to link the urban and rural greenspace areas, as in Rome and Bergamo.

Despite the evident enthusiasm for green belts and greenways, their implementation has not been without difficulty. The initiatives that were taken before 1993 were limited by a lack of enforcing legislation through the main planning document, the General Municipal Regulatory Plan (GMRP) and can therefore be deemed to have had limited success.

The green belt within Ravenna's plan (1993) however, was a watershed initiative that was subsequently highly influential on greenspace planning for other cities in Italy. It was the first plan that attempted to make provisions for purchasing land as part of the green belt and for controlling development through a transfer of development rights schemes. The plan was thus able to balance the conflicting private and public interests in its implementation.

In the future it is likely that greenspace initiatives will proliferate further. There will continue to be a need for limiting the urban growth of areas as there will be for using green belts to retain the identity of areas. It is likely that cities will increasingly look to their green belt areas as those for cultivating typical or specialised regional products for which individual cities are famous. Finally, it is important to note the impact of wider shifts in Italy's local political landscape. The 1999 legislation to authorise the bottom-up creation of metropolitan areas (European Economic and Social Committee, 2007), has allowed 14 cities (Bari, Bologna, Cagliari, Catania, Florence, Genova, Messina, Milan, Naples, Palermo, Rome, Turin, Trieste and Venice) to have increased political autonomy from the national government. It is therefore likely that these cities will continue to attempt innovative greenspace schemes in the future.

The Effectiveness of Greenspace Planning in Milan

We now turn our discussion to a detailed examination of one of the most important greenspace planning schemes in Italy, the South Milan Agricultural Park. The following work aims to do this by analyzing the impact of protected areas on the urban expansion.

The Problems of Urban Expansion in the Metropolitan Area of Milan

The planning schemes that guided the development of the city of Milan until the 1980s were based on the city-capital as centre of all territorial issues in the metropolitan area (Beltrame, 1989). The model was that of the centre-to-periphery development, that brought a pattern of growth that resembled an 'oil stain', driven by speculators who balanced between the land value (that increases closer to the centre of the city) and location economies (for example, proximity of markets, of merchandise, for the residents and inputs for production). Milan has taken on a sprawling shape: a shape that clearly demonstrates the hierarchy of the centre.

The initial development of this model brought, on the one hand, a city that became a reference point for innovation and production, while on the other hand, the outskirts remained dependent on the centre, with a qualitative decrease of social functions. Milan's growth was characterized by a hurried and disorderly process of establishing settlements in outlying areas driven by a greater availability of land and relatively lower costs. The metropolitan area assumed the typically dispersed shape of the 'diffuse city' with a high waste of land and a fragmentation of areas not yet developed.

Scattered urban growth caused various abnormal situations, most importantly the formation of 'fringe areas' as connection areas between the urban and rural system, where the urban system does not yet demonstrate its own organizational qualities, while the rural system became contaminated by episodes of urbanisation that compromised its identity. Even the areas between buildings and land under development represent an abnormal situation resulting from the presence of abandoned industrial areas due to the relocation of the production structures to the outskirts of the city.

Within this context, an understanding developed over time regarding the role that agriculture can play in the outlying urban areas subjected to strong development pressure, not only from the productive point of view, but also from a landscape, ecological, and recreational one and as a balancing factor in territorial development.

The agricultural areas have undergone changes not only in terms of loss of land, but also in terms of structure and landscape: the mesh of the fields, the irrigation and rural road networks, and the tree rows have been changed as a result of the intense agricultural practices. The heart of the provincial agriculture (made up of the irrigation areas located south of Milan) has been able, until now, to partially defend itself from the growth pressure; however the impact from construction and the high density of the infrastructure and technology networks and their connection points is evident.

The Experience of the South Milan Agricultural Park

The idea to create a green area around the city of Milan goes back to the 1960s with the origin of planning at the super-municipality and metropolitan area level; in fact, in some studies of the Milan Inter-municipality Plan (or in Italian *Piano Intercomunale Milanese* – PIM) the creation of recreational green areas in the southern part of Milan were proposed. In the 1970s, the idea began to spread of a park oriented to the protection of agriculture and in 1983 the Lombardy Region included the area in the Regional Law no. 186 of the 1983 'General Plan of the Regional Protected Areas' identifying it as an 'area of particular natural and environmental relevance'. After seven years (in which, however, the urban expansion was slowed by its inclusion among the areas of environmental relevance), and thanks to the work of a committee composed of the municipalities involved, Regional Law 23 April no. 24 was approved in 1990, that created the Metropolitan Belt Regional Park named 'South Milan Agricultural Park' (Figure 11.1). Article 2 of the law, in compliance with the objectives of the parks of the metropolitan belt,[1] specifies that

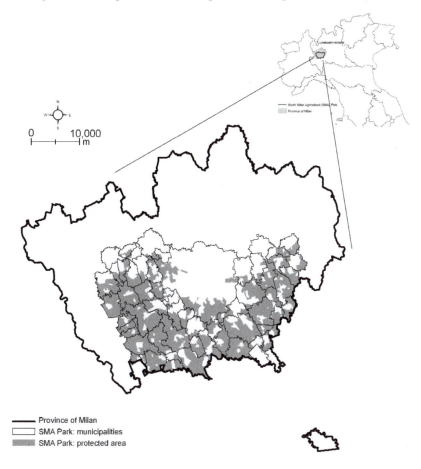

Figure 11.1: South Milan Agricultural (SMA) Park and the municipalities concerned

1   The 'Metropolitan Belt Parks' are, as provided by the Regional Law 86/83 modified by he Regional Law 41/85, 'areas of strategic importance for the ecological balance of the metropolitan area, the protection and the scenic and environmental recovery of the connection zone between the city and the countryside, the connection of the outlying areas with the urban green areas system, the recreation by the citizens, through a more effective landscape management, with particular regard to the agricultural activities'.

the goals of the park, in consideration of the prevailing agricultural nature of the territory at the border with the major metropolitan area of Lombardy are

● the protection and the scenic and environmental recovery of the connection zone between the city and the countryside as well as the outlying areas with the urban green areas system
● the ecological balance of the metropolitan area
● the protection, qualification, and the strengthening of the agricultural activities in coherence with the characteristics of the area
● the cultural and recreational enjoyment of the area by the citizens.

The park has a surface of 46,300 hectares, including 61 municipalities that cover a total area of 86,600 hectares and form, in effect, a green belt, of an approximate width of 15 kilometers, that surrounds the southern part of Milan from east to west (Figure 11.1).

The borders of the protected area were decided by the municipalities at the local level who reached a compromise that guarantees them a set expansion of the urban area in subsequent years (Figure 11.2). This characteristic of the process, while initially limiting the ability of the park to slow urban expansion, at least guaranteed an eventual containment of the land fragmentation and construction in the long term.

The planning system provided by the law comprises: a Master Plan (known as a

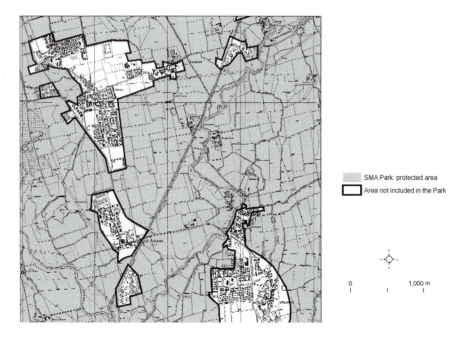

Figure 11.2: Example of Park borders in the municipality of Mediglia

Piano Territoriale di Coordinamento in Italian), the Management Plan and the Sector Plans, and, in particular, the Agricultural Sector Plan.

The Master Plan, approved with Regional Council Decision 3 August 2000, no. 7/818, represents the reference document for planning of the park; article 3 made it mandatory for the municipalities to conform their town planning schemes to the park's Master Plan by identifying the activities that are incompatible with the use of the area as a park. The Park Management Agency (in this case the Province of Milan) expresses opinions, authorizations, and concessions in cases that arise under Article 21 of law no. 86/83, (for example, on the town and city planning schemes, the agricultural plans, the quarry plans, etc.). It also takes decisions that are not covered by the Master Plan (for example, locating and choosing routes for national-level public works).

The territory of the park, 'in relation to the more complex objectives of protection and development of the agriculture, the environment and the enjoyment of the park' was subdivided into three types of area for which specific protection rules are provided:

Agricultural areas of the metropolitan belt   Includes the areas characterised by a high level of agricultural productivity constituting the core of the agricultural production system, for which the primary objective is the practice and conservation of agriculture.

Agricultural and green areas of the urban belt   Includes areas located between the city and the 'agricultural areas of the metropolitan belt'. These areas provide for the protection and restoration of the landscape and the environment, the protection of remaining agriculture and the development of infrastructure to enjoy the park (for example, green areas, recreation equipment and sports structures).

Connection areas between the city and country leisure zones   Includes the connection band between the 'areas of the metropolitan belt' and the urbanised areas outside the park that are not part of the 'urban belt areas'; specific measures are provided for the 'leisure zones' (cultural, recreational, and sporting) and for the 'transitions zones' between the external areas of the park and the 'agricultural areas of the metropolitan belt'.

In addition, the plan highlights the areas that should be preserved for environmental, scenic and ecological reasons, as well as precise areas of environmental, scenic, architectural and monumental significance (heritage buildings, springs, water flows, trails, and wetlands). Sixteen years since its establishment, the park remains an important means for safeguarding agriculture against the indiscriminate expansion of urban areas and a way of restoring the environmental and scenic values of an area that has been highly compromised by human activity.

Evaluating the Ability of the South Milan Agricultural Park to Control Urban Expansion

Study Objectives

The policy of preserving rural areas through the South Milan Agricultural Park represents an indirect instrument for controlling residential, manufacturing, and infrastructure development. The municipalities when defining planning schemes or other changes must seek the permission of the Park Authority, who can therefore guide the planning process based on the guidelines laid out of the Park Master Plan.

The objective of this study was to evaluate the effectiveness of the South Milan Agricultural Park as a green belt for limiting Milan's urban growth. The following reports on the results of an analysis to compare the extent of urban growth in the Province of Milan, which broadly contains Milan's metropolitan area, with the urban area in the park over time. Specifically the study looks at the effect of the park by examining the urban growth before the establishment of the protected area, until the moment of establishment, and up until present.

Materials and Methods

A quantitative method was chosen to compare data obtained from maps and statistical data over time. Maps from different periods represent a useful source in this type of analysis (Chilò and Tosi, 1992), to which data from other media such as aerial photos, satellite imagery, digital ortho-photography, digital maps can be added and processed using a Geographical Information System. Information technology provides an effective support for assessing of urban expansion (Paracchini, 1994; Jensen, 1996). The study was carried out in two phases:

1 An evolutionary analysis of the urbanised areas in the recent past (from the establishment of the park to the present);
2 An analysis of urban expansion in the period pre-dating the establishment of the park.

The objective of the first phase was to quantify urban expansion and compare it in the Province of Milan as a whole and the areas of the north and south of Milan separately. The choice of time horizons was determined by the availability of information sources that, for the purpose of this study, were produced by the Lombardy Region. In particular, the data chosen were:

● For the analysis of the situation at the time of the establishment of the park, the data relative to land use from the CT10 database (derived from the Regional Technical Map on a scale of 1:10,000), updated for the study area in 1994 (four years after the establishment of the park)
● For the analysis of the current situation, the data relative to the urbanised areas

from the DUSAF database (Agricultural and Forest Land Use, at a scale of 1:10,000), updated in 2000 (currently the most recent data source available regarding land use in Lombardy).

In order to identify the urbanised areas to compare in the two periods, the following classes of chosen databases were considered: 'urbanised residential areas'; 'industrial areas'; 'communication networks and related spaces'; 'construction sites related to areas under transformation'; 'sports facilities' and 'camp sites and tourist structures'. The 'parks and green areas' were, however, excluded from the comparison even if they were included in the urban context (Figure 11.3).

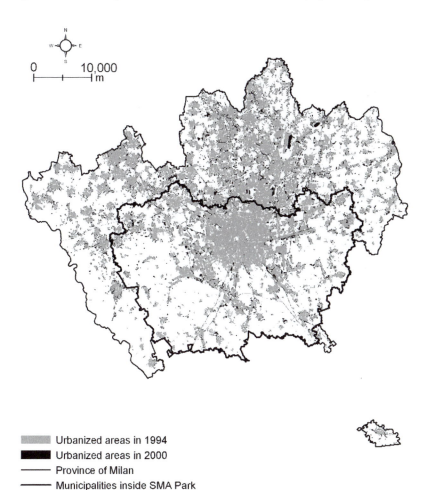

Urbanized areas in 1994
Urbanized areas in 2000
Province of Milan
Municipalities inside SMA Park

Figure 11.3: Expansion of the urbanised areas in the Province of Milan between 1994 and 2000

To make the information in the two databases comparable, an operation of 'cartographic generalization' was deemed necessary, because the smallest unit of representation of the area is 10,000 square meters in the case of the 1994 database, and 1,600 square meters in the case of the 2000 database. From the latter, the polygons were deleted if their surface area was smaller than 10,000 square meters or if they were isolated and not contiguous to the polygons of urbanised area already present in the map from 1994.

Furthermore, it was decided to compare the trend of the urbanised areas with those of the population in the same time period. For this purpose the population data from the Italian National Institute of Statistics (in Italian *ISTAT* or *Istituto Nazionale di Statistica*), from the General Census of the Population for 1991 was used (Istituto Nazionale di Statistica, 1991, 2001). Both the map data and the alphanumeric data were recorded and analyzed using the GIS software ArcGIS 9.1.

In the second phase the urbanisation before and after the establishment of the park were compared at the level of the whole province and for the North and South areas of Milan, separately. This was done to verify if the evolution of the land use noted in the south of Milan after the establishment of the park shows a different trend with respect to the prior period, also in comparison to the area north of Milan and to the entire Province.

The choice of time horizon was again determined by the availability of information. It was decided to refer to the period between the 1960's and 1980's, extrapolating the information contained in a study conducted by the Milan District Research Centre (Centro Studi Comprensorio Milanese, 1982) in reference to the period 1936–1980, on the area of the cities taking part in the Milan Intermunicipality Plan. This study has the advantage of having already been used for other evaluations (Toccolini, 1989), even if the data between 1963 and 1980 were not directly comparable with the data analyzed in the first phase, as they referred to a smaller area of 91 municipalities that comprised the Milan Intermunicipality Plan at the time. To overcome these limitations, the analyses were conducted for the area that corresponded with these municipalities, divided in two sub-regions: the municipalities located north of Milan and those located to the south (Figure 11.4).

Results and Discussion

In the first phase the total urban area in 1994 and 2000 was calculated for

● the whole Province
● the municipalities not part of the South Milan Agricultural Park
● the municipalities of the Park, including Milan
● the municipalities of the Park, excluding Milan.

This last classification was made to highlight the dynamics of the area south of Milan, without considering downtown Milan . The values obtained are included in Table 11.2.

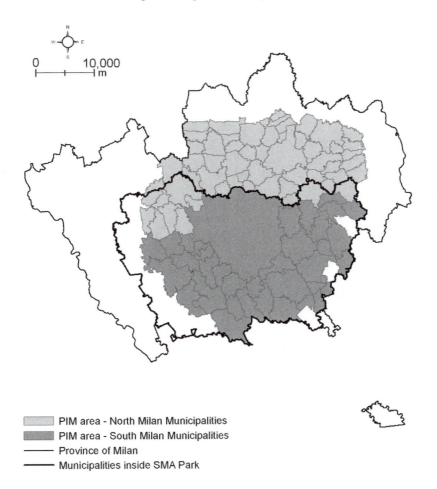

PIM area - North Milan Municipalities
PIM area - South Milan Municipalities
―――― Province of Milan
━━━━ Municipalities inside SMA Park

Figure 11.4: Expansion of the PIM area with respect to the Province of the South Park

As can be seen in the data in the table, despite the establishment of the park the increase in urbanisation is higher in the municipalities of the Park than for the province in total and the municipalities to the north of Milan. This result, which contrasts with the park's goal is understandable because of the following considerations:

- as the map (Figure 11.3) shows, the area north of Milan was already much more saturated in 1994 than the south.
- the process of including areas in the park pragmatically excluded areas that were considered to already be susceptible to urbanisation (Figure 11.2). This allowed in fact an expansion of building in those areas.

Table 11.2: Variation of the urbanised area 1994 to 2000 for the Province of
Milan and sub-areas of interest

	Total area	Urbanised area				Urb. area increase (1994–2000)	
		(1994)		(2000)			
	Km²	Km²	%	Km²	%	Km²	%
Province of Milan	1980.1	585.0	29.5	674.0	34.0	+89.0	+15.2
Municipalities outside the SMA Park	1113.9	335.4	30.1	390.6	35.1	+55.3	+16.5
Municipalities inside the SMA Park	866.2	249.7	28.8	283.4	32.7	+33.7	+13.5
Municipalities inside the SMA Park excluding Milan	684.4	139.9	20.4	166.6	24.3	+26.7	+19.1

Source: GIS processing on Lombardy Region data

To obtain a clear idea of the impact of the park it would be necessary to follow the method used by Longley et al. (1992) and compare the expansion that actually occurred with a modeled expansion. It would have been interesting to compare the expansion that actually occurred with that had the park not existed. Evidently this hypothesis is not possible until several decades have passed and it would become possible to examine urban expansion in the context of a wider analysis of regional development. It remains, then, even more difficult to extrapolate the changing dynamics of the city of Milan from those of the other municipalities of the park, by identifying the dynamics of the latter that are influenced by the former.

However, in order to reach a better understanding of the current phenomenon, the expansion of the urbanised areas was disaggregated by municipality by overlaying. The vector layers containing the urbanised areas were overlaid with the boundaries from the municipality layer in the Province of Milan. For each municipality the urbanised area was calculated for 1994 and 2000 as well as the absolute and percentage value increments (Figure 11.5a and Figure 11.5b)

The results emphasize how between 1994 and 2000 the city of Milan has slightly increased (+6.4%) its urbanised area. The results also show the slow growth in the municipalities located to the north of the metropolis which were already saturated because of the expansion that occurred in the 1960s–1980s. As far as the southern part of the Province, one can observe that the municipalities inside the Park have been able to better contain the expansion in comparison with those outside the Park, even if in some cases marked increases of urbanised areas can be noted. These municipalities are located on the external border of the belt. A large proportion of their territory is not included within the perimeter of the park however.

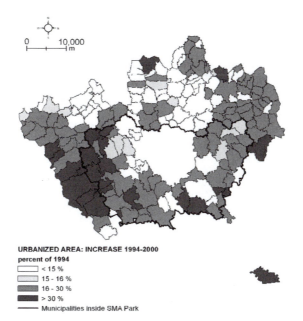

Figure 11.5a: Increase in the urbanised area in the municipalities of the Province of Milan 1994 to 2000

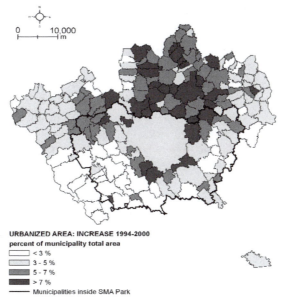

Figure 11.5b: Increase in the urbanised area relative to land area in the Province of Milan 1994 to 2000

If these increases are shown as a proportion of the available land area in the municipalities, the urbanisation in municipalities contained within the park appears less significant than for many of municipalities in the north of the province (Figure 11.5b). This confirms the hypothesis that the strong increase in urbanisation in southern Milan is primarily due to the greater land availability in the south compared to the north.

In a further attempt to better understand the current dynamics, the expansion of the urbanised areas was compared with the trend of the population in the same time period. To accomplish this, the population data relative to 1991 and 2001 Censuses from ISTAT were used, held to be approximately comparable with the map data of 1994 and 2000 (Table 11.3).

Table 11.3: Population changes 1991 to 2001 in the Province of Milan and sub-areas of interest

	Population (1991)	Population (2001)	Pop. difference (2001–1991) %
Province of Milan	3,738,685	3,707,210	–0:84
Municipalities outside SMA Park	1,670,085	1,728,994	+3:53
Municipalities inside SMA Park	2,068,600	1,978,216	–4:37
Municipalities inside SMA Park excluding Milan	699,369	722,005	+3:24

Source: ISTAT

It is interesting to note that, against a general increase in the urbanised areas (Table 11.2), the population of the Province of Milan has decreased, even if only slightly. In point of fact, the phenomenon was helped, as is typical in almost all Western cities, by a transfer of the population from the city to the surrounding countryside ('rurbanisation'). While the municipalities of the park in the south recorded a decrease in population on the whole, the population increased if the city of Milan is not included in the data.[2]

Further analysis compared, for each municipality in the province, the data relative to the increase in urbanisation with that relative to the population trend. This analysis should be considered carefully, since it is not rigorous because the time periods that were compared do not correspond precisely. Despite this, the results obtained are interesting and at least give a basic idea of the phenomenon (Figure 11.6). One can observe that in some cases an increase in the urbanised area is recorded which is not accompanied by an increase in the resident population that on one hand indicates the

---

2   The city of Milan has experienced a decisive loss of residents in the last decade.

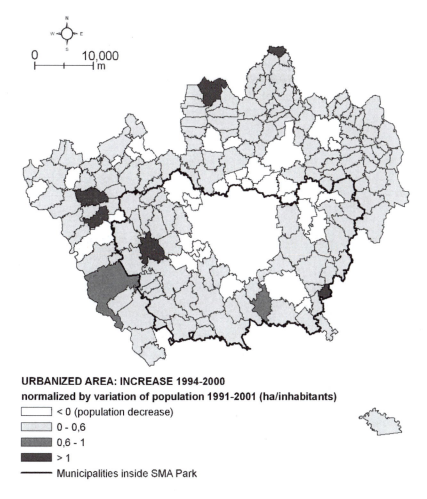

URBANIZED AREA: INCREASE 1994-2000
normalized by variation of population 1991-2001 (ha/inhabitants)
☐ < 0 (population decrease)
☐ 0 - 0,6
▨ 0,6 - 1
▪ > 1
── Municipalities inside SMA Park

Note: areas indicate urbanisation compared to population increase

Figure 11.6: Increase in urbanisation qualified by the variation in population
for each municipality in the Province of Milan

development of structures for production, services or infrastructural uses, but on the other hand denotes a policy that is not attentive to conservation of land resources.

In the second phase of the work, we wanted to analyze the trend of urbanisation and population for the period prior to the establishment of the South Milan Agricultural Park. As stated, the lack of available data led the research toward the following choices:

- reduction of the study area to the 91 cities of the PIM area (Figure 11.4), accordingly divided into north and south of Milan;
- considerations of the time thresholds relative to 1963 and 1980 (with data from the Centro Studi Comprensorio Milanese, CSCM) and 1994 and 2000 (with Lombardy Region data) for the urbanisation trend (Table 11.4a);
- considerations of the time thresholds relative to 1961, 1981, 1991, and 2001, with ISTAT data (Istituto Nazionale di Statistica, 1985, 1991, 2001) for population trends (Table 11.4b).

To better compare the trends of the phenomena, graphs show (Figure 11.7):

- the trend of the resident population,
- the trend of the urbanised area.

From the analysis of the data in Tables 11.4a and 11.4b and from Figure 11.7 it seems that in the study area, similar to what has happened in all developed countries, the curve of the urbanised area tends generally to grow at a greater rate with respect to that of the population. In order to better investigate the phenomenon, the following two indicators were calculated:

- Intensity of Use index, equivalent to the number of inhabitants per hectare of urbanised land (Ambiente Italia Research Institute, 2003) (Figure 11.8);

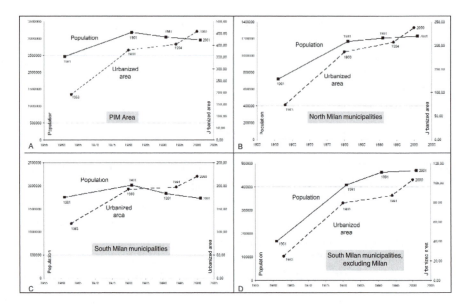

Figure 11.7: Comparison of the trend of resident population and that of the urbanised area. Data derived from Tables 11.4a and 11.4b

Table 11.4a: Changes in the urbanised area (absolute and percentage) between 1963 and 1980 (with CSCM data), and 1994 and 2000 (with Lombardy Region data) for the PIM area

	Area¹	Urbanised area (1963)	Urbanised area (1980)	Urb. area increase (1963–1981) %	Urbanised area (1994)	Urb. area increase (1981–1994) %	Urbanised area (2000)	Urb. area increase (1994–2000) %
Province of Milan	1104.02	191.79	34.36	+97.78	404.24	+6.57	458.05	+13.31
North Milan Municipalities	485.66	73.58	186.47	+153.42	207.16	+11.10	237.86	+14.82
South Milan Municipalities	618.36	118.21	192.85	+63.14	197.08	+2.19	220.19	+11.73
South Milan Municipalieies, excluding central Milan	436.61	24.79	79.49	+220.65	87.30	+9.93	103.39	+18.43

¹ All areas in (Km²)

Table 11.4b: Changes in the population between 1961 and 2001

	Population (1961)	Population (1981)	Population difference (1981–1961) %	Population (1991)	Population difference (1991–19810) %	Population (2001)	Population difference (2001–1991) %
PIM Area	2,470,059	3,182,189	+28.83	3,041,059	−4.43	2,957,439	−2.75
North Milan Municipalities	720,350	1,168,905	+62.27	1,208,462	+3.38	1,230,972	+1.86
South Milan Municipalities	1,749,709	2,013,283	+15.06	1,832,597	−8.97	1,726,467	−5.79
South Milan Municipalities, excluding central Milan	167,288	408,510	+144.20	463,366	+13.43	470,256	+1.49

Source: ISTAT

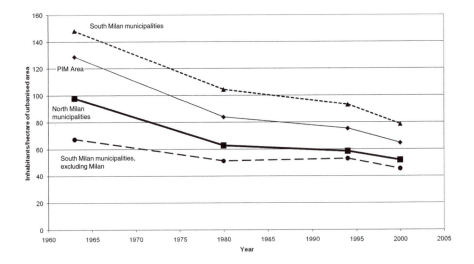

Figure 11.8: Changes in the density in the different parts of the study area

● urbanisation Index, equivalent to the percent of urbanised land in a given municipality (Figure 11.9).

Considering the two indicators together it is possible, for example, to distinguish 'compact and dense areas'. These have a large unbuilt area and a high density in the built-up area (for example, Zaragoza, with 5% of urbanised area and 112 inhab./ha) (Ambiente Italia Research Institute, 2003).

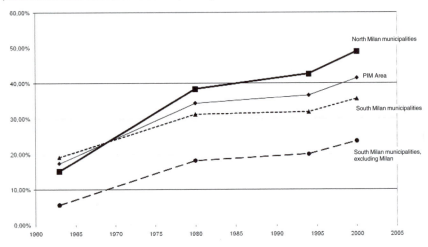

**Figure 11.9: Changes in the urbanisation index in the different parts of the
study area**

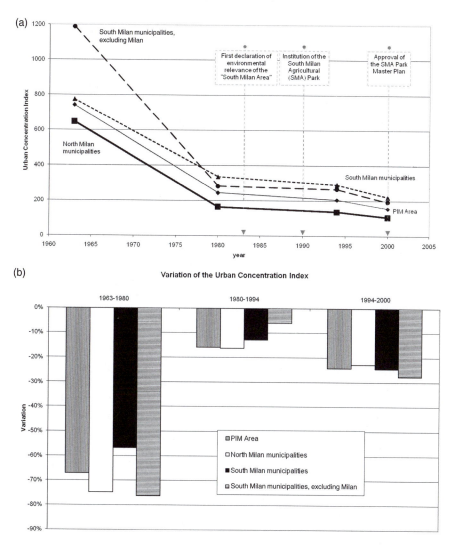

Figure 11.10: Changes in the Urban Concentration Index in the different parts of the study area

- Areas with 'low or medium intensity' of land use (for example, Ferrara, with 10% of urbanised area and 31 inhab./ha).
- Areas of 'high or medium saturation' (for example, Stockholm with 53% of urbanised area and 76 inhab./ha) (Ambiente Italia Research Institute, 2003).

Figure 11.10 shows that in the period 'mid-80s to 90s' the area of the 'municipalities south of Milan, excluding Milan' show a different trend to the rest of the study area.

Even without useful information available to study the causes in depth it is possible to say that the South Milan Agriculture Park could be a contributing factor. In order to combine these indices the Urban Concentration Index was calculated by dividing Intensity of Use Index by the Urbanisation Index.

The period of uncertainty regarding the fate of the area south of Milan began in 1983 with its inclusion in the Regional Law on protected areas as an 'area of particular natural and environmental relevance'. This period ended in 1990 with the establishment of the park (even if it was definitely concluded in 2000 with the approval of the park Master Plan). This uncertainty period seems to have produced a certain slowdown in urbanisation, that seems to have restarted after the borders of the park (that, as stated previously, excluded in the establishment phase the expected areas of expansion) gave certainty regarding the availability of unconstrained land, thereby giving a push to urbanisation. If these hypotheses are true, it is reasonable to expect that, once the available land provided for by the park Master Plan is saturated, the urban expansion will slow down, demonstrating the benefits of the Metropolitan Belt Park. But for that it will be necessary to wait for a few years.

Conclusions

This chapter has reviewed the employment of green belts in Italy. It has shown that a number of greenspace initiatives and planning schemes exist that aim to control urban expansion by highlighting the importance of agricultural and forest areas.

In some cases, green belts have been employed to preserve the historical character of the countryside, linking the urban and rural greenspace areas. The South Milan Agricultural Park can be considered a positive example of green belt implementation for protecting agricultural land loss in the face of indiscriminate urban expansion. The study evaluated the ability of the South Milan Agricultural Park to control the southern expansion of Milans metropolitan area. The results shows that the green belt contained urban expansion in southern Milan when compared with expansion in the north. The study also argues that local municipalities would benefit ecologically and socially by further limiting urban growth. With further data the role and function of the South Milan Agricultural Park in containing urban growth could be assessed. New sources of multi-scale geospatial information are needed in order to monitor urban expansion. Further studies are also needed in order to predict urban expansion through modelling techniques and new set of indicators assessing land-use changes.

References

Ambiente Italia Research Institute (2003), *European Common Indicators: Towards a Local Sustainability Profile* (Brussels, Rome: European Commission, Ambiente Italia).

Beltrame, G. (1989), 'Territorio, organizzazione urbana e risorse fisiche', in Irer Centro Studi PIM and Istituto di Geografia Umana dell'Università degli Studi di Milano (ed.), 'Trasformazioni territoriali e organizzazione urbana', (Milan: Franco Angeli).

Centro Studi Comprensorio Milanese (1982), *l'evoluzione dell'agricoltura milanese nell'ultimo trentennio, tra suoli in trasformazione e acque inquinate* (Milano: CSCM).

Chilò, L. and Tosi, A. (1992), *Cartografia e territorio rurale. L'uso dell'informazione cartografica in alcuni casi di studio* (Brescia: Grafo Edizioni).

European Economic and Social Committee (2007), 'European metropolitan areas: socio-economic implications for Europe's future', ECO/188 European metropolitan areas, Opinion of the EESC, Brussels.

Istituto Nazionale di Statistica (1985), *Popolazione residente e presente dei comuni-censimenti dal 1861 al 1981* (Roma: ISTAT).

—— (1991), *Censimento della popolazione e delle abitazioni* (Roma: ISTAT).

—— (2001), *Censimento della popolazione e delle abitazioni* (Roma: ISTAT).

Jensen, J.R. (1996), *Introductory digital image processing: A remote sensing perspective* (Upper Saddle River, NJ: Prentice Hall), 2nd edn.

Longley, P., Batty, M., Shepherd, J., and Sadler, G. (1992), 'Do Green Belts Change the Shape of Urban Areas? A Preliminary Analysis of the Settlement Geography of South East England', *Regional Studies*, 26(5), 437– 52.

Paracchini, M.L. (1994), *Integrazione tra telerilevamento e GIS per l'analisi del territorio rurale*, Ph.D. thesis, Università degli Studi di Milano.

Toccolini, A. (1989), 'Agricoltura periurbana e governo del territorio nel sistema metropolitano milanese', *Genio Rurale*, 12(12), 35–47.

CHAPTER 12

The Paris-Ile-de-France *Ceinture Verte*

Nicolas Laruelle and Corinne Legenne

Introduction

The Paris-Ile-de-France new regional master plan – at least in its current draft version (Région Ile-de-France, 2007) – has put a new emphasis on the underestimated charms of the green belt (or *ceinture verte* in French).

In this chapter, the *Ceinture Verte d'Ile-de-France* will first be explained, considering it successively as a specific area of the Ile-de-France region (section 12), as an ambitious – though not always easily understood – project led in this area by the Ile-de-France Regional council (part 2), and as an innovative and efficient policy implementing this project (part 3). Then, the original contribution of the new regional master plan to the future of the green belt will be discussed (part 4).

The Green Belt as a Specific Area of the Ile-de-France Region

The green belt area is a belt located between 10 and 30 kilometres away from the relatively small (10,500 hectares) city of Paris. It is about 266,000 hectares, which accounts for 22 per cent of the region's total surface area. It is therefore about twice as small as the London metropolitan green belt area, which has long been a strong reference for regional planners in Ile-de-France. Apart from being a belt, the main characteristic of the green belt is – not unsurprisingly – being green, due to a proportion of woodland and farmland adding up to 60%.

A Green Belt as Green as the Trees

Parks and, most of all, well-preserved woods, form an almost continuous string around the central urban area. Ten of these woods are more than 750 hectares each and are now publicly accessible, such as the Ferrières regional forest in the Seine-et-Marne county or the St-Germain national forest in the Yvelines county.

When moving from the most rural and distant parts of Ile-de-France into the green belt area, one will notice that the proportion of built-up area is quadrupled, while the proportion of woodland and parks remains surprisingly the same, at a relatively high level internationally of 28 per cent.

A Green Belt as Green as Salad

With a proportion of farmland reaching 32 per cent, the green belt area accounts for 13 per cent of the region's farmland but, due to a significant presence of intensive market gardening besides large-scale farming, it actually represents more than 20 per cent of the region's farms and 25 per cent of the region's jobs in agriculture.

Of course, time has passed since the 1920s, when the term green belt was first used to name an area of thriving fruit, vegetable and even flower farming around the central urban area, as opposed to the closer *Ceinture Rouge* (or 'Red Belt') of industrial communist municipalities located just outside Paris: in the 1920s the Montmorency cherries or the Arpajon beans were famous all over France. Over the last 20 years, the total amount of farmland in the green belt area has decreased by 20 per cent and the part of this farmland dedicated to market gardening has decreased by 34%.

Nevertheless, this global decline hides divergent trends in market gardening. Of course, the main trend is the strategic withdrawal or the mere disappearance of market gardening, making room for either urbanisation or large scale cereal farming, which often appears to be more flexible in a peri-urban context. But another trend is the increasing diversification or reorientation towards local markets or select Parisian restaurants, organic or integrated farming, alternative distribution networks or pick-your-own sites.

The Green Belt Area is Also Slightly 'Grey'

Even though this specific feature is not always well understood, the green belt area has a proportion of built-up area of about 40 per cent. Furthermore, this 'grey' part of the green belt area does not only consist of older historical cities, like Versailles or Saint-Germain-en-Laye, but also – for some reasons that are explained below – of the region's main urban developments since the 1970s: the region's five new towns (launched in the early 1970s), the third regional motorway ring (started in the mid-1970s and not completed yet), the region's main airport platform (Roissy-Charles de Gaulle, opened in 1974), the TGV interconnection stations (Massy, opened in 1991, Chessy and Roissy, opened in 1994) and the region's main tourist attraction besides Paris (Disneyland, opened in 1992). Because of the great variety of urban fabrics and socio-economic contexts in these built-up areas, and in spite of the similarity of their open space environment, the green belt area is not recognised by the vast majority of the region's inhabitants. None of them would say 'I live in the green belt' or 'house for sale in the green belt' or 'let's go for a day out in the green belt' or even 'I am the mayor of a green belt town'.

The Green Belt as a Project

In the second half of the 1970s, the idea of a green belt project for the preservation

Photo: D. Prat/AEV

Figure 12.1a: Célie wood (Seine-et-Marne county), regional estate since 1999, 20km away from Paris

Photo: L. Reynaert/IAURIF

Figure 12.1b: Val-de-Seine regional sports and recreation park (Yvelines county) 31km away from Paris

Photo: C. Legenne/IAURIF

**Figure 12.1c: The green triangle of the Hurepoix market gardening towns
(Essonne county) agri-urban project 20km away from the city of
Paris**

and valorisation of woodland and farmland around the Ile-de-France central urban
area gradually arose, as a joint answer to rapid urban growth, new leisure practices
and emergent environmental awareness.

In its long awaited second regional master plan (Préfecture de la région d'Ile-de-
France, Service régional de l'équipement de la région d'Ile-de-France, 1976), the
Central Government wanted to promote a major change in the regional 'urban
pattern', with the notion of regional urban polycentricity, based on the creation of five
satellite new towns. At the same time, the management of the region's open spaces,
i.e. all the areas that were neither urbanised nor 'urbanisable' according to the new
master plan, was decentralised to the newly-created regional authority (1976). Soon
afterwards, the regional authority, later to become the Regional council (1982),
started to consider basing its open space policy on a regional 'green pattern' that
would fit with the new regional 'urban pattern'.

But this proved to be quite a difficult equation to resolve. Of course, the Central
government services knew which 'urban pattern' they did not want: the 'Finger plan'
(see Figure 12.2a), for which the corresponding 'green pattern' would have been the
'green wedges', like in Greater Copenhagen. They also knew what they wanted: the
polycentric metropolis (see Figure 12.2b), for which the corresponding green pattern
would have been the 'green belt' between the central urban area and the five new
towns, like around London – even though the new towns were planned much closer to

Figure 12.2a: The *Finger Plan* with its green wedges

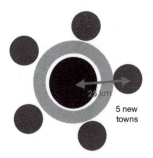

Figure 12.2b: The polycentric metropolis with its green belt

Figure 12.2c: The mix

the central urban area in Paris, when compared to London. But they knew even better that because of an early tendency towards urban coalescence between the central built-up area and the neighbouring new towns (mostly due to high speculation in the fringes of the long-awaited new towns), they were about to obtain a mixture of both, for which idealised planning scheme was much more difficult to find (see Figure 12.2c).

A green ribbon had to find its way through the urbanised fingers, the green wedges had to find their way through the motorway rings, and the new towns, with their expectedly high proportion of urban open space, were considered as an opportunity for 'greening' this complex green pattern and, thus, had to be linked together.

Although the picture was complex – all the more complex because it was never summarised by a sole explicit diagram –, the objectives of the green belt project were clearly expressed by the Regional council. There were 'spatial' objectives, regarding the general interactions between built-up areas and open spaces: to contain urban sprawl, to prevent the breaking up of open spaces by new roads and railways, to increase the understanding of large landscapes and to improve the visual quality of entrances to the central urban area. There were also 'functional' or rather 'multifunctional' objectives, regarding the specific roles that open spaces had to play in the green belt area: to protect and extend publicly accessible woodland, to create new recreational facilities, to prevent the decline of peri-urban farming and to protect the regional fauna, flora and natural heritage.

In order to share these regional objectives with the counties and towns of the green belt area, five very precise green belt studies were carried out by the IAURIF (Institut d'Amèragement et d'Urbanism de la Région d'île-de-France) for the Regional council (Région d'Ile-de-France, Agence des Espaces verts de la région d'Ile-de-France, 1995a; Région d'Ile-de-France, Agence des Espaces Verts de la Région d'Ile-de-France, 1983, 1985, 1986; Région d'Ile-de-France, Agence des Espaces verts de la région d'Ile-de-France, 1989). These studies assessed the strength of urban pressure on every single piece of open space, and the reasons and means for its preservation and preservation as green belt. The study asked a series of questions (for example): should this fallow orchard or former quarry be transformed into a park? Should this field be publicly purchased in order to prevent farmland speculation? Should this wood be made publicly accessible?

On the basis of these studies, many local authorities (from small boroughs to big counties – seven of the eight counties of Ile-de-France being directly concerned by the green belt area) have shown more interest in the preservation and preservation of their neighbouring open spaces. But, meanwhile, some of these local authorities and most of the others have forgotten the complex overall picture of the green belt project and many links of major regional interest between open spaces have been spoiled through development. In some cases, like in the North, between Paris and the Roissy-Charles-de-Gaulle Airport, the third regional master plan of 1994 (Préfecture de la région d'Ile-de-France, Direction régionale de l'Equipement, 1994), still the responsibility of the Central Government, clearly led to this development.

The green belt project found its most complete expression in the *Plan vert régional* (Région d'Ile-de-France, Agence des Espaces verts de la région d'Ilede-France, 1995a), which first considered the green belt as an interface between the central urban area 'green grid', the outer 'rural outer ring' and the valleys and green links running through this concentric pattern. The *Plan vert régional*, literally 'regional green plan' was first published in 1994 but finally not voted by the Regional council, and was thus re-issued in 1995 as a mere working document.

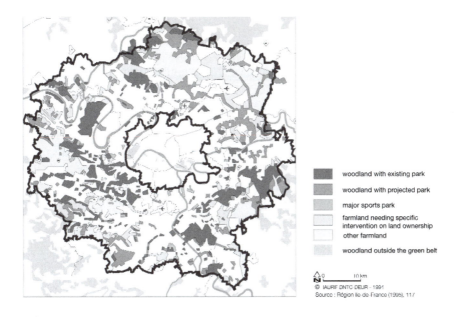

Figure 12.3a: The green belt open spaces as identified by the regional green plan of 1994

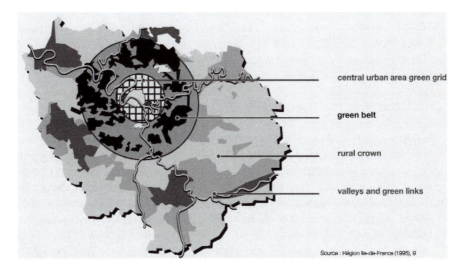

Figure 12.3b: The regional green plan general diagram

The Green Belt as a Policy

If, in spite of the complexity of the green belt project, the green belt area has not become too 'grey' over the last decades, it is certainly due to the innovative and efficient green belt policy.

More Than Partnership: 'Supportive Subsidiarity'

To preserve and valorise the open spaces of the green belt area, the Regional council had no legally prescriptive tool, like land-use plans that would have been imperative to other local authorities, and no territorially dedicated tool, like special measures that would have applied only to the green belt open spaces.

But the Regional council has used an extensive toolbox ranging from woodland acquisition and laying-out, farmland ownership watch, support to peri-urban farming projects, thematic measures on water-management, bio-diversity or innovative farming practice. Most of these tools have been intensively mobilised inside the green belt area, simply because it was there that the urban pressure on open spaces was the highest.

But most of all, the Regional council has built a tight network of partners who were ready to mobilise their own tools. This network is based on the notion of 'supportive subsidiarity': for instance, a county council may delegate its pre-emptive right to the Regional council to enable it to purchase a piece of open space of regional interest; on the other hand, the Regional council may subsidise a town council to help it to create a new publicly accessible local park. The high number of stakeholders and tools is an opportunity rather than a problem.

The essential networking task is carried out by the highly-motivated 'territorial' officers of the '*Agence des espaces verts*', the regional agency that was created in 1976 to implement the Regional council's open space policy, with a significant annual budget of 20 million euros. This budget is mainly dedicated to the purchase of land and the laying-out of publicly accessible woods and parks, and to subsidies to local authorities in order to enable them to do the same at their own level.

A Major Tool in the Hands of the Agence des Espaces Verts: the PRIF

A *périmètre régional d'intervention foncière* (PRIF), literally 'perimeter for regional intervention on land ownership', is almost nothing. It is just a line drawn on a map, covering an average surface area of 500 hectares, in a place that is considered as of regional strategic interest. It is almost nothing, but the Regional council voted on it, after both the County council and the Town council had also voted to express their approval. Therefore, the PRIF is recognised as an area of co-ordination and negotiation between all partners, public and private, and as an area of integration between all tools that are likely to be mobilised, inside the perimeter itself or close to it.

Table 12.1 shows, in the left column, the types of partners that are likely to

Table 12.1: Partners, actions and tools for the implementation of the green belt policy

	Scientific recognition	Protective regulation	Action on land ownership	Incentive measures and contracts	Planning documents
Central government and European Union	ZNIEFF (nature zones of ecological faunistic and floristic interest), ZICO (important bird areas), Natura 2000 sites	Nature (national) reserves, Sites classés (protected sites), Sites inscrits (listed sites), ZAP (protected forest), protected water	National forests, ZAD 'de protection' (deferred development zones – pre-emption zones used for protection)	Peri-urban agri-environment measures	Regional master plan
Regional council (*Conseil régional*)	*Charte régionale de la biodiversité* (charter for biodiversity), studies, heritage inventories	Regional nature reserves	PRIF (decision), *base de plein air et de loisirs* (sports and recreation parks)	Various types of contracts and charters between the Regional council and other local authorities; PNR (Regional nature parks); subsidies to good agricultural practice	Regional master plan, opinion on local planning documents (PLU, SCOT)
Agence des espaces verts	Prospective studies before PRIF proposals, ecological inventories		PRIF (proposal and implementation)	Subsidies to other authorities for open space acquisition and laying out	Contribution to regional opinion on local planning documents (PLU, SCOT)
County councils (*Départements*)	ENS ('sensitive nature areas') inventories, way-marked paths, County investment plan		ENS ('sensitive nature areas', pre-emptive zones, County forests	Various types of contracts and charters between the County councils and other local authorities, subsidies to other local authorities for open space acquisition and laying out	Opinion on local planning documents (PLU, SCOT)
Municipalities (*Communes*)	Landscape charters		Municipal ZAD (deferred development zones), open space acquisition		Local planning documents (PLU, SCOT), Chartes PNR (charters for regional nature parks)
Non-governmental organisations (*Associations*)	Inventories, (natural) heritage audits		Open space aquisition	Agri-urban cooperation programmes	

participate in the implementation of the green belt policy inside a PRIF or close to it and, in the top line, the types of actions that they are likely to take.

The Green Belt and the New Regional Master Plan

The New Master Plan is a Major Opportunity to Reconcile Urban Planning with 'Green Planning'

Between 1960 and 1976, regional urban planning and 'green planning' in the Paris-Ile-de-France region were both the responsibility of the Central government. After 1976, 'urban planning' remained a prerogative of the Central government, while the Regional council was gradually consolidating its commitment to open spaces, and thus to regional 'green planning'. In 1994, the *Plan vert régional* ('regional green plan') was published (but never voted) by the Regional Council while a revised *Schéma directeur régional* (regional master plan), of which the Regional council had expressed its disapproval mainly because of a lack of consideration for the green belt issues, was issued by the Central Government.

According to the 1995 law for planning and development, the elaboration of the regional master plan is now the responsibility of the Regional council, in association with the Central government services. Shortly after the 2004 regional elections, the Regional council decided to launch a new revision of the regional master plan.

The revision appeared as an opportunity to reconcile 'urban planning' with 'green planning' – now both the responsibility of the Regional council – which was particularly needed in the green belt area. The Regional council was deeply aware of this major issue and, from the beginning of the revision period until the completion of the planning document, the need for a better integration between the built-up environment planning and open spaces planning has been clearly asserted.

The Main Strategic Challenges of the New Master Plan all Question the Green Belt Issues

The three main strategic challenges that the revised regional master plan has chosen to address have a clear link with the green belt issues. They have thus re-questioned the green belt area and project, most often in a rather dialectic way, considering it as an 'area of higher tensions' between:

> the will to protect open spaces which are much appreciated for their proximity to the central urban area and to support peri-urban farming which is partly responsible for the sustainable maintenance of these open spaces,the need to allow urban extensions in the immediate vicinity of the central urban area where, because of their proximity to existing business districts and public transport facilities, they are more likely to reduce land consumption [because of higher building densities] and commuting (Région Ile-de-France, 2007, 145).

Challenge number 1 – 'Promoting social and territorial equity in order to improve social cohesion: towards a supportive region' (Région Ile-de-France, 2007, 29). On one hand, there is a strong urge to protect and, in some cases, to regain open spaces for gardens and parks in areas hit by social deprivation, poor public transport service and noise and air pollution, particularly in the North-East and South-East of the green belt area. On the other hand, there is a need to offer affordable housing to underprivileged households, in the central urban area or in its immediate vicinity, i.e. in the green belt area.

> Over the last decades, the tendencies in regional planning – urban sprawl, spatial mismatch and poor public transport servicing of some areas – have had negative social effects. Underprivileged households are particularly struck by the inconsistencies of regional planning and notably by the high cost of transport. The part of household budget dedicated to transport varies from 7 per cent in the core-city to 25 per cent in the most rural and distant parts of Ile-de-France. The consequences of poor public transport servicing are stronger for those whose jobs are more scattered and less accessible by public transport, with odd working hours, poorer qualification and higher precariousness (Région Ile-de-France, 2007, 31).

Challenge number 2 – 'Anticipating major crises and mutations, notably climate change and the rise in the price of fossil energy: towards a resilient region' (Région Ile-de-France, 2007, 35), resilience being the ability of a 'system' to resist disruptions but also to rapidly recover after major crises. On one hand, there is a need to protect and, in some cases, to regain open spaces in order to reduce the effects of heat waves, storms and river floods that will result from climate change. Green corridors are also vital for the necessary northward migration of species and ecosystems. On the other hand, there is a need for a 'compaction' of urban development, with urban extensions located in the vicinity of the central urban area rather than further away – where commuting distances are longer and public transport servicing is poorer – in order to reduce the dependence on fossil energy and to slow down climate change.

Challenge number 3 – 'Developing a dynamic region which preserves its global influence' (Région Ile-de-France, 2007, 41). On one hand, there is a need to offer new well-located business sites on the outskirts of the central urban area. On the other hand, there is an opportunity to use the potentially renewed prestige of the green belt open spaces as a real asset for the international attractiveness of the region.

The Green Belt Appears as an Alternative to Green Belts as Usually Understood

Thanks to the in-depth debates initiated by the Regional council all along the revision period, the ambivalence of the green belt area and project – that is, the fact that there should be a fair 'grey' part in the green belt – has been better understood and accepted. The *green belt/Ceinture Verte* is now considered as a sensible alternative to green belts as usually understood (in the UK). The urban extensions that are still needed, in spite of the high densification of the central urban area, should predominantly be located in the green belt area, rather than further away. But, as a counterpart, they should both offer higher building densities and respect the principles of the *Système Régional des Espaces Ouverts* ('Open Space Regional System').

Table 12.2 shows that the proportion of urban extension sectors which are located in the green belt has remained the same between the 1994 and the draft 2007 regional master plan, but that, as a counterpart, the total surface area of urban extension sectors has been reduced by more than a third.

Table 12.2: Urban extension sectors: a comparison between the 1994 and the draft 2007 regional master plans

	Central urban area %	Green belt %	Rural outer ring %	Region total %	Region total (ha)
Surface area of the urban extension sectors in the 1994 regional master plan	4	63	33	100	39,100
Urban extension sectors in the draft 2007 regional master plan	0	63	37	100	16,100
Surface area of the urban densification sectors in the draft 2007 regional master plan (pro memoria)	54	35	11	100	18,500
Total surface area	5	22	73	100	1,207,200

The Green Belt is a Key Element of the Système Régional des Espaces Ouverts *(SREO)*

The *Système Régional des Espaces Ouverts* is aimed at the protection and valorisation of opens spaces all over the region, through a clear definition of their vocation – woodland, farmland, park, ... – and a recognition of the multiple functions that they are likely to fulfil, individually or, as much as possible, collectively ... – production of farming and forestry products, sustainable management of natural resources (water, air, materials), protection of bio-diversity, structuring of the built-up areas, contribution to living environment quality (calm, beauty), reinforcement of community cohesion, regional attractiveness, cultural heritage (Région Ile-de-France, 2007, 73).

Its major innovation has been the clear assertion that, in a systemic approach, 'the capacity of open spaces to fulfil their multiple functions depends not only on their intrinsic qualities but also on the qualities of the links between themselves and with the built-up environment, on the various scales of the system'.

On the regional scale, the overall structure of the *Système régional des espaces ouverts* is clearly expressed by the A4-size open space strategic map (see Figure 12.4). It is a radio-concentric structure, with three concentric areas run-across and linked together by large open-space penetrating wedges, the 'grandes pénétrantes'.

The three concentric areas are:

- the central urban area *Trame verte* ('green grid'), which covers 5% of the region's total surface area, with a proportion of open spaces of 10%;
- the green belt, which covers 22% of the region's total surface area, with a proportion of open spaces of 60%;
- the *Couronne rurale* ('rural outer ring'), which covers 73% of the region's total surface area, with a proportion of open spaces of 90%.

The *grandes pénétrantes* will

ease the way of nature back into town through ecological corridors of regional concern consisting of main river valleys and green continua, tighten the functional links between the green belt's peri-urban farmland and the *Couronne rurale*'s bigger and stronger farmland entities, and further away, will renew the connections between the region's and its neighbour's open spaces' (Région Ile-de-France, 2007, 73).

As an interface area between the *Trame verte*, the *Couronne rurale* and the *grandes pénétrantes* the green belt is a key element of the radio-concentric structure of the *Système régional des espaces ouverts*.

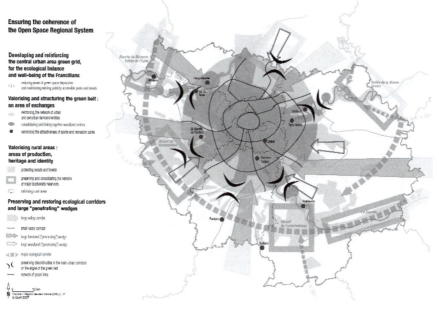

Figure 12.4: The new regional master plan open space strategic map

Source: Région Ile-de-France, 2007

The Land-use Map offers a Faithful and Concrete Translation of the SREO

At a more local – though nevertheless of regional concern – level, the 1:200,000 land-use map of the regional master plan appears as a faithful translation of the *Système Régional des Espaces Ouverts'* main principles into concrete items that are imperative to local planning documents. Not only does the map use 'traditional' patches of colour to express the main vocation of the open spaces which have to be protected and valorised as coherent entities: yellow for farmland, dark green for woodland and natural heritage, light green for relaxation, leisure and tourism. But it also uses some 'innovative' linear items which, even though not all exclusively dedicated to the green belt, are largely concentrated in the green belt area:

- urban front of regional concern, to be maintained (dotted lines – see Figure 12.5),
- (wide) ecological continuity, to be protected (thick double-headed arrows),
- (thinner but effective) farming continuity or leisurely continuity, to be created or strengthened (thin double-headed arrows).

Figure 12.5: The new regional master plan open land-use map sector located between Roissy-Charles de Gaulle airport and Marne-la-Vallée new town

Source: Région Ile-de-France, 2007

These linear items are expected to be easily understood and adopted by the future local planning documents, but also to be used by the *Agence des Espaces Verts* as a practical agenda for its future commitments in the green belt. For instance, new PRIF should be sensibly located in areas with at least one green doubled arrow.

Conclusion

Throughout the Paris-Ile-de-France new regional master plan elaboration process, reinforced political will and technical expertise have brought new hopes for a better preservation and valorisation of the Ile-de-France green belt. Yet, this better preservation and valorisation still needs public awareness of the open spaces issues at a regional level. Over the last few years, local environmental non-governmental organisations have shown more interest in the notion of green belt as a pertinent regional frame for their inch-by-inch and day-to-day commitments. In the future, this may raise public awareness and lead to a better recognition of the many amenities that the green belt open spaces can offer.

References

Préfecture de la région d'Ile-de-France, Direction régionale de l'Equipement (1994), *Schéma directeur* (Paris: IAURIF).

Préfecture de la région d'Ile-de-France, Service régional de l'équipement de la région d'Ile-de-France (1976), *Schéma directeur d'aménagement et d'urbanisme de la région d'Ile-de-France* (Paris: IAURIF).

Région d'Ile-de-France, Agence des Espaces Verts de la Région d'Ile-de-France (1983), *Projet de Ceinture verte de Paris et sa banlieue secteur 2: de la forêt de Bondy à la forêt de Sénart* (Paris: IAURIF).

—— (1985), *Projet de Ceinture verte de Paris et sa banlieue secteur 3: de la forêt de Sénart à la forêt de Verrières* (Paris: IAURIF).

—— (1986), *Projet de Ceinture verte de Paris et sa banlieue secteur 4: de la forêt de Verrières à la forêt de l'Hautil* (Paris: IAURIF).

Région d'Ile-de-France, Agence des Espaces verts de la région d'Ile-de-France (1989), *Projet de Ceinture verte de Paris et sa banlieue secteur 5: de la forêt de l'Hautil à la forêt de Montmorency* (Paris: IAURIF).

—— (1995a), *Projet de Ceinture verte de Paris et sa banlieue secteur 1: de la forêt de Bondy à la forêt de Montmorency* (Paris: IAURIF).

Région Ile-de-France (2007), *Schéma directeur de la région Ile-de-France Projet arrêté par délibération du Conseil régional le 15 février 2007* (Paris: IAURIF).

Index